Peter Hunter Blair is Fellow of Emmanuel College and Reader in Anglo-Saxon History in the University of Cambridge. He was educated at Durham School and Emmanuel College, Cambridge. His publications include *An Introduction to Anglo-Saxon England*, *The Moore Bede*, *The World of Bede* and a number of articles in various journals.

Front cover: Romano-British jet pendant found at York (Yorkshire Museum, York)

Back cover: Gold fibula from the seventh-century Sutton Hoo ship burial (British Museum: photo Michael Holford)

A HISTORY OF ENGLAND

A series edited by
C. N. BROOKE, M.A., F.R.Hist.S.
Professor of History, London University
and
D. M. SMITH, M.A.
Fellow and Tutor, Peterhouse, Cambridge

Also available

FROM ALFRED TO HENRY III 871–1272
by Christopher Brooke (*Professor of History, London University*)

THE LATER MIDDLE AGES 1272–1485
by George Holmes (*Fellow of St Catherine's College, Oxford*)

THE CENTURY OF REVOLUTION 1603–1714
by Christopher Hill (*Master of Balliol College, Oxford*)

FROM CASTLEREAGH TO GLADSTONE 1815–1885
by Derek Beales (*Lecturer in History, Cambridge University*)

MODERN BRITAIN 1885–1955
by Henry Pelling (*Fellow and Lecturer in History, St John's College, Cambridge*)

ROMAN BRITAIN AND EARLY ENGLAND 55 BC – AD 871

ROMAN BRITAIN AND EARLY ENGLAND 55BC–AD871

Peter Hunter Blair

CARDINAL edition published in 1975
by Sphere Books Ltd
30/32 Gray's Inn Road, London WC1X 8JL

First published in Great Britain
by Thomas Nelson & Sons Ltd 1963

First Sphere Books edition 1969

Set in Linotype Times

Printed in Great Britain by
Hazell Watson & Viney Ltd, Aylesbury, Bucks

ISBN 0 351 15318 7

CONTENTS

MAPS AND PLANS

GENERAL EDITORS' PREFACE

Knowledge and understanding of English history change and develop so rapidly that a new series needs little apology. The present series was planned in the conviction that a fresh survey of English history was needed, and that the time was ripe for it. It will cover the whole span from Caesar's first invasion in 55 B.C. to 1955, and be completed in eight volumes. The precise scope and scale of each book will inevitably vary according to the special circumstances of its period; but each will combine a clear narrative with an analysis of many aspects of history —social, economic, religious, cultural and so forth—such as is essential in any approach to English history today.

The special aim of this series is to provide serious and yet challenging books, not buried under a mountain of detail. Each volume is intended to provide a picture and an appreciation of its age, as well as a lucid outline, written by an expert who is keen to make available and alive the findings of modern research. They are intended to be reasonably short—long enough that the reader may feel he has really been shown the ingredients of a period, not so long that he loses appetite for anything further. The series is intended to be a stimulus to wider reading rather than a substitute for it; and yet to comprise a set of volumes, each, within its limits, complete in itself. Our hope is to provide an introduction to English history which is lively and illuminating, and which makes it at once exciting and more intelligible.

C. N. L. B.

D. M. S.

AUTHOR'S PREFACE

This volume spans more than nine centuries of Britain's recorded history. While writing it, I became increasingly aware that any merit which it might be found to possess would be due less to its author than to those many scholars whose published works are the tesserae from which the mosaic itself must be constructed. They will recognise their own craftsmanship and I gladly acknowledge my debt. My own task, mainly that of selection, synthesis and arrangement, has been greatly eased by much helpful advice and criticism from the general editors, Professor C. N. L. Brooke and Mr Denis Mack Smith.

Not everyone will agree with my views on controversial topics. In a period where there is so much uncertainty widely differing conclusions can be drawn from the same body of evidence, and opinions which at one time seem to be well founded are apt to be rudely overthrown by the new evidence which accumulates so rapidly. If my hope that the book may be found free from factual error is likely to prove a vain one, I know at least that there are many fewer blunders than there would have been but for the generous response made by Professor I. A. Richmond and Professor D. Whitelock to my exacting demands upon their time and patience. I am deeply grateful for their help.

I should also like to thank the following for permission to draw upon reference material in the preparation of maps and plans: the Society of Antiquaries of London (*The Antiquaries Journal*, vol. xviii, p. 376); the British Academy and Oxford University Press (*Offa's Dyke* by Sir Cyril Fox, fig. 121); the Clarendon Press (*English Romanesque Architecture before the Conquest* by A. W. Clapham, fig. 6); the English Place-name Society (vols. xxv–xxvi, map 4); Professor I. A. Richmond and the Society of Antiquaries of Newcastle upon Tyne (*Archaeologia Aeliana*, 4th ser., vol. xxix, p. 31); the Controller, H.M. Stationery Office (Ordnance Survey *Map of Roman Britain*, 3rd ed., 1956, Crown copyright reserved); and Messrs. Thames and Hudson Ltd. (*East Anglia* by R. Rainbird Clarke, fig. 32).

P. H. B.

PREFACE TO THE THIRD IMPRESSION

A great deal of fresh evidence has been recovered in recent years by excavation, especially in the period down to *c.* 600 A.D., but since much of this evidence has not yet been published I have thought it best to leave the text as it stands, making only a few minor corrections. In the section BOOKS FOR FURTHER READING I have referred to more recent editions of old books and have added a short list of new works of a general kind. The reader will thus be able to form his own conclusions about the ways in which earlier views may require modification.

P.H.B.

(1974)

CHAPTER ONE

THE NATURE OF THE SOURCES

Since the battle of Hastings was fought in the year 1066 Britain, though often attacked, has never been successfully invaded from overseas. William the Conqueror's victory was the decisive event in the fourth and last of the invasions of Britain which are recorded in historical sources—first the Romans, then the Anglo-Saxons, next the Vikings and finally the Normans. Julius Caesar's exploratory visits in 55–4 B.C. were followed in A.D. 43 by the landing in Kent of a powerful, highly trained professional army whose objective was the military conquest of Britain. Unlike the Roman legions, the next invaders, the Anglo-Saxons, did not come as soldiers in the pay of a great empire but as men greedy to possess themselves of a country whose wealth and prosperity, acquired under the shield of the *pax Romana*, offered a tempting contrast with their own unsettled, overcrowded and at times half-waterlogged homelands. Their occupation of that part of Britain which they turned into England was a long and slow process beginning before 400 and not yet completed by 600. This was the migration of a people, part of that great upheaval of European peoples whose effects spread as far east as the Black Sea and as far south as Spain and North Africa. The movement of the Anglo-Saxons into Britain was not marked by any one decisive event comparable with the landing of the Roman army at Richborough in A.D. 43 or of William's knights at Pevensey in 1066.

For about two centuries from A.D. 600, Britain enjoyed freedom from external attack while the new states of western Europe were taking shape within the spaces left by the collapse of Roman rule, but before 800 some of its outlying parts were visited by raiding Vikings. The scale and intensity of the Viking attack steadily increased until, in 865, there came to the shores of East Anglia a Danish army which within a few years took possession of much of eastern England. Shortly afterwards, the north-western parts of Britain began to suffer from attacks delivered by Vikings whose homes were in Norway.

The Vikings, like the Anglo-Saxons, came in search at first of loot and then of land. Long years of fighting, both at sea and on land, eventually gave them a degree of military supremacy in north-western Europe almost as great as that which the Roman legions had once enjoyed, and it was this supremacy that led in 1016 to the establishment of a foreign king, Cnut, on the English throne. Finally, in 1066, came the Normans, a well-organised fighting force able to defeat their enemies in pitched battle and thereafter, like the Romans, to impose a system of military government upon the country which they had conquered.

The interval between the raid on Britain by Julius Caesar in 55 B.C. and the accession of Alfred the Great in A.D. 871 is less only by a century than half the span of Britain's recorded history. Caesar's raid was preceded by an immensely long period of human activity in Britain about which we can learn only from the methods of archaeology. His assault, which brought increasingly close contact between Britain and the civilisation spread by Rome, leads us gradually into an era in which written records supplement, though they by no means supersede, the different kinds of material evidence which can be recovered by excavation. A written account of the military campaigns of a governor of Roman Britain will certainly be of the greatest value, but the existence of such an account will not lessen the value of what is to be learned by looking at the roads along which his soldiers marched, the camps in which they lived and the fields on which they fought. A written description of the seventh-century church of St Peter and St Paul in St Augustine's monastery at Canterbury will be neither less nor more valuable than the detailed plan of that church recovered by excavation. Each will supplement the other, each make the other more intelligible.

Those who interest themselves in this period of British history between 55 B.C. and A.D. 871 will find that as their knowledge grows they become more and more fascinated by this problem of evidence, by the means of discovering new sources of information and by the reinterpretation of the old. Not for them the unopened sacks of letters and documents piled high in a record office. Yet they can remember that less than thirty years have passed since the most important discovery that has ever been made in the field of west European archaeology—the finding of a royal burial chamber intact at Sutton

Hoo—that the first excavation of an Anglo-Saxon royal palace has but recently been completed, and that what is, from a textual point of view, the best surviving manuscript of Bede's *Ecclesiastical History* is only now being used for the first time in a new edition of that outstanding work. If at times they must lament the seeming impossibility of solving some particularly vital problem, at other times they may take heart from the continuing and rapid growth in both the quantity and the quality of the evidence from which the centuries between Julius Caesar and Alfred the Great can now be studied. And so the varying nature of this evidence shall be our first concern.

The value to be attached to the different sorts of evidence will depend upon the particular problems to be solved. Where the problem is that of establishing the simple narrative of events the most valuable kind of evidence is likely to consist of contemporary accounts written by eye-witnesses of the events which they describe, provided always that such accounts have been preserved in early and trustworthy manuscripts, or, if the manuscripts themselves are late, at least in trustworthy copies. It is important to realise that there is no single episode in the whole history of Roman Britain for which we have written evidence deriving directly from two or three of its eye-witnesses, and moreover that there are not more than one or two episodes for which we have even a single account that can be regarded as that of an eye-witness.

Julius Caesar wrote as a participant in the events which he described. His vivid account of the midnight sailing from the shores of Gaul, the difficulties faced by the heavily armed Roman infantry as they struggled for a foothold on the shelving beaches, the sudden storm that dispersed the cavalry transports, the hazards of the unfamiliar spring tides of the Atlantic and the strong currents of the Channel—all these brightly illuminate the first direct military contact between the peoples of south-eastern Britain and the soldiers of Rome, at the same time as they remind us of a more recent invasion in the other direction. Even so, it is to be remembered that this record puts the point of view of the Roman military commander and that we have no account of Caesar's expeditions written by any military leader of the forces which opposed him. Indeed the whole narrative of Roman military conquest in Britain can be told only from the Roman point of view. Tacitus wrote from first-hand knowledge of Agricola, the most prominent of the governors of Roman Britain. To him we owe a vivid account of hard-fought battles among the Welsh mountains, of the passage of the Menai Straits to Anglesey and of the rebellion of Boudicca which brought the Roman legions in Britain near to disaster. Again it is only the Roman tale that has been told, for the speech which Tacitus puts into the mouth of the Caledonian chief, before the assembled tribes of the Scottish Highlands were defeated at the battle of Mons Graupius, is no more than a literary device. Nor must it be forgotten that Tacitus was the son-in-law of Agricola, and anyone who reads the account which the former wrote of his father-in-law must ask himself whether Agricola owes his fame to the chance which gave him a distinguished writer as a son-in-law or to his real skill as a soldier and administrator. The question need not be asked in vain since other kinds of evidence can be found to give an answer.

Taken as a whole, the written records of Roman Britain are very slight in their bulk, and it is only during the period from Caesar's first expedition in 55 B.C. until the end of Agricola's governorship in A.D. 84 that they come near to providing a connected narrative. The *Agricola* of Tacitus survives complete, but unfortunately most of his two other major historical works, the *Annals* and the *Histories*, has been lost. His account of the invasion of Britain by Claudius in A.D. 43 is among the missing parts of the *Annals* and this misfortune is only partly made good by the survival of another account which was written in Greek by Cassius Dio in the third century. The *Histories* which originally covered the period 69–96, now survive only for the year 69 and part of 70, but much of this period is covered by the *Agricola*.

At no time in the later history of Roman Britain can the narrative be told in such detail from written record as it can for the period of Agricola's governorship. For the most part, references to Romano-British affairs in the second and third centuries are no more than the occasional sidelong glances of writers whose prime concern was with Rome and her emperors. The chance that Vespasian, the future emperor, was in command of the legion which fought on the south-western front during the Claudian invasion enables us to associate him with the capture of two in particular of the many Iron Age hill forts which still dominate the landscape of Thomas Hardy's Wessex—Maiden Castle and Hod Hill. Several writers contributed to a collection of lives of some of the later emperors, a work known as the *Historia Augusta*, and occasionally there may be a brief reference to British affairs, but even the briefest of such references can be of the first importance when it is considered in association with relevant archaeological material. Written evidence becomes more detailed for a short period after the middle of the fourth century when the disasters which overwhelmed Roman authority in Britain in 367, and the reconstruction which followed, are described by Ammianus Marcellinus, the last of the great Roman historians.

Excepting the times described by Caesar, Tacitus and Ammianus Marcellinus, the narrative history of Britain from 55 B.C. to A.D. 400 is derived only to a small extent from written sources. We value the more highly what we have largely because it is scarce, but we value it also because it does at times bring independent witness to confirm a conclusion which may have been reached by other means. Considered in isolation, the few words in which Capitolinus attributed to Lollius Urbicus, a governor of Britain in the second century, the building of 'another wall of turf' (*alio muro caespiticio*) could give rise to endless and not very profitable discussion, but when they are associated with inscriptions and other archaeological evidence found in the debris of that very wall, they acquire force and meaning. So also, some centuries later, the account of Scyld's burial in the opening lines of the Anglo-Saxon poem *Beowulf* acquires new and more vivid meaning when it is associated with the discoveries made at Sutton Hoo.

The reconstruction of narrative is only one aspect of historical studies, though it may seem a very important one in the age of transition from prehistoric times. The economic, social and agrarian history of Roman Britain, the daily lives, thoughts and beliefs of those who lived in its towns and countryside or patrolled its frontiers—these are not revealed to us by written sources, a fact which makes the search for other sorts of evidence bearing on these aspects of Romano-British history all the more challenging. We have no written records about the management of the imperial estates in Britain or about the running of the waterways along which grain was carried from the fenland of East Anglia to the military centres farther north. We have no account books from the lead-mining or pottery industries. We know nothing in detail about the organisation of the cloth industry at Winchester, nor have we any playbills from the theatres at Canterbury, St Albans or Brough-on-Humber.

There is, however, one small group of written sources which is of the first importance in giving life and reality to the map of Roman Britain. At about the middle of the second century A.D., Ptolemy, writing at Alexandria in Egypt, completed his great work on the geography of the world as he knew it. This work consisted partly of maps and partly of long lists of geographical names with the latitude and longitude of each name. The maps have perished, but the lists of names survive and from the data accompanying each name fresh maps can still be reconstructed. Using Ptolemy's data it is possible to draw a map of Britain, a little surprising in the shape of its northern part to be sure, but nevertheless containing the names of many of its principal natural features—bays, headlands, rivers and so forth—as well as those of many of its towns, tribal centres and military forts.

The road system of Roman Britain is known primarily from the surviving traces of the roads themselves, but valuable written evidence about it is preserved in a document of the third century known as the *Antonine Itinerary*. This is a route book, analogous to those compiled in modern times by some motoring organisations, but concerned with matters of public policy such as the organisation of the Imperial Post and perhaps also the movement and supply of troops. This document covers the whole of the Empire, and for Britain in particular it gives details of sixteen routes radiating from London with the names of places along them and the mileages from one place to the next.

Thirdly there is a valuable geographical work which was compiled by an unknown geographer who lived at Ravenna in the seventh century and is therefore known as the *Ravenna Cosmography*. Despite its late date, it is concerned with the geography of the Roman world only and from it there is much to be learned about the names of rivers, towns and military forts.

Quite different in kind, and still the subject of much dispute, is the work known as the *Notitia Dignitatum* which contains important details about the military organisation of Britain in the later days of the Roman occupation and especially about the names and garrisons of the Saxon shore forts along the eastern and southern coasts.

These and other sources have preserved rather more than 250 names of places and natural features, some of them in forms not greatly changed since Roman times. River names in particular have survived more commonly than other sorts of name. Thames has changed very little since Julius Caesar called it *Tamesis*, and the *Sabrina* of Tacitus is still easily recognisable as the modern Severn. Ptolemy's *Tava* remains close to the modern Tay. Thanet and the Isle of Wight still closely resemble the ancient forms of their names, *Tanatus* and *Vectis*. A few of the names of the larger towns have also survived, notably London (*Londinium*), Lincoln deriving from *Lindum Colonia*, and Gloucester to whose Roman name *Glevum* the Anglo-Saxons added the element *ceaster* which they had adapted from the Latin *castra*; but the names of most of the lesser places have vanished. It is not from the Romans but from the Anglo-Saxons and the Vikings that we have inherited the place-names of our countryside.

It has long been a common practice to label the two centuries between the end of organised Roman rule in Britain and the arrival of Augustine at Canterbury in 597 with such obscurantist titles as the Dark Ages or the Lost Centuries, as though we neither knew anything about these two centuries nor had any means of learning anything about them. The plain fact is that the written sources of British history for the fifth and sixth centuries are more plentiful than those for the second and third centuries. Moreover, for the first time we have written sources growing out of a west European and not a Mediterranean environment, some of them written in Gaul, some of them in Britain itself. Their authors may have lacked the literary skill of a Caesar or a Tacitus, but they were more directly involved in the world about which they wrote. This change, the gradual growth of literacy within Britain itself, was a direct consequence of the spread of Christianity. To this we owe what we may count among the very earliest native sources of British history, the works of St Patrick, written about the middle of the fifth century. From about a century later, as most people think, comes the work called *De Excidio et Conquestu Britanniae* written by Gildas the Wise. The self-imposed task of Gildas was to rebuke backsliding Christians, not to write a history of his times, but at least his work is that of a native of Britain, a man who had some historical awareness of the nature of the times through which he was living. Thus a little light comes not only from those parts of Gaul where books were still being read and written but also from the rapidly growing centres of Celtic Christianity in western Britain.

The Anglo-Saxon invaders of Britain came from a part of north-western Europe which had experienced very little direct contact with Roman civilisation and they were themselves illiterate in the sense that they had no written books, though they may well have possessed an oral literature expressed in songs and poetry. No Anglo-Saxon was capable of keeping a written account of any part of the invasion of Britain in the way that Julius Caesar recorded his own expeditions five centuries earlier. There were undoubtedly people among the natives of Britain who could have kept such an account, but if any was kept, none has survived save the work of Gildas. The great change came with the arrival of Christian missionaries among the Anglo-Saxons—Augustine at Canterbury in 597, Paulinus at York in 625 and Aidan at Lindisfarne in 635—and with the gradual spread of Christianity among the Anglo-Saxon kingdoms during the seventh century.

Christian services could not be held without service books and copies of the Scriptures. There is still in the library of Corpus Christi College at Cambridge a copy of the Gospels which is believed to have belonged to St Augustine himself, but this was a book written in Italy, not an Anglo-Saxon book. Among the documents which would be needed at the more important centres of Anglo-Saxon Christianity were the tables containing data about the phases of the moon and other matters necessary for calculations to be made about the date of the most important festival of the Church's year—Easter Sunday. These tables played a vital part in the growth of historical record among the Anglo-Saxons. So also did the Church calendar whose function was not simply to keep before some private owner details of the date and day of the week, but to remind officiating clergy of other Church festivals, of the seasons of rejoicing and the seasons of fasting, of the festivals of saints whose memory was to be observed by the appropriate prayers. Such festivals might be those of the Virgin Mary, St Stephen or St John the Baptist, but as the years passed they might also be those of new local cults—of St Patrick, St Chad or St Cuthbert, or even St Oswald, a king in his lifetime and not a cleric. The day of sainted bishop or sainted king recorded in an ecclesiastical calendar might become the occasion for preaching a commemorative sermon and such a homily could be the foundation for a written *Life* of the person commemorated. These two sources, chronology and what we call hagiography, or the writing of saints' *Lives*, were important elements in the beginnings of Anglo-Saxon historical record.

The *Lives* of three English saints of the seventh and early eighth centuries still survive, though there were certainly others that have been lost. The three surviving are those of Cuthbert who reluctantly abandoned his lonely hermitage among the Farne islands for the bishopric of Lindisfarne, Wilfrid whose favourite monasteries were Ripon and Hexham where the church was reputed to be the grandest on this side of the Alps, and Guthlac who made his lonely home among the watery wastes of the East Anglian fens. These works are all written in Latin, which remained the language of scholarship until the time of Alfred. *Lives* of saints such as these can be regarded as a form of literary composition and as such they can be read today with pleasure and profit. They can also be regarded as important historical sources, but those who use them for this purpose need to know something about the background and the conventions of this particular kind of writing.

Saints' *Lives* are primarily of interest for ecclesiastical history, although separation of the affairs of Church and State from one another is a modern historical convention which has no reality for Anglo-Saxon history in the times before Alfred. There were certainly other kinds of historical record being kept in monasteries in different parts of the country from an early date. Among the more important of these were the lists of successive kings who reigned in the several kingdoms of the early Anglo-Saxon period. The names of the kings in these lists were commonly accompanied by numerals denoting the number of years reigned by the king in question. Though exceedingly simple in their form, these lists are of great historical importance because they are the basis upon which can be established the succession of rulers in Kent, Mercia, Wessex, Northumbria and other kingdoms, in some instances as far back as the fifth century. It needs to be realised that the custom of the Christian world in reckoning the passage of years *Anno Domini*, which has now been the practice for many centuries, was virtually unknown in England before Bede adopted it in his *Ecclesiastical History* which he completed in 731. We think now, for example, of the Germanic invaders Hengest and Horsa traditionally arriving in Kent in A.D. 449 or of Edwin, king of Northumbria, beginning to reign in A.D. 616. But these dates *Anno Domini* arise from calculations made later, in part perhaps by Bede himself, and it was mainly the regnal lists, giving the number of years ruled by the successive kings that made such retrospective calculations possible.

Bede's *Ecclesiastical History of the English Nation* is one of the most important single sources of information about the Anglo-Saxon period as a whole and on any count it must hold a very high place among the literary monuments of the European Middle Ages. Written at Jarrow, where Bede passed almost the whole of his life, it spans nearly eight hundred years from the earliest contacts between Britain and the Romans until A.D. 731, four years before its author's death. This book is the first major historical work to have been written by an Englishmen and it still remains one of the greatest. Finding his material in earlier written sources, including the work of Gildas, using documents of which copies were brought to him from Canterbury and other places, and drawing upon ancient traditions as well as upon his own direct knowledge, Bede surveyed the whole with an acutely critical mind developed by a lifetime of theological studies in the great library at Jarrow. To find another historian comparable with Bede in powers of synthesis and breadth of historical understanding we should need to look backwards to some of the great historians of classical times or forwards to such a one as William of Malmesbury in the twelfth century. The *Ecclesiastical History* is now, and will always remain, the chief source of information about the conversion of the English to Christianity and the growth of the Christian Church in England during the seventh and early eighth centuries.

Bede's *History*, a work compiled by one man from a variety of sources and covering several centuries, across which its author looks from his own particular standpoint, is without even inferior parallel in the Anglo-Saxon period. As a form of historical record it may be contrasted with annals such as constitute the *Anglo-Saxon Chronicle*. Annals record the occurrences of the immediate past. They are a kind of diary, but the unit of record is the year, not the day. Annals are threads, history a fabric. Whereas such a history as Bede's is likely to reveal some of the interests and prejudices, as well as the character, of it author, annals are anonymous and they will tend to be dry, factual, precise. The particular advantage of an annalistic chronicle is that it can be set aside by the writer and taken up again by himself or by another as circumstances suggest and opportunities arise. It is not necessarily dependent on the lifetime of any particular individual.

There can be little doubt that some records of significant events were being kept in different parts of England almost as soon as Christianity had become established, although these very early records now survive, if at all, only in later collections. The chief collection of annals relating to the Anglo-Saxon period, the work known as the *Anglo-Saxon Chronicle*, is in reality a group of several chronicles written at different times and places, but based on a common stock of entries and therefore standing in close relationship to one another. There is one important respect in which these chronicles are distinguished from the common run of European annals compiled during the Middle Ages. They are written in the vernacular, that is to say in Old English, and not in Latin, and so possess the very greatest interest and importance for the light which they throw on the historical development of the English language. Among the earliest substantial passages of English prose that now survive are the entries describing Alfred's wars against the Danes in the latter part of the ninth century. These entries are found in what is called the A-text of the *Chronicle* which was written near the end of Alfred's reign, that is shortly before A.D. 900. Although the A-text cannot be directly associated with Alfred himself, its compilations and the distribution of copies of it to other centres, may be regarded as a consequence of the stimulus which Alfred gave to educational and historical interests, and, perhaps more particular, to his belief that English could be a written as well as a spoken language.

The authority of the *Chronicle* is greatest when its entries represent the work of contemporary witnesses, as was the case in the ninth century, and perhaps also in the eighth, but some compilers had access to earlier sources which no longer survive independently. It was thus possible to carry the record much further back, although it must not be supposed that a statement about the movement of Anglo-Saxon invaders in the fifth century can have the same authority as a statement about the movement of Danish armies in the reign of Alfred. The latter is a contemporary record, perhaps even of an eye-witness, and the former is a tradition, though a tradition, it may be, of great value. It is known that the A-text of the *Chronicle* was at Winchester in the tenth century where it was continued by various writers until 975 when it ceased to be an effective record. It was at Christchurch, Canterbury, in the eleventh century, and after coming into the hands of archbishop Matthew Parker in the sixteenth, it passed into the possession of Corpus Christi College, Cambridge, in whose library it is still preserved. Although the different texts of the *Chronicle* are the main source of annals for times before the reign of Alfred, there is also some information to be gathered from the works of certain writers of later ages who had access to early materials now lost, such men as Florence of Worcester, Symeon of Durham and Roger of Wendover. It is mainly from such material as this that the narrative of Anglo-Saxon history has been reconstructed.

Bede was primarily a teacher in his own age, and when he wrote his *History* it was in the hope that the past lives of good men might inspire those who came after towards godly living and help them to shun the ways of evil. The same instructive purpose prompted the writing of saints' *Lives*. But there are other sources which were written by authors whose main aim was neither to instruct nor to commemorate. The fame of Bede's Jarrow or Cuthbert's Lindisfarne should not be allowed to obscure the fact that during the seventh and eighth centuries there were, scattered widely over the country, a large number of monasteries whose occupants, both men and women, attained a high state of education. They were able to correspond freely in fluent Latin not merely with the occupants of other monasteries in England, but also with their own brethren who had set out to work as missionaries among the pagan peoples of north-western Europe. Many of these letters still survive, some of them written in England, rather more of them written home from abroad. With their expressions of the hopes and fears, the joys and sorrows of their authors, they give to this chapter of Anglo-Saxon history a sense of the realities of daily life such as is not to be found in the more formal sources of history.

The saint who immersed himself up to his neck in the chilly waters of the North Sea, while reciting the penitential psalms, may nowadays excite no more than questioning surprise at his manner of worship, but we can sympathise at once with the scribe whose hands were so numbed by the bitter cold of an exceptionally severe winter that he had not been able to complete his task of copying books. Even so, his abbot had been able to send overseas at least some of those books for which the missionaries had asked. A less austere scene rises to our imagination as we picture the nuns of Minster-in-Thanet making ready to meet the request of Boniface who had asked them for a copy of the Epistles of St Peter, all written in letters of the purest gold, so that the heathen to whom he was preaching might be the more impressed by the worth of God's holy word.

Less deserving than either of these are the Northumbrian nobles of whom Bede writes in a letter to Egbert, shortly to become archbishop of York, men who by royal charter incorporated themselves, their wives and families as monasteries so that they might secure exemption from taxation and from military service. The letter in which Bede gives an account of these and other matters touching the state of the Church in the early part of the eighth century brings us, for a brief moment, into even closer touch with his age than does his own *History*.

To illustrate the functions of another group of sources, royal charters, we may turn to the words in which Eddius describes the ceremonial dedication of Wilfrid's new church at Ripon shortly after 670.

> Then St Wilfrid the bishop stood in front of the altar, and turning to the people, in the presence of the kings, read out clearly a list of the lands which the kings, for the good of their souls, had previously, and on that very day as well, presented to him with the agreement and over the signatures of the bishop and all the chief men, and also a list of the consecrated places in various parts which the British clergy had deserted when fleeing from the hostile sword wielded by the warriors of our own nation.

A formal document attested by the ruler in whose name it was made, as well as by a varying number of spiritual and lay dignitaries, the royal charter seems to have come into use in England shortly after the middle of the seventh century. Its ancestry is to be sought in Roman practice and it may well have been introduced by Theodore of Tarsus who was consecrated archbishop of Canterbury in Rome in 668 and reached England in the spring of the following year.

Charters could be issued by persons other than kings, but most of those which survive from Anglo-Saxon times are in fact of royal origin. All the earliest charters—and the oldest genuine examples to have survived date from *c.* 675—serve the purpose illustrated in Eddius' description of the dedication of the church at Ripon, namely the granting of land to religious persons or bodies for the endowment of a church or other form of religious foundation. The charter itself becomes evidence that land so granted has been alienated from the king and that the new owner is entitled to the dues and benefits from it which had formerly been received by him, save for certain common obligations which continue to be due to the crown. From times before the birth of Alfred genuine charters survive from the kingdoms of Kent, Sussex, Essex, Wessex and Mercia, but there are none from East Anglia or Northumbria. Documents such as these, which conveyed substantial economic benefits to their recipients, offered great inducement for forgery and it is not always an easy task even for an expert to distinguish the genuine charter from the forgery, especially when there are so many documents which are neither wholly genuine nor wholly forged.

Also formal in kind, but having affinity in their content with Germanic rather than Roman custom, are the codes of law which were promulgated by the rulers of some of the Anglo-Saxon kingdoms, usually after consultation with the leading members of their nobility met in formal assembly. Three Kentish codes survive from the seventh century, and as a group they represent the oldest surviving body of Teutonic law written in a vernacular tongue, although they are preserved only in a late manuscript. There is also one seventh-century West Saxon code, but there is none of early date from any of the other kingdoms. These early codes of law are for the most part concerned with regulating the penalties for offences against God and the Church, but they are also an important source of information about the social structure of the kingdoms of Kent and Wessex in the seventh century. The lack of any comparable body of evidence for Mercia and Northumbria leaves serious gaps in what can be learned about the social organisation of the midlands and the north in the times before the Danish invasions in the ninth century.

Saints' *Lives*, narrative history, annals, letters, charters—all these are types of writing inherited from parts of the world which either were or had once been within the boundaries of the Roman Empire. These sources of Anglo-Saxon history are ultimately in the same line of historical tradition as the written sources of the Romano-British period. There is, however, one major group of written sources which stands wholly outside this imperial and ecclesiastical tradition. Tacitus, writing of the *Germani* in the first century A.D., refers to their songs and poetry, saying that these formed the only kind of historical tradition which they possessed. The Anglo-Saxons shared this common Germanic love of minstrelsy, and their poets told of Gothic and Burgundian heroes as well as about men of their own race. Oral tradition of this kind can only be known to us now in so far as it was at some time committed to writing, yet there is good evidence for believing that in the days before the Anglo-Saxons could read or write there was a considerable bulk of oral literature circulating amongst them.

The story of Cædmon, the cowherd who lived at Whitby in the seventh century and who is the first English poet known to us by name, rightly finds a place in the nursery history books. Only a little less familiar is William of Malmesbury's tale of the wily Aldhelm, bishop of Sherborne early in the eighth century, who used to take up his stand on a bridge in the manner of a professional minstrel and sing songs to those who passed by in the hope that he might thereby persuade them to listen to weightier discourse in church. To these references from Northumbria and Wessex may be added another from East Anglia. An entry in the *Chronicle* for the year 792 records briefly the execution of a king of East Anglia by Offa, king of Mercia. A later work describes how, on his journey to the Mercian court, the East Anglian king was preceded by young men who sang songs about the deeds of his ancestors. This Offa, who built the dyke which still bears his name, was a descendant of another king of the same name who ruled over the Angles before they migrated to Britain and who figured prominently in the heroic traditions of the Anglo-Saxons. Some of these stories lingered on in current English tradition until they were written down at St Albans in the thirteenth century. There is, then, plenty of evidence—not forgetting the harp found in the Sutton Hoo burial ship—for the widespread currency in Anglo-Saxon times of stories about men and women of the Germanic Heroic Age, even though times, places and people were apt to become confused over the centuries. Most of these stories have been lost utterly, and others are known to us now only in part, through allusions which would have been fully understood in their own day, but whose full meaning now escapes us.

The Church monopolised the transmission of written documents in early Anglo-Saxon times, and it is probably for this reason that most of the surviving poetry is religious in kind, drawing for its subjects upon the books of the Old and New Testaments and upon other early Christian literature. The traditional forms and the ancient poetic skills, developed through centuries of use, were a means which could be adapted for the instruction of an aristocratic audience, no less than humbler people, in the fundamental teachings of Christianity. Cædmon, as Bede tells, was divinely inspired to compose a hymn in praise of God the Creator. This work, which still survives, is the oldest Christian hymn in the English language. Thereafter he abandoned his secular way of life and entered the monastery at Whitby, where he was fully instructed in the Holy Scriptures. His lesson completed, he would go away and chew upon it, as a cow chews the cud—the metaphor is Bede's—and then, returning to his teachers, he would recite it to them, all turned into the sweet-sounding song of his own language. The subjects of his poetry were taken in part from the books of Genesis and Exodus, but he sang also of the Incarnation, the Passion, the Resurrection and Ascension, the coming of the Holy Spirit and the teaching of the Apostles. Although there are a number of surviving religious poems whose content resembles that of some of the poems attributed to Cædmon by Bede, it is not at present believed that any of Cædmon's own work remains except for his hymn to the Creator.

Later than the times of Cædmon, though exactly how much later is not certain, are the poems of Cynewulf of whose personal history nothing is known, save that he was a skilled poet who was very widely read in Latin religious works. Such a man must have been an ecclesiastic. There are four poems which bear his signature—*Juliana*, the legend of a Christian martyr, *Elene*, which describes the vision of the Cross seen by Constantine the Great and the finding of the Cross itself by Helena Augusta, a piece entitled *The Fates of the Apostles* based ultimately on the Greek *Acts*, and a poem on the *Ascension*. Although there are noble passages to be found in these and other religious poems of early Anglo-Saxon times, as a whole they are scarcely to be reckoned as still being part of the living body of English poetry, largely because they rest upon a double translation, from Latin into Anglo-Saxon as well as from prose into verse, rather than upon the first-hand emotional experiences of their authors. Even so, they are of high value for the light which they throw upon the means used for spreading the knowledge of Christianity among the Anglo-Saxons. It is these poems, not the Bible and their other sources, which reflect for us today the image of Christianity as it was presented to the common Anglo-Saxon people in early times. From them we can also learn something about the religious books which were circulating in the monasteries, and they are of course a major source of information about the vocabulary of the Anglo-Saxon language as well as the technique of its verse-making.

A close approach to the deeper emotions of the Anglo-Saxons is not likely to lie through this kind of religious poetry which has for its setting times and places known to the poets only at several removes. No doubt there were many men and women who underwent deep spiritual experiences, and there was certainly one who brought the highest poetic skill to the expression of such experience in the poem called *The Dream of the Rood*. The narrator of this poem is the Cross itself appearing to a sleeper in a vision and telling its own fearful and wonderful story from the time when it first grew as a tree in a wood until, after it had borne aloft the crucified Christ, it was thrown down and buried in a pit, only to become in the end a jewel-decked symbol honoured among men the world over. This moving poem is known to us now from a manuscript which was written in southern England in about the year A.D. 1000, but a similar poem was known in Northumbria at least two centuries earlier. Visitors to Ruthwell on the northern shore of the Solway Firth can see some extracts from it carved in the runic alphabet upon the great sculptured cross which is now housed within the church.

Comparable with *The Dream of the Rood* in the living intensity of the emotions which they express are other poems touched, and perhaps more than touched, by Christian thought. In such poems—*The Wanderer, The Seafarer, The Ruin*—the miseries and loneliness of a man without friends or home, the struggles of the sailor against the pitiless storms of the winter sea, and the transient nature of mere earthly joys, are themes which have lost none of their poignancy in this present world.

Such works, like the *Riddles*, those brief and sometimes enchanting miniatures in which common objects of the world around are drawn in deep disguise, may present problems to critics. We do not know by whom they were written and we cannot do much more than guess where or when. They contribute nothing to the understanding of narrative history, the development of government or changing economy, but as giving insight into the hearts and minds of men and women, they must be reckoned among the most important of the historical sources.

Almost all the surviving body of Anglo-Saxon poetry is preserved in one or other of four manuscript books which were written in England within a decade or so of the year 1000: the Exeter Book which is still at Exeter where it has been since the eleventh century, the Junius Manuscript which is now in the Bodleian Library at Oxford, the Vercelli Book which had reached Italy by the latter part of the eleventh century, and finally the Beowulf Manuscript which is in the British Museum and which contains the unique copy of the only surviving Anglo-Saxon poem written on an epic scale. *Beowulf* is the oldest narrative poem on such a scale in any European tongue outside the classical world, and as a source of information about the Anglo-Saxons it ranks with Bede's *Ecclesiastical History* and the *Anglo-Saxon Chronicle.* This great poem was first published by Thorkelin in 1815, and although many scholars have worked upon it since, it has not received sustained and detailed study until comparatively recent times.

Recalling the revolutionary consequences of the Sutton Hoo discoveries for Beowulf's studies as a whole, it would be foolish to suppose that the judgments of scholars about the poem have moved so near to finality that they are unlikely to be altered substantially by further study. We do not know, and have little prospect of ever knowing, who wrote the poem, but most scholars now think, as they have not always done, that it is the polished work of one poet who was wholly Christian in his own outlook, well read in the literature of his day and highly skilled in his poetic art. It is difficult to think that the poem can have been composed earlier than *c.* 650 or later than *c.* 850, and if this wide stretch of time can be narrowed, perhaps the eighth century seems the most likely period. The scene of the poem is set in Denmark and Sweden. Beowulf himself, the hero, is a wholly fictitious character, and as fiction also, based on folk tale, we must regard the narrative as a whole which rests upon the struggles of Beowulf against three creatures of evil. His first adversary was Grendel, a monstrous creature who had brought grief and misery to the Danish court by his nightly attacks on Heorot, the great hall of the Danish king Hrothgar. His second fight was against Grendel's mother whom he attacked and slew in a lair hidden deep beneath a pestilential mere whose bloodstained waters were filled with venomous reptiles. Beowulf's third and final victory, which cost his own life as well as his opponent's, was over a dragon which had been enraged by an attempt to rob it of part of a treasure which it guarded.

Beowulf's struggles against these evil creatures are placed in a setting which seems to be based at least in part upon historical fact. The tribes who figure most prominently in the poem—Swedes, Geats and Danes—were real people who lived in Sweden and Denmark. Archaeological evidence, together with the study of other literary traditions, mostly preserved in late Scandinavian sources, makes it reasonably certain that the characters who figure as members of their ruling dynasties were also real people, living late in the fifth century or in the first half of the sixth. There is a sense in which *Beowulf* may be described as the earliest written source for the history of Scandinavia, although the historical material in the poem takes the form of allusions to past or future events rather than the form of continuous narrative.

If *Beowulf* is only to a limited extent a source of history, and Scandinavian rather than Anglo-Saxon history at that, the information to be won from it about other aspects of its age is of many different kinds. The vivid account of Scyld's burial with which the poem opens, might serve, with only slight change, for a poetic description of the Sutton Hoo ship burial. The description of Heorot, the great hall of the Danish king, is a literary counterpart of the royal palace recently excavated at Old Yeavering in Northumberland. The account at the close of the poem of Beowulf's own funeral reflects scenes which we may believe to have been enacted at many heathen burial mounds in different parts of England. On these, and on many smaller points of detail about swords and armour, royal standards and battle helmets, swimming, horse racing, seafaring, hunting, court ceremonial and such life, *Beowulf* is an invaluable source of information which can be neglected by no historian or archaeologist whose interests lie in the Anglo-Saxons and their times. At another level we look to the poem for expressions of mind and temper, of moral standards and human ideals. Murder and vengeance, courage and faith, honour and generosity, the bloodthirsty violence of the powers of evil and the gentle strength of ennobled virtue, all these find their expression in what remains in the last resort a great poem whose tragic theme is enlightened by its implicit message of the victory of Christian light over pagan darkness.

Roman Britain was a small part of a great empire and those who looked towards it from Rome were looking outwards to the very edge of the western world. Anglo-Saxon England was politically its own master, not subject to any external governmental control. To Bede, at least, the great mercantile centre to which men of many nations came to buy and sell was London. Rome was a far distant place. The written sources of the two ages reflect this difference of outlook. For Roman Britain they are small in bulk and they are the record of matters that primarily concerned, not Britain, but Rome, its rulers, its military governors and its soldiers. Mere natives provided the means of triumph for some and defeat for others, but otherwise they were of no importance to imperial historians. For Anglo-Saxon England the written sources are not only much larger in quantity, they are also much more richly varied in kind, largely because Britain, the remote province, had given way to a new country which lay at the centre of its own world and whose inhabitants had for the first time become articulate. Yet despite this difference in both quantity and quality, there are some aspects of Britain's history about which we are better informed for the Romano-British period than we are for the early Anglo-Saxon period. For example, a much more detailed account can be written of the conquest of Britain by the Romans in the first century than can be told of the invasion of Britain by the Anglo-Saxons in the fifth and sixth centuries, and if we are to understand why this should be so, we must look at other kinds of evidence.

The most important single source of information about the history and organisation of Roman Britain is of a kind which in its form is written, but in its context is archaeological—namely inscriptions. These stone documents have many of the best qualities of both written and purely archaeological sources. They provide for the Romano-British period the contemporary, authoritative, eye-witness record such as is lacking in the written histories, and they can very often be exactly dated. Moreover, the names of peoples and places to which they refer offer the best witness to the usage of their times, being wholly free from the kind of corruption which may easily arise in manuscript transmission through the mistakes of copyists. Most Romano-British names are, as we have seen, derived from the work of geographers or from imperial roadbooks, but there are many others known from inscriptions recovered on the very site of the place to which they refer. Such witness, comparable to that of the modern road sign recording the name of the village by which it stands, has authority of quite a different order from that of a Mediterranean geographer whose work has been preserved only in late manuscripts.

The modern practice of laying inscribed foundation stones to mark the beginning of work upon an important building is paralleled in Roman times by the setting up of inscriptions, often in quite elaborate terms, to mark the construction, or the restoration, of civil or military buildings. Such inscriptions were frequently placed, like that of modern London's Admiralty Arch, over a gateway where they would catch the eye of those who passed through. The building of the new city hall and market-place at Wroxeter, the tribal capital of the Cornovii, was so commemorated in 129–30 by a splendid monumental inscription of which the greater part still survives. Agricola's fame as governor of Britain rests mainly on his military achievements in the north, but the words in which Tacitus comments on his contribution to the cultural life of the province have taken on new meaning in the light of the discovery at St Albans of an inscription bearing his name and evidently commemorating the erection of a monumental gateway in the city market-place in A.D. 79. Inscriptions bearing the name of the legate Aulus Platorius Nepos are the basic evidence upon which the building of the Roman frontier wall, with its turrets and milecastles, can be attributed to the reign of Hadrian. As the building of this wall, and of its companion across the Forth-Clyde isthmus, went forward, the military units engaged upon the work left their marks behind in the form of brief inscriptions from which it is now possible to learn a great deal about the way in which these immense undertakings were organised and carried to completion.

The history of this frontier zone, the repeated attacks which it suffered and the successive restorations which were thereby made necessary, has been reconstructed very largely, from inscriptions. Altars dedicated to Neptune and Ocean by members of a legion anxious to placate the deities of river floods and tides, the arrival of reinforcements from Germany to make good losses suffered by the legions in a barbarian uprising, the building of a new fort at Brough in Derbyshire or the repair of an old one at Birrens in Dumfriesshire in the second century, and rebuilding from the foundations of a gateway and walls at Risingham in Northumberland in the third century, the restoration in the fourth century of severely damaged buildings at Birdoswald in Cumberland—this is the kind of groundwork, all of it recorded on inscriptions, upon which the narrative of Romano-British history chiefly rests. And to such inscriptions as these may be added others which have a little to tell about the government of Roman Britain, its organisation into provinces, its local administration and the status of some of its towns, a little also to tell about the workings of the lead industry, and a great deal to tell about the deities worshipped by its inhabitants. Building inscriptions were already becoming less common in the third century, and although they are not unknown in the fourth, they are no longer a principal source of its history. Taking a long look forward to the middle of the ninth century, we can find from the whole of the early Anglo-Saxon period only one building inscription in any way comparable with those from the forum at Wroxeter or St Albans, and that one is the dedication stone of the church at Jarrow, dated 23 April 685. There are, indeed, a considerable number of inscriptions from the early Anglo-Saxon period, but most of them are Christian tombstones and only one or two of them can be closely dated.

Roman military forts, whether intended to house a legion, a cohort or a mere military patrol, were designed according to certain standards laid down in military textbooks and prevailing throughout the Empire as a whole. When a Roman fort was damaged by attack, it was the normal Roman practice not to clear the whole site, but to carry out only such levelling as was needed to produce a building surface and to use the debris of the old as foundation for the new. Such debris would certainly contain large quantities of broken pottery, probably a few coins and perhaps some fragments of an inscription. A fort which was severely damaged three or four times at fairly long intervals during its occupation will thus disclose to an excavator three or four layers of debris, each layer resting upon an earlier floor and each layer save the last covered by a later floor. When such a pattern is found to be repeated over a wide area at, for example, each of the forts of Hadrian's Wall, and perhaps also at each of its milecastles, making almost a hundred separate sites in all—it becomes possible to associate the layers of debris with particular and exactly dated occasions known to historians. When it is known that a particular site was destroyed *c.* 196, again *c.* 296 and a third time *c.* 367, and that it was rebuilt or repaired after each destruction, it then becomes possible to give dates to material found in the layers of debris, such as coarse pottery, which is not datable by its own nature. Once the changing types of pottery have been established within moderately close limits, these types can be used as a chronological yardstick upon other sites, not necessarily military ones, whose occupation does not reveal the same pattern of destruction and repair.

This, reduced, let it be said, to terms of extreme simplicity, is the basis of Romano-British archaeology in the military zone of Britain. The excavator of such a site as the Claudian auxiliary fort at Hod Hill in Dorset or the Agricolan legionary fortress at Inchtuthil in Perthshire can bring to the difficulties of his task the knowledge that much of what he finds will conform to an imperial pattern and that he may be able to draw upon comparative material from Spain, Africa or Romania. Some measure of this conformity to a standard will also occur on sites in the civil zone away from the centres of military occupation. The street pattern of a town may be regular in plan and its defensive walls may reflect conditions which were not peculiar to itself, but were shared by other towns over a wide area, perhaps conditions of public investment in impressive buildings, perhaps conditions of insecurity arising from the threat of external attack. A farmhouse may likewise conform to one of a small number of easily recognised types, with a standard heating system and a regular layout of its rooms. Yet materials of this kind cannot easily be made to tell so much about the social and economic life of the countryside, its phases of prosperity or depression, as military sites can be made to tell about the history of a frontier zone. A well-directed excavation can recover the plan and, with luck, much of the history, of a five-acre fort in a matter of weeks, especially if the site is still open land. Even though such a fort may have been occupied for only a decade and then systematically dismantled it can still be made to tell its tale. A town site, maybe of a hundred acres and probably encumbered with buildings of every age to the present day, offers much more difficult problems, and it is even more difficult to discover how many acres of land belonged to a particular farm in the country, what was the size of its fields, what its methods of cultivation and what the crops it grew.

The material remains of Roman Britain reflect, as we might expect them to do, some of the qualities of that Empire from which most of them derive. They are exact and precise in their military aspects, they conform to a common pattern over much even of the civilian area, and they were made to last. Economically the change from Roman Britain to Anglo-Saxon England was a disaster. The newcomers, although skilled as shipwrights and workers in metal, lacked many of the techniques and almost all the resources which had been at the service of the Roman Empire. They built mainly in wood, using stone only where old Roman buildings offered quarries of ready-cut material, they did not coin money and they were incapable of carving any but the very simplest of inscriptions, and even then only in the runic alphabet. Those kinds of archaeological evidence which give chronological precision to the history of Roman Britain are almost entirely lacking from the age of the Anglo-Saxon invasions. The urns containing the incinerated remains of men and women, the weapons and jewellery from inhumation burials are not promising material from which to reconstruct the course of an invasion, yet it is of such that most of the archaeological evidence from the pagan days of Anglo-Saxon England at present consists.

Although such evidence has much to tell about the origin of the invaders, as well as about the force and direction of their movements into Britain, we must remember how great has been the element of chance in its discovery. The farmer's plough, the picks and shovels of builders' labourers, and more recently the mechanical excavator, have been the chief instruments in bringing Anglo-Saxon burials to light. We cannot even guess how much evidence of this kind was destroyed during the rapid growth of industrial towns, especially in the area of Greater London, during the eighteenth and nineteenth centuries. But it is not only in the urban areas that the evidence may present a distorted picture. Whether or not dead men's bones survive in the ground depends mainly upon the nature of the soil in which they are buried. In one place a skeleton can remain in an excellent state of preservation for centuries or even millennia. In another it can vanish so completely as to leave no visible trace.

The pagan Anglo-Saxons usually buried their dead in shallow pits dug into the ground. Sometimes the remains were first cremated and the ashes then placed in an urn; sometimes the bodies were buried unburnt. But in either case it was unusual for a pagan burial place of the Anglo-Saxon period to be marked by a mound or any other kind of surface memorial. A small group of barrows which lie on the sandy heath called Sutton Hoo, overlooking the estuary of the river Deben and the town of Woodbridge in Suffolk, form a notable exception (see map on p. 191). As a group they seem to represent the burial ground of a royal dynasty, and in one of them, during the summer of 1939, when this same eastern coast was once more being threatened by invasion, there were discovered the contents of a royal burial chamber, untouched since their deposition at about the middle of the seventh century. The soil was not of a kind favourable for the preservation of bones, so that after even the most careful excavation had failed to reveal any trace of a human being, chemical tests were necessary before it could be established beyond reasonable doubt that no body had ever lain in the burial chamber itself.

The Sutton Hoo memorial was a cenotaph constructed from a great open rowing boat, 80 feet long and 14 feet wide at its greatest beam. Propelled by 38 oarsmen, it was perhaps the kind of boat in which some of the ancestors of those who hauled it up the steep slope from the river below had crossed to England from the mainland of Europe. Its journey from the river bank to the immense grave which had been dug to receive it was one of about half a mile, rising a little over 100 feet in vertical height. When the boat had been lowered into the grave, a wooden chamber with gabled roof was built amidships and within this chamber there was laid a treasure of such splendour that it is without parallel in the archaeology of western Europe. Here was gold jewellery- of the highest excellence both technically and aesthetically, silver plate of which at least one piece was of Byzantine origin, weapons, some of them thought to be of Swedish origin, gold coins imported from Merovingian Gaul, and a great quantity of iron work, fragments of textiles, leather and many other objects, including the remains of a small harp. When this splendid treasure had been laid within the burial chamber the whole ship was covered with a great mound of sandy soil.

Years of study will be needed before the significance of the discoveries made at Sutton Hoo can be fully understood. We do not yet know, and perhaps we shall never know for certain, the identity of the person commemorated by this monument, nor can we at present be more precise about its date than to say that the ship and its treasure were probably buried within twenty years of 660. Whatever answers may yet be given to these and other puzzling questions it is certain that no-one can take an intelligent interest in them without making more than a passing acquaintance with that other great monument of the Anglo-Saxon age—the poem *Beowulf*. Each of the two illumines the other at innumerable points. Neither of the two can be understood in isolation.

Another recent and important excavation provides a further example of this interdependence of archaeological and literary evidence, and an example also of the immensely important body of new evidence which has been won in recent years by means of aerial photography. This site, at Old Yeavering in northern Northumberland, was at first no more than a group of variegated marks, invisible on the ground, but conforming to a regular pattern when seen from the air. While in process of being excavated, it was very little more than a complex arrangement of holes in the ground left where timbers had decayed, but from this evidence it has been possible to recover in very considerable detail the history of a royal palace in late pagan and early Christian times, from its first foundation in the sixth century through succcessive destructions and rebuildings to its final abandonment in the seventh. The remains at Old Yeavering are illuminated by the poetical descriptions of the hall in *Beowulf* called 'Heorot' no less than the finds at Sutton Hoo are illuminated by the account of the burial of Scyld and by other passages in the same poem. (See Appendix B, pp. 285–6.)

The site at Old Yeavering when discovered by aerial photography was under grass. The growth of corn crops or of grass can be variously affected by the earlier disturbance of the soil beneath them. Stone walls or paved streets, lying just far enough below the surface to escape the destructive action of the ploughshare upon them, alter the moisture content of the soil above them so that when the season of ripeness approaches, more particularly in times of drought, crops lying over structures of this kind will have a more stunted growth and will ripen sooner than those which can draw moisture from a greater depth of soil beneath them. If, on the other hands, crops are planted in a field beneath which lie the remains of ditches or of wooden buildings, the effect upon them may be quite the opposite. Ditches enclosing a military fort, a civil town or even a farm building were often dug to a considerable depth, and if, after remaining open for a while, they gradually became filled by the natural processes of erosion and silting, they might in many cases provide a richer, or at least a contrasting, subsoil for the crops grown above them at the present day. So also with wooden buildings whose posts and beams were left to rot over the years. In this way the varying growth of vegetation can reveal the pattern of disturbance lying beneath, the pattern it may be of streets and buildings belonging to a town of which little or no trace remains above ground, the pattern of defensive ditches enclosing a military site or the outline of post holes which once formed part of a wooden temple or a farm building.

Marks such as these are usually too slight to be seen from ground level, but in favourable conditions they show up with startling clarity from the air. The play of light and shadow, or the lie of snow affected by eddying currents of air over slightly undulating ground, may also reveal shallow banks and hollows which are too slight to be detected by anyone on foot, or if they should be noticed, too confused to give any suggestion of a regular, artificial pattern. Even where surface remains may be prominent, an aerial view can sometimes give fresh detail that may help to solve an old problem or pose a new one. The use of aerial photography has already transformed the map of Roman Britain in many areas, adding to it new sites, both civil and military, and offering more detailed information about some of those already known. Farming in the East Anglian fens and the distribution of military forces in the south-west of Scotland are two important aspects of Romano-British history about which virtually nothing was known before the days of aerial photography.

The site at Old Yeavering is that of a royal palace, and its construction, though wholly of timber, was on a scale commensurate with its function. Moreover, after its abandonment, it was never subsequently reoccupied. Even aerial photography has so far been able to make very little contribution to the problem of identifying the homes and houses, the farms and villages of those who are now known to us only from their graves. Perhaps it is that the building materials which they used were too slight to have left their mark and their foundations too shallow to have survived after centuries of ploughing. Perhaps it is also that many of the sites on which they first settled have remained in occupation ever since and lie beneath the foundations of today's farms and villages. The study of place-names, which is essentially a linguistic study, has gone some way towards filling this gap.

Place-names reflect the language used by those who gave the names. The languages spoken in Britain as native tongues before the time of Alfred the Great fall into two groups—the Celtic and the Germanic. The Celtic can be subdivided into a British language from which are descended Welsh, Cornish (now extinct) and Breton, and a Goidelic language which was the ancestor of Irish, Scottish and Manx Gaelic. The primitive Germanic language was the ancestor of a west European group comprising Old High German, Old Saxon, Frankish, Old Frisian and Old English. This last is the name given to the language spoken by the Anglo-Saxon invaders, and it has developed through Middle English into the Modern English which we speak today. The primitive Celtic language was once spoken over a very wide area of Europe, and it was only in comparatively recent times that its descendants came to be confined to the western fringes of Britain and to north-western France. During the Roman occupation of Britain most of those who lived in the occupied part of the country spoke the British language, but when Britain passed out of Roman control and was possessed by the invading Anglo-Saxons, the British language gradually retreated towards the west where it underwent a process of rapid change and development. During and after the time of Alfred the Great another descendant of the primitive Germanic language was introduced into Britain. This we call Old Norse. It was spoken in those northern, eastern and midland parts of England which were settled by the Danes—the Danelaw—and also in north-western England, as well as in parts of the mainland of Scotland and in the neighbouring islands where there were extensive settlements of Vikings from Norway.

While Britain formed part of the Roman Empire Latin was spoken by some elements in its population, notably by the governing classes, by those concerned with administration, the army and trade, and probably by the better educated among those who lived in towns. But Latin was a second language, a mark of mannered society, and there can be no doubt that the population as a whole was not Latin-speaking. Latin, however, was the only written language current in Roman Britain. Literacy, and therefore the use of Latin, was destroyed in those parts of the country occupied by the Anglo-Saxons and it survived only in the west. After the conversion to Christianity Latin came back into use among the Anglo-Saxons as the language of scholarship and learning. Old English was not extensively used as a written language until the time of Alfred.

There is much to be learned from the study of place-names about the pattern of settlement arising from successive invasions and about the geographical relationship of the newcomers in one age to their predecessors of another. Devon and Cornwall take us back through Old English forms to the Celtic *Dumnonii* and *Cornovii*, but the *Trinovantes* and the *Iceni* who lived in the eastern part of Roman Britain have been wholly overlaid by Norfolk, Suffolk and Essex, all of them English names in origin, just as the Old English name *Norpworpig* was later overlaid by the Scandinavian Derby. Other names of a type represented by Angmering in Sussex, Godalming in Surrey and Barking in Essex have been made to yield important evidence about the nature of the earliest Anglo-Saxon settlements. Others, such as Harrowden and Weedon, both containing elements referring to heathen worship, or such as Thunderfield, Tuesley and Wednesbury, which refer to the heathen gods Thunor, Tiw and Woden, tell us something about old pagan practices. Other kinds of name throw light on institutions—Mutlow refers to a hill on which a local assembly held its meeting; on the classes of society—Aldermanbury is the ealdorman's manor; on agrarian customs—Buckland is *boc land*, that is land granted by royal charter; and upon innumerable other aspects of life in the towns, villages, farms, woodlands, downs and fens of Anglo-Saxon England.

CHAPTER TWO

FROM JULIUS CAESAR TO BOUDICCA

The inhabitants of Britain have learned to look upon their island as a 'fortress built by nature for herself against infection and the hand of war', but their long respite from overseas invasion, since William of Normandy landed nine centuries ago, has been due at least as much to their own exertions as to the waters by which they are surrounded. The Spaniards, the French and the Germans were not repelled by natural obstacles; neither were the Celts, the Romans, the Anglo-Saxons, the Danes or the Normans. Britain is indeed an island, but an island which, on a clear day, lies within sight unaided by telescope of the neighbouring mainland. This distant view of Britain's white cliffs was no doubt the spur which set in motion many successive movements across the narrow Channel, some of them on a scale large enough to be called invasions, others no more than incursions of small bands of adventurers or traders. Prehistoric studies have now so altered our perspective view of the past that we can see Britain's recorded history from Julius Caesar to the present day as no more than a small fraction of the long ages during which men of the human race have lived within the country. The colossal horseshoe setting of lintelled trilithons which is now the dominating feature of Stonehenge is thought to have been set up by people whose arrival in Britain, from about 1900 B.C. was accompanied by that rapid expansion in the use of bronze for tools and weapons which led to the epoch's being designated the Early Bronze Age. Yet these trilithons themselves mark a comparatively late stage in the development of this unique monument whose beginnings lie in far distant neolithic times when no metal was yet being used in Britain.

No close date can be given to the first arrival in Britain of men who used iron for their weapons and tools. The transition from Late Bronze Age to Early Iron Age was a gradual process varying no less in its thoroughness than in its pace, but the process seems to have begun in parts of southern Britain in the fifth century B.C. Over a period of about four hundred years successive groups of people, racially much alike perhaps, but showing distinctive features in their culture, crossed the narrow seas from homes which lay as far west as Brittany or as far east and north as the Rhine mouths. The age was characterised by periodic warfare as this or that dynasty sought to establish its authority over its neighbours, in much the same way as the Anglo-Saxon kingdoms struggled among themselves in the sixth and seventh centuries A.D. By the time of Caesar's first expedition to Britain in 55 B.C. migratory movements had established close ties of kinship and common interest between the peoples who lived in Gaul and some of the inhabitants of Britain. The *Parisi* who lived where now lies the East Riding of Yorkshire were kinsmen of those who gave their name to the capital of modern France. Yet it was not merely that parts of Britain and Gaul were inhabited by men who were akin to one another and who spoke a common language. There was a time when that Celtic language might have been heard as far east as Constantinople, and community of language was a feature of a large part of Europe in the last four or five centuries B.C.

What was of greater importance than this for both Britain and Rome was that the earlier homelands of some at least of the Iron Age migrants to Britain were absorbed into the Roman Empire to form the provinces of Belgica and Gallia Lugdunensis. Herein lay one of the more compelling reasons which led to the conquest of Britain itself by the Romans. British incitement to rebellion against Roman authority in Gaul, or a search for Roman support by an exiled chieftain seeking to overthrow his enemies in Britain, are manifestations of a degree of military and political intermingling between the peoples on the two sides of the Channel which would make it difficult for the Romans, having conquered the one, to defer for long the conquest of the other. Moreover, if a large army was needed to secure Gaul against insurrection prompted from Britain, that same army could as well be used to secure Britain and thereby bring other advantages to Rome.

Yet increased security for Gaul, or fresh triumphs for the Roman legions, were incidental to the more substantial gains from which Rome might expect to profit eventually by the conquest of Britain. Those parts of the country about which Caesar knew at first hand, or about which he had been informed by his agents, were thickly populated according to the standards of the day. Hopes that a country which was known to have deposits of tin in the south-west and iron ore in the south-east might also have other minerals in areas as yet unknown to the Romans, were fulfilled in that exploitation of the rich deposits of lead in the Mendips which followed swiftly upon the Claudian conquest. Although the inhabitants of the island were still dominated by its natural vegetation, by the distribution of forest, scrub and marsh in their natural state, some at least of them were beginning to profit from the new methods of ploughing which enabled them to attack the heavier soils whence richer crops might be harvested. Yields beyond the needs of mere subsistence were beginning to leave a surplus for export. Such increasing prosperity found expression in the coinage of the Catuvellauni who symbolised the source of their wealth, which they won from these heavier soils, by using the corn ear as decoration for one side of their coins.

The Catuvellauni were not the only people of Roman Britain who had reached that stage of economic development in which goods could be bought and sold for coined money. Neither was corn Britain's only export. Strabo (who died *c.* A.D. 21), names also cattle, iron, hides, slaves and dogs. The export trade in slaves was still flourishing in St Patrick's day in the fifth century and English dogs were still highly prized in Italy in the eleventh. Back to Britain came glass-ware and pottery from Gaul or from Italy itself, as well as luxuries such as amber and bracelets or necklaces made of ivory. Belgic Gaul was the source whence coinage was introduced to Britain, and coined money came to play a significant part in the economy of the country, primarily in the south-east among the Trinovantes of Essex, among their western neighbours, the Catuvellauni, among the Cantii of Kent and the Atrebates whose capital lay at Silchester. Coins were also used by more distant tribes who were less directly subject to continental influences, such as the Iceni of East Anglia, the Coritani of the Trent basin and the Dobunni of the lower Severn area. The economy of these more distant people rested, according to Caesar, primarily upon stock-raising rather than upon corn-growing.

Although Caesar describes the people of Kent as being the most highly civilised of Britain's inhabitants, it was the Catuvellauni who were the most powerful and aggressive tribe in the south-eastern part of the country. Their ruler, Cassivellaunus, had killed the king of the Trinovantes who thereupon became suppliants for Roman help. Caesar's second expedition, in 54 B.C., took him as far as the stronghold of Cassivellaunus, which he found to be stoutly defended by forest and marsh, and well supplied with both men and cattle. The site is thought to be represented by the massive defences at Wheathampstead in Hertfordshire which, supplementing natural protection offered by heavy forest, enclose an area of about a hundred acres, more than twice the area of a legionary fortress designed to house six thousand men.

Caesar's troops had learned that their opponents had evolved methods of fighting on open ground which made them formidable enemies. In particular, their use of the horse-drawn chariot had, by long and arduous training, given them a degree of mobility which placed the more heavily armed and cumbersome legions at some disadvantage. The swift and sudden onslaught at full gallop down a steep slope, followed by quick withdrawal, gave them, as Caesar put it, the mobility of cavalry and the staying power of infantry. But an assault against a set position, however strong its defences, was a different proposition for the Romans, and one of which they had had much experience in Gaul. The stronghold of Cassivellaunus was taken, along with many prisoners, and Cassivellaunus himself, after a final fling, came to terms. Among the terms imposed upon him was an undertaking that he would cease from his aggression against the Trinovantes, an undertaking which was not likely to be observed unless it was enforced. When next we can get a glimpse of the political situation in this part of Britain, shortly after the beginning of the Christian era, the Trinovantes had been completely absorbed by the Catuvellauni whose ruler, Cunobelinus, had transferred his capital to Camulodunum at Colchester, in the heart of Trinovantian territory. Here, a little to the north and west of the medieval and modern city, on a stretch of firm ground near to what was probably the lowest tide-free ford across the river Colne, lay the nucleus of a great fortified area of some twelve square miles. Its prosperity, to which its remains bear witness, rested partly on overseas trade, and as the largest and richest city of south-eastern Britain it became the first objective of the invading armies of Claudius which landed in Kent in A.D. 43.

The invasion was carried out by four Roman legions under the command of Aulus Plautius, the Second Augusta, the Ninth Hispana, the Fourteenth Gemina and the Twentieth

Valeria Victrix, a body of about twenty-five thousand men if the legions were all at full strength. To these must be added a number of auxiliary regiments, as well as those whose task it was to ferry such formidable numbers across the Channel. After some difficulties with troops brought to the verge of rebellion against being shipped to what they regarded as the ends of the earth, the expedition set off in three separate divisions, seeking thereby to confuse any possible opponents by spreading their initial assault more widely. One of the points at which they came to land was Richborough, where a fortified bridge-head was established for the landing and housing of stores. Other landings may have been made at Dover and Lympne which offered good harbourage, but they have not so far yielded any positive evidence of Roman occupation at this moment of invasion.

The landings, which were unopposed, were followed by preliminary skirmishes in Kent against British forces led by Togodumnus and Caratacus, but the first serious opposition to the Roman advance came at the crossing of the river Medway, a crossing which was achieved only after two days of heavy fighting. The British, perhaps divided in their counsels by dual leadership, withdrew across the Thames. At this point Aulus Plautius called a halt, so that there might be time for the emperor Claudius to come up and himself direct not only the crossing of the Thames, but also the subsequent advance to their prize, Camulodunum, a trophy which might be held to deserve the honours of a military triumph in Rome.

The next stage of the Roman advance across Britain cannot be told in detail. The tracks are as those of a fox or a hare running across a field on which there is a patch or two of snow, now showing an imprint sharp and clearly cut, now a little blurred at the edges, now vanishing completely, and leaving a doubt, when they reappear, whether they are the tracks of the same animal or those of another which passed that way later in the day. The tracks of the Roman army may take the form of a Roman soldier's tombstone with an epitaph naming the military unit to which he belonged, such as may be seen in the museums at Colchester or Shrewsbury. They may take the form of pottery of Claudian date found, somewhat unexpectedly, at the bottom of a well half-way between Lincoln and Leicester. Or again they may appear as the remains of military earthworks marking the Roman occupation of an

Iron Age hill fort in Dorset. Or, perhaps most forcefully of all, we may find them as roads cutting purposefully across the English plain from London. The Thames could be forded near Westminster, but a bridge gave obvious advantages to a marching army. It was the near approach of gravel beds to the river banks on either side which made the building of a bridge an easy task for Roman engineers, and which also made the fortunes of London. From London the roads strike northwards to Lincoln, north-westwards to Wroxeter and Chester, and south-westwards to Silchester, Old Sarum and Dorchester. Such roads, unlike the trackways of pre-Roman Britain, were the work of military engineers whose aim was to provide ease of communication and the means of moving troops rapidly from one part of the country to another. The blazing of at least the more important of these roads is likely to have proceeded concomitantly with the advance itself and so their general direction may have something to tell about the principal lines upon which that advance was made.

The Ninth Legion Hispana may have been the one responsible for building much of the road known now as Ermine Street—an ancient name, though not quite as old as Roman times, for it derives from a small group of Anglo-Saxons called the *Earningas* who settled near it on its passage through what is now southern Cambridgeshire. Farther north this road strikes the Lincoln Edge, the chalk ridge which leads on, with two breaks, to the wolds in the East Riding of Yorkshire. The major of these two breaks is formed by the Humber estuary. The lesser of the two is made by the Witham which, after flowing northwards on a course parallel to that of the Trent, then turns sharply eastwards through a gap in the chalk to make its way down to the Wash. Here, at the gap, high above the left bank of the river on a site now dominated by the great medieval cathedral of Lincoln, tracks of the legion are clearly revealed to those who know where to look.

Tombstones, coins and pottery of Claudian date were strong presumptive evidence for the existence of a legionary fortress on this site from very early times in the occupation. Excavation has now located its defences on each of its four sides. Something still remains of the massive ditch cut through the rock and also of the earthen rampart laid upon timber strapping and with revetted timber front which enclosed an area of rather more than 43 acres. The occupation began about the year 48, five years after the first landing, and the timber defences were of such stoutness that in some places they were still in use a hundred years later, though by that time Lincoln had long ceased to be a legionary base.

Another of the four invading legions, the Second Augusta, was operating on the left flank, towards the south-west, under the command of Vespasian who was later to become emperor. Under his leadership, says Suetonius, it conquered two very powerful tribes and more than twenty fortified strongholds (*oppida*), as well as bringing the Isle of Wight into subjection. The tribes can be identified with the Belgae and the Durotriges whose lands corresponded roughly with Wiltshire, Somerset and Dorset. An *oppidum,* in those parts of south-eastern Britain known to Caesar, was a densely wooded area fortified with a rampart and ditch, but the *oppida* assaulted by the Second Legion in the south-west of the country were something very different.

Westwards from the Hampshire Avon across Cranborne Chase and the Dorset Downs, leading on towards the borders of Devonshire, lies a belt of upland country where broken stretches of woodland emphasise by their contrast the sweeping expanse of open chalk down. Within this area, dominating the landscape much as did the baronial castles of Stephen's reign in the twelfth century, and a witness to similar conditions of insecurity, there lie more than seventy hill forts, some of them with two or three lines of defence and elaborate outworks to protect the main entrances. The most famous of them, Maiden Castle, enclosed at its greatest extent about 45 acres, a little more than the legionary fortress at Lincoln. Although this site was first occupied in neolithic times, the final elaboration of its defences belongs to the later stages of the Iron Age. The defences of many other Wessex hill forts were being strengthened at the same time and many are known to have been in occupation at the time of the Roman invasion. Strongholds such as these were not merely places of refuge in times of need, neither were they, like the Anglo-Saxon *burh* of Alfred the Great's time, the result of some uniform design imposed upon the area by a controlling authority. They were permanently occupied as the stronghold of individual groups whose leaders had considerable resources at their command. These were the *oppida* with which the Second Legion was faced in its westerly advance, and among them there are some at which the Roman tracks are deeply cut.

Lying on the line of advance from Southampton Water, in a commanding position which later made it the focal point of several Roman roads, is another of the Wessex hill forts, Badbury Rings. This great circular fortification is thought to have been the scene of a battle in which the native British defeated Anglo-Saxon invaders late in the fifth century, a battle which later romancers associated with Arthur. There is at present no evidence of a Roman assault upon Badbury Rings about the middle of the first century, but the evidence from Maiden Castle and Hod Hill will hardly permit us to suppose that the Romans allowed it to remain in hostile hands. At Maiden Castle itself the major assault took place at the eastern end, where the defences were a little less formidable than those at the west. The iron-shod ballista bolts, the ashes and post holes of the burned huts, the roughly hewn graves with victims of the Roman assault, some with sword cuts on their skulls, one with an arrowhead embedded in a vertebra, another with a skull pierced by an iron spearhead, some holding joints of meat in their hands, others accompanied by food vessels and drinking cups – all these, together with the minutely detailed study of the lie of overthrown and tumbled defences, are the foundations upon which we can now reconstruct an account of the storming of the eastern gateway of Maiden Castle in itself no less vivid than the accounts written by Tacitus of later episodes in the conquest of Britain by the Romans, of the assault by Ostorius Scapula on a strongly defended hill fort among the Welsh mountains, of the attack against Anglesey led by Suetonius Paulinus, or of Agricola's final battle against the Caledonian tribes at Mons Graupius in north-eastern Scotland.

Twenty miles by crow's flight to the north-east of Maiden Castle, the Stour cuts through a gap between the chalk uplands of Cranborne Chase on the one side and the Dorset Downs on the other. Two of the hills which flank the northern side of this gap are fortified, and in the corner of one of them, Hod Hill, there lies embedded a Roman fort which makes use of the Iron Age defences for two of its four sides. Excavation at this site has told a very different tale from that of Maiden Castle. The defences of the Roman fort have been examined and one after another its internal buildings identified and planned—the headquarters building, the commandant's house, barracks for a contingent of legionaries, stables for a detachment of cavalrymen's horses, granaries for the feeding of both: all these displaying the characteristic Roman conformity to a pattern and yet yielding something unique in Britain, a military encampment intended for something more than merely transitory occupation and belonging to the Claudian period. Maiden Castle was wholly abandoned after the Roman assault, but the appropriation of Hod Hill in this fashion may suggest that here there lay, for as long as was needed, a military centre from which a close watch could be kept upon the whole of the Wessex uplands and swift action taken should there be any sign of resurgence of that military strength represented by the hill forts. For the rest of the Roman period these chalk downs were a land of farms, not of fortresses. Elsewhere in the south-west, traces of Roman military occupation in the Claudian period have been found at Waddon Hill, north of Bridport, and beneath the later Roman streets of Cirencester.

The Ninth Legion's tracks at Lincoln, like those of the Second at Maiden Castle and Hod Hill, are clear enough, but these places account for not more than half the legionary strength of the invading army. If we ask where the other two legions were quartered during these early years, and also what was happening on the hundred mile stretch between Lincoln and Maiden Castle, it is not easy to find a clear answer. Yet this midland front was undoubtedly of great importance to the Roman high command and there ought to be tracks somewhere across it, if only to show the route taken by the forces which were preparing for the assault upon Anglesey in 61. Perhaps the line of Watling Street crossing the midlands through St Albans, Towcester, High Cross, Wall and Wroxeter is such a track.

To the west of Maiden Castle there lies the southern end of a road which crosses the midlands in the opposite direction, from south-west to north-east, from Exeter to Bath, Cirencester, Leicester and Lincoln. This road, the Fosse Way as it has been called since at least the tenth century, for all that it remains one of the most striking monuments of Roman road-making in the country, is still over much of its length little more than a narrow country byway, if we judge it by modern standards. That it has not been widened to meet the needs of present-day traffic is largely due to the fact that, unlike most of the other major Roman roads of Britain, it does not follow natural lines of communication, perhaps because it was intended to serve some different purpose. Such a purpose might have been to act as the main lateral line of communication at a time when most of the lowland plain of Britain had fallen into Roman hands, but no substantial advance had yet been made into the more difficult country farther north and west.

A road such as the Fosse Way might have formed part of a frontier zone extending as far north as the Humber estuary and as far west as the southern shore of the Bristol Channel, with the valleys of the Trent and the Severn lying beyond, the one overlooked by Lincoln, the other commanded by Gloucester. Such a frontier might have been fortified in some depth, though perhaps not with the solidity of later frontier zones if it were intended merely to mark a temporary stage of consolidation before a further advance was made. This may be one reason why traces of fortifications are not easy to find. Another may be that they have been buried beneath some of the midland towns. Yet several military sites lie in the triangle between Leicester, Cirencester and Wroxeter, and at some of them, as at Greensforge and Metchley, traces of occupation in the first century have come to light. Sites such as these, and others at Wall, Penkridge and Red Hill, lie along the watershed dividing the streams which eventually run north-eastwards into the Humber from those which make a swifter passage to the Bristol Channel. On the southern shore of the Humber, at Wroxeter and at Cirencester the outer limits of the lowland zone of Britain had been reached.

Wroxeter was the chief city of the Cornovii whose canton, formally styled *civitas Cornoviorum* on the monumental inscription which commemorated the building of its forum early in the second century, included Shropshire, Cheshire and Staffordshire. From it have come some tombstones of the Fourteenth Legion. Military ditches lie beneath some of its later buildings and it may be that the growth of the town which came to rank among the largest in Britain, was stimulated in its early days by the previous existence upon the site of a legionary base. Its relation to Watling Street as well as to the Fosse Way makes it a likely centre for troops operating on the midland front and a probable predecessor to the fortress which came to lie farther north in the same canton at Chester.

Cirencester (*Corinium*) was the cantonal capital of the Dobunni, the southern neighbours of the Cornovii. The pleasant lands of Gloucestershire and Worcestershire brought them such prosperity as made them the wealthiest community in the country and their capital its second largest city. Nowhere else in Roman Britain did the homes of prosperous farmers come to lie so thickly on the ground.

These people, the Cornovii and the Dobunni, experienced much of the rising standard of living which could be enjoyed under the protection of Roman arms. So long as the fortress at Chester was there and garrisoned, as it was for most of the Roman occupation of Britain, the Cornovii at least were not likely to forget the conditions upon which their security depended. Among the Dobunni, too, lay a legionary base for a short while, to be succeeded later by a more advanced position. However much farther the Romans advanced, henceforward they would seldom be out of sight of moorland and mountain amid which there lived people who, at a heavy price in man-power, could be dominated for a while, but who could never be brought to abandon their hostility towards what remained to them an unwelcome occupying power. In this highland zone only two areas on the map of Roman Britain are free from the symbols indicating the presence of soldiery serving as permanent garrisons. One lies deep in the north, where the mountains of the Scottish highlands were far beyond any Roman control, and the other in the far south-west where lived the Dumnonii of Devon and Cornwall. These latter enjoyed a softer climate, as well as a reputation for being hospitable towards the traders who came from as far away as Spain. Certainly the import of wine jars, not empty we may suppose, from the Mediterranean had begun before the Romans came and did not cease when they left.

For the rest, almost beyond the civilising agency of either climate or Roman influence, there lay round the outer rim a group of tribes or loosely knit confederacies who became subject to direct military government for as long as Britain remained part of the Roman Empire. In Wales there were the Silures of the south, the Ordovices farther north and the Deceangli of Flintshire. In northern Britain were those who eventually proved to be the most formidable of all the Romans' opponents, the Brigantes.

We cannot as yet define exactly the limits of the Roman advance by the year 47 when Aulus Plautius, the leader of the invasion four years earlier, laid down his office, nor can we say exactly how much of the Fosse Way frontier was drawn by him or how much by his successor, Ostorius Scapula. It was Ostorius Scapula, however, who made the first assault against the peoples of Wales, not in the south, but in a campaign undertaken in the year 49 against the Deceangli of Flintshire. Diverted from his objective by a summons for help from one of two contending sides among the Brigantes, Ostorius subsequently moved against the Silures of southern Wales among whom Caratacus, leader of the British opposition to the Romans in the earliest days of their advance across Kent, had found a refuge. Some of the people of eastern Britain had already begun to chafe under Roman restraint, and a movement deep into the difficult country of southern Wales could not wisely be undertaken unless preceded by measures designed to provide security in the rear. It was with this end in view that a *colonia*, a settlement of veteran soldiers, was founded at Colchester in 49, and the building of the legionary base at Lincoln served the same purpose. Nor would it have been wise to commit large forces to what were likely to be long and bitter campaigns in Wales if the right flank was exposed to attack, and in the light of later events we may fairly conclude that Cartimandua, queen of the Brigantes, had entered into a treaty with Ostorius Scapula. A necessary preliminary to the opening of a Welsh campaign in the south was the establishment of a base from which operations could be directed, and this was met by the building of a new legionary fortress at Gloucester.

Smoked out from the Silures, Caratacus moved northwards to the Ordovices where, in a pitched battle fought from chosen positions, the British suffered a heavy defeat, whereupon Caratacus fled northwards for refuge to Cartimandua who handed him over to the Romans, an act which may have seemed to the victim a shameful betrayal, though perhaps to the queen herself it was no more than the fulfilment of treaty obligations to Rome. The war against the Silures was resumed, but in 52 Ostorius died, worn out by the cares and anxieties of his military campaigns. Little has been recorded of the activities of his two successors of whom the first was an elderly man, content if existing limits could be maintained, and the second in office for only one year.

The next governor of Britain, Suetonius Paulinus, was an eminent soldier who brought to the direction of the war against the Welsh tribes experience gained in campaigning under somewhat similar conditions in north Africa. His tenure of office was not long, but associated with it are two momentous episodes, the assault on Anglesey and the rebellion of the Iceni and Trinovantes under the inspiration of Boudicca, queen of the Iceni. After some time spent in preliminary campaigning and in the strengthening of garrisons, Suetonius stood ready, by the year 60, to cross the Menai Straits. The crossing itself was made partly by infantry carried in flat-bottomed transports built specially for the purpose, and partly by cavalry who were able to swim or make use of shallow fords. As the Roman forces advanced they were met by a spectacle which may have caused even the most stout-hearted among them to pause in fear. Shrieking women with long flowing hair ran wildly about with blazing torches as they sought to arouse the defenders to a similar pitch of frenzy. Priests invoked the aid of their gods and called down maledictions upon their enemies. But these efforts did not avail. The island was taken and its religious sanctuaries destroyed.

If we are to have any understanding either of the reasons which prompted the Roman attack on Anglesey or of the community of druids whose home lay on the island, we should do well to look beyond the account given by Tacitus. Anglesey was at this time a wealthy island, for there, and on the nearby parts of the mainland, lay Britain's richest deposits of copper. The rich and varied hoard of Iron Age objects discovered on the island at Llyn Cerrig Bach suggests that exploitation of the copper mines had brought to the Anglesey community not merely economic wealth, but also political power which might well have been great enough to organise serious opposition to further Roman progress not only in Wales, but also among the Brigantes. The scene described by Tacitus has undoubtedly given rise to distorted views about the nature of druidism and it is therefore well to remember that the druids of Gaul had formerly been men having important judicial and political functions, and being deeply concerned with the philosophy of religion. If Anglesey was in fact the centre of such a combination of economic wealth and political power, sustained by the zeal of a priestly caste, it is hardly surprising either that

Paulinus should have deployed such force or that Tacitus should have used his pen to such effect.

Paulinus was making his arrangements for the security of Anglesey when news reached him of revolt among the Iceni in East Anglia. At the time of the Roman invasion Prasutagus, king of the Iceni, submitted to the Romans and was allowed to remain in his kingdom with the status of client-king. Upon his death he left a widow, Boudicca, and two daughters. His considerable wealth was divided into two shares of which one went to the Emperor and the other for division between the daughters, but officials of Roman government, encouraged by the procurator, Catus Decianus, began to plunder the kingdom of the Iceni with great ferocity. Boudicca herself and her daughters were brutally treated and the property of the Icenian nobles was confiscated. While the Iceni were in this way driven to the point of rebellion, their southern neighbours, the Trinovantes, suffering under the heavy burden of taxation laid upon them for the maintenance of the temple at Colchester where the living emperor was worshipped, were finally brought to open revolt by the rude behaviour of the veteran soldiers in the *colonia*. The two tribes united against the common enemy. The small garrison at Colchester, which as yet had neither ditch nor pallisade to protect it, sought refuge in the temple itself, but it was quickly overwhelmed, and after all the captives had been slaughtered, the *colonia* was laid waste. The Ninth Legion, commanded by Petilius Cerialis, a future governor of Britain, hastened to bring relief from Lincoln, but the infantry were severely handled by the victorious rebels and the commander barely escaped with his cavalry. As soon as news of the revolt reached Paulinus he made what haste he could from Anglesey towards London, sending word to the Second Legion in the south-west. Paulinus reached London ahead of his main body, but realising that he had no hope of holding it against the rebels with his own small numbers, he withdrew northwards again, abandoning not only London, but also St Albans. In both cities a widely spreading layer of burnt ash still marks the destruction worked by the rebels. No help came from the Second Legion, and Paulinus was left to handle this dangerous situation as best he could with his own forces. Seeking for a favourable position, he drew up his men on a site which gave good protection to his flanks, and in their excess of confidence the advancing rebels blocked their line of retreat with their own wagons. Here was a situation in which superior discipline and heavier armament made up for any disadvantage which the Romans suffered from their inferiority in numbers. The attack was launched and the rebels were driven back on to their own wagons where they were quickly cut to pieces.

CHAPTER THREE

FROM BOUDICCA TO AGRICOLA

The occupants of lowland Britain presented the Roman armies with no more formidable military difficulties than the woodland strongholds of the Catuvellauni or the great hill forts of Wessex. Once the people had been conquered and their fortifications slighted or evacuated, there remained no natural features, nor any unity of command, which might have enabled the tribes to organise continued military opposition. They could be driven into rebellion by oppression or economic exploitation, but the victory won by Suetonius Paulinus in 61 is a measure of their real military weakness, and as the occupying troops moved away into more distant parts of the country, there are likely to have been steadily increasing numbers who began to perceive that it was not only the Romans who might profit from the inclusion of Britain within the Empire. The penetration of the highland zone was a very different matter. A mere movement of armies into this kind of country was not enough. Initial penetration had to be followed by the construction of a system of communications and the building of permanent, strongly fortified positions, as well as by the definition of frontiers in a manner very different from that suggested by the Pennine Chain pushing southwards beyond York and Chester to the Peak of Derbyshire, the Cheviots and the southern uplands of Scotland, with the remote highlands lying beyond—here lay the natural strongholds of backward peoples whose warlike habits were an ever-present threat to the greater prosperity of the lowland plain. The Romans were, so far as we know, the first invaders of Britain who succeeded in giving security to the lowlands by imposing military government upon part at least of the uplands. There are few periods in the later history of Britain when successive governments, whether Norman, Plantagenet or Tudor, were able to avoid at least some measure of fortification in these mountainous areas.

We have no very exact information about the political frontiers of the various peoples who inhabited northern Britain. Most of northern England as far at least as the Tyne Gap, but excepting the East Riding of Yorkshire, was occupied by the Brigantes, believed by Tacitus to have been the most numerous single people in the whole of Britain and described by Ptolemy as stretching from sea to sea. The Roman capital of their canton lay at Aldborough, between York and Catterick, both of which were within their boundaries. It is probable that their lands stretched westwards across the Pennines to the shores of Morecambe Bay, as well as northwards to the Solway Firth and the Tyne. This is a very large area and one which shows marked differences of physical feature in its various parts. Perhaps we ought to think of it less as the home of a single homogeneous people, than as a land inhabited by groups of people who were more or less isolated from one another, but held together, though with some difficulty, by a single dynasty, much as this same area, but with a big extension to the north, was held together by the Northumbrian dynasty in the seventh and eighth centuries.

In these remote northern areas the changes of the Iron Age which are so plainly marked in southern England had little noticeable effect. The Bronze Age lingered on until the Roman period. Signs of habitation are abundant enough. Hill forts, some of them strongly defended, are numerous, and even more numerous in some areas are the groups of hut circles which may be loosely described as the sites of British settlements. Material remains on such sites as these, whether of pottery or metalwork, are often so slight that it is sometimes difficult to determine even approximate dates of occupation. Yet it would be easy to underestimate the economic importance of this area to the Romans, particularly of its stock farming, probably of cattle rather than sheep, upon which its economy mainly rested. In the East Riding of Yorkshire where the Parisi lived, there are signs of greater wealth. These people had come from the north-eastern parts of Gaul and their culture, represented by a number of richly equipped chariot burials, suggests a fighting aristocracy more alike in its kind to some of the Iron Age peoples of southern Britain than to the less civilised Brigantes and their northern neighbours.

The conquest of the Brigantes, the occupation of the southern uplands of Scotland and a penetration even deeper into the north took place between 71 and 84 under the direction of three successive governors, Petilius Cerialis, Julius Frontinus and Julius Agricola. Tacitus has left us a full and detailed account of the military campaigns of Agricola, but there is nothing comparable for his two predecessors. During the fifteen years in which these three distinguished men were successively in office the Romans advanced from Lincoln to far beyond the Tay. Excavation at many sites has done much, and will yet do more, to trace the progress of this advance, but its results can hardly be so precise, saving the discovery of new epigraphical evidence, that we shall be certain of always being able to distinguish the work of Cerialis from that of Frontinus or perhaps even that of these two from the achievement of Agricola himself.

Advance beyond Lincoln could follow two separate lines, either due north along the ridge to the Humber estuary, or in a swinging curve first westerly and then northerly across the open country lying between the inner edge of the flood plain of rivers draining into the Humber on the one side, and the lowermost slopes of the Pennines on the other. The first route involved the difficulty of crossing the Humber estuary itself at a place where the tide flows strongly, but it was more direct. The second route avoided this most formidable difficulty, but it was more circuitous and there were some half-dozen lesser rivers flowing eastwards across its path. Both routes were later followed by Roman roads and perhaps both were used in the first advance. Traces of a Roman foothold on the northern side of the Humber have come to light at Brough which was in Parisian territory. Here the remains of a turf rampart, with a defensive breastwork seemingly constructed of woven osier hurdles, proves Roman occupation during the governorship of Cerialis. Remains of a similar age have come to light at Malton, midway between York and the coast, a site which was later the hub of an important Roman road system. York itself has yielded a layer of occupation debris which suggests the use of the site as a campaigning base at this time.

The Vale of York offered then, as it still offers now, the easiest and most direct route towards the north, but at its northern end, shortly after the crossing of the Swale, the Roman soldier, like the modern traveller, found himself faced with a choice. He could continue northwards into the county of Durham or he could turn north-westwards across the Pennines through the gap marked by Greta Bridge, Bowes, Rey Cross, Brough and Kirkby Thore. In either case he would leave the easy marching of the Vale of York behind and have before him an altogether sterner prospect. This parting of the ways was no less important for the Brigantes than for the Romans, for it was here, if anywhere, that the lie of the land gave them the opportunity of holding up the Roman advance by resolute defence. At Stanwick, a few miles north of Richmond and overlooking these two natural routes to the north, there lies a site which, shortly after the middle of the first century A.D., suddenly expanded from the modest native settlement that it had formerly been into a fortified position of such immense size that it came to contain within its six miles of defensive rampart an area of no less than 850 acres, almost twenty times as large as that enclosed by the defences at Maiden Castle. Its defences, though much less elaborately developed than those of the Iron Age hill forts of Wessex, were formidable enough, but its occupation seems not to have been long lived. Here in all probability lay the stronghold which was hastily fortified by the northern tribes to meet the threat of the advancing Roman armies. There is no written reference to this site, nor, as yet, is there any evidence of any Roman assault upon it, but if this was indeed the place from which the Brigantes hoped to direct prolonged opposition against the Romans, it seems to have failed in its purpose. There are other indications, in the form of temporary camps set up for a brief halt by troops on the march, which point to the continuing advance of Cerialis across Stainmore and onwards perhaps even as far as Carlisle. There was no longer any need for the legionary base at Lincoln, now left far in the rear, and a new fortress was built at York for the Ninth Legion.

York was one of the three permanent legionary bases of Roman Britain. The other two, which lay at the two ends of the Welsh border, were the principal military memorials of the governorship of Julius Frontinus who succeeded Petilius Cerialis in 74 and in the years which followed carried out measures designed to secure the final conquest and pacification of Wales. At the southern end of the frontier Frontinus abandoned the earlier base at Gloucester and moved across the Severn into the country of the Silures where, at Caerleon upon Usk, a new fortress was built to house the Second Legion Augusta. It was later balanced at the northern end of the frontier by a similar fortress at Chester on the Dee in whose neighbourhood Julius Agricola, commander for a time of the Twentieth Legion Valeria Victrix, gained some military experience which he found of great value when he himself became governor of Britain a few years later. These two great bulwarks were the base supports upon which rested the whole military organisation of the Welsh front, and it may be that each had special responsibilities, and perhaps even some independence of command, within its own area. Beyond this baseline there was built a series of lesser fortifications, from which patrols could police the roads which were pushed along the coastal belts so as to encircle the central mountains or along the river valley into the heart of the mountains themselves.

Upon his arrival in Britain in the autumn of 78 Agricola found himself confronted with a situation which demanded prompt and stern action if much of the ground secured by his predecessor in North Wales was not to be lost once more. He was informed that the Ordovices had attacked and almost destroyed a regiment of cavalry which had been stationed on the borders of their territory. Although the season was late and ill-suited for campaigning in such mountainous regions, he took to the field at once at the head of a punitive expedition whose assault was so vigorously executed that almost the whole fighting force of the tribe was annihilated. His subsequent occupation of Anglesey may suggest that the diversion caused by Boudicca's rebellion in 60 had prevented Suetonius Paulinus from driving home his own assault to the point at which a renewal of danger from this area was no longer to be feared. With the Welsh tribes now enmeshed within a net of roads, supported by strong-points strategically placed for ease of communication between garrisons, and with the fortresses at Chester and Caerleon holding strong reserves which could be used both for support against a local threat within Wales or more widely to prevent any irruption into the midland plain, Agricola was able to turn his attention to the north.

The next campaigning season was spent in repeated harrying attacks against hostile forces, a process which was accompanied by widespread reconnoitring for the purpose of choosing sites suitable for military camps. Tacitus tells us that during this season many tribes which had hitherto been independent now submitted to Roman rule and, though he does not tell us the names of any of them, we may fairly infer from the account of Agricola's third campaigning season, that the Votadini and the Selgovae were among them. In this third season Agricola reached the Firth of Tay, but not without learning that in these remote areas the climate could prove as formidable an enemy as any other that might be encountered. Although his troops were severely buffeted by continuous storms in the open field, they found good protection against the onslaught in the encampments which they built. This swift advance was succeeded by a year of consolidation in which the large areas overrun in the two previous seasons were secured by the placing of garrisons at strategic points. In particular the narrow isthmus between the Firths of Clyde and Forth was firmly gripped in this fashion.

Agricola had now campaigned for three seasons in Scotland, and from many of the sites which he chose for his garrisons the northern outlook will have given him a not so distant glimpse of what an Elizabethan translator of Bede called those 'high and hideous ridges of hylles' that form the Central Highland massif. The sight may well have given him pause to think, and perhaps it was as a consequence of his thoughts that he turned away from this view towards a part of Scotland which he had hitherto left untouched. This was what Tacitus described as the side of Britain facing Ireland, and we now know, largely through discoveries made by aerial photography, that he was referring to south-western Scotland, particularly to the shires of Dumfries, Kirkcudbright and Ayr. Agricola's campaign opened with a sea passage which we can perhaps regard as an exploratory voyage undertaken for the purpose of discovering whether there was a practicable land route towards the north. A series of actions was fought against the south-western tribes, and garrisons were established among them. The results of his voyage of exploration were perhaps discouraging to Agricola since we find him in the next year back at the Forth-Clyde line and moving beyond it with infantry and cavalry supported by marines. Considerable opposition was met and the Ninth Legion had a narrow escape from disaster. In the sixth and last of his northern campaigns Agricola reached what was clearly regarded by Tacitus as his crowning achievement, the utter defeat of the assembled tribes of Caledonia in a pitched battle at Mons Graupius. It was now the year 84 and after having held office for longer than was normal, Agricola was recalled.

This account of Agricola's seven seasons of campaigning, one in north Wales and the other six in northern England and Scotland, is derived from Tacitus. There is no subsequent period in the history of Roman Britain, or even in the early history of Anglo-Saxon England, for which we have a similarly detailed narrative from a written source. Indeed if we wished to find a parallel, we should need to look as far forward as the ninth century to the account given in the *Anglo-Saxon Chronicle* of the movements of the great Danish army which landed in East Anglia in 865. The movements of Agricola's armies could have been reconstructed in some measure of detail even without the written account left by Tacitus, but, setting aside the written sources, we should have been able to recognise only the consequences of the ninth-century Danish invasion, knowing virtually nothing of its progress in detail. Two factors have contributed to the relatively great abundance of archaeological evidence for the movements of the Roman armies in the north during Agricola's period of office. First, a great many of the sites which he chose for his garrisons are in upland country of a kind which has not been greatly disturbed either by agricultural activites or by the imposition of modern buildings. Such sites, even where they are not at once visible to the naked eye, can often be located from the air, though the site itself may be no more than a hastily built marching camp occupied for only a very brief time. Secondly, many of the sites were chosen with such a good eye for the tactical and strategical needs of their neighbourhood that they were found suitable for reoccupation later in the Roman period and thus, although the Agricolan occupation may itself have been short, its remains may yet be preserved beneath those of a later age.

Cerialis, we have seen, crossed the Pennines from the Stanwick area by Bowes and Brough, whence the Eden valley leads on to Carlisle, but he, or perhaps more probably a successor, drove another road due northwards on the eastern side of the Pennines to cross the Tees at Piercebridge and make its way through County Durham by Binchester and Lanchester to the crossing of the Tyne at Corbridge. Here, leading westwards to Carlisle some forty-five miles away, lay the great break in the hills known to geographers as the Tyne Gap, and through it, to form a link between the eastern and western sides of the country, Agricola built the road which we now call the Stanegate. It lay some little way south of the line followed by the Hadrianic frontier and, like other roads through areas actually or potentially hostile, it had fortified positions at intervals along its course. The Tyne Gap and the peculiar conformation of the hills along its northern side provided conditions particularly favourable for frontier defence, and here in fact the northern frontier of the province lay for most of the Roman occupation. But the point of stability had not been reached yet and there may have been some hope that by continuing to press northwards the armies might still be able to encompass the uttermost limits of the island.

The lie of the roads, no less than the remains of the marching camps and more permanent forts along them, seems to suggest that Agricola's passage through the southern uplands of Scotland was made on two fronts, or perhaps rather in two columns, one on the eastern side continuing the route from Piercebridge and Lanchester, and the other on the western side with its starting point at Carlisle. Now the Great North Road of modern times coincides with the Roman road through the Vale of York, but shortly after Catterick the two diverge from one another, the modern road swinging away eastwards to find easier gradients. Foot soldiers, or at least their commanding officers, may have been more concerned with reaching their objective by the most direct route possible than with avoiding steep ascents and descents. Even so, it is a little surprising that the Roman engineers preferred the more difficult route across the westerly parts of Durham where snowfalls are frequent and heavy in winter, to one nearer the coast. Across the Tyne there is an even more striking contrast between the line followed by the modern road along the flat coastal plain of Northumberland and the abrupt and rugged route, much of it near or above the thousand-foot contour, by which the Romans chose to cross the Cheviots which they could so easily have circumvented. Corbridge is, to be sure, the starting point of two roads to the north, and the more easterly of these, the Devil's Causeway, takes a much easier passage across Northumberland to the mouth of the Tweed, yet, so far as we know at present, this was not the route followed by Agricola.

The tracks of his armies lie along the road which runs from Corbridge to Risingham, High Rochester and Chew Green, the latter offering the site for an encampment which is lost in the clouds for much of the summer and snowbound for most of the winter. The difficulties of keeping open such a road as this and of supplying the garrisons along it seem poor compensation for the gain in directness of route, and we are left to wonder what may have been the circumstances which made such a choice preferable. This, however, was the way that Agricola went, and from Chew Green the road led on to Cappuck, down to Newstead in the valley of the Tweed and finally, after crossing another moorland belt, down to the Forth at Inveresk. It may be that Agricola's two columns converged here, for Inveresk is also the northern terminal of the road which runs up the more westerly side of the southern uplands from Carlisle, climbing over Beattock Summit on its way and then dropping down into the valley of the upper Clyde. For part of its course this road was paralleled by another and more westerly road running up Nithsdale. The many fortified sites along these two roads, as well as others even farther west along the northern shores of the Solway Firth, represent the archaeological expression of Agricola's fifth campaign when, as Tacitus says, he lined the side of Britain facing Ireland with his troops, but of this there is much yet to be learned.

The southern uplands offer no passage between their eastern and western sides comparable with the Tyne Gap, yet some of the tributaries of the Tweed rise in moorland whose farther slopes fall away to Annandale or upper Clydesdale, thus pointing the way to cross-roads linking the main eastern and western routes. Beyond the Forth-Clyde isthmus, secured during Agricola's third Scottish campaign by the construction of a number of strong-points, there runs only a single Roman road. It strikes northwards from Camelon to cross the Forth at Stirling, and thence north-eastwards through Strathallan and along Strathmore, the wide and fertile valley that lies between the south-eastern edge of the Grampians on the one side and the Ochil and Sidlaw Hills on the other. Here the camps and signalling stations that line the road itself, the outlying forts skilfully placed to block any sudden irruption from the Highland glens and, above all, the great legionary base at Inchtuthil, bear witness to the weight of Agricola's advance during the last two of his Scottish campaigns. Beyond the point at which this road can now be traced a series of marching camps leads onwards across Aberdeen almost to the shores of the Moray Firth. Somewhere in these parts, the exact site itself unknown, lay the scene of Agricola's victory at Mons Graupius.

When Agricola was recalled from his office of governor, Roman soldiers had been in Britain for just over forty years, now pushing swiftly forwards across easy country, now fighting hard against stubborn opposition and now slowly erecting the whole apparatus of military government in a conquered area. It is time that we turned aside momentarily from the narrative of events to take a closer look at the army by which these tasks were carried out. Six legions, though never more than four at any one time, as well as small detachments from two or three others, participated at one time or another in the occupation of Britain, but, after various changes, arising in part from the situation in Britain itself and in part from the demands of the Empire elsewhere, the permanent army of occupation was reduced to three legions, with an appropriate number of auxiliary regiments. The three legions were the Twentieth Valeria Victrix whose base was at Chester, the Second Augusta stationed at Caerleon and the Sixth Victrix at York. The total strength of a legion at the time of the occupation was a little less than 6,000 men, subdivided into 10 cohorts and 64 centuries. It was commanded by a legate or general (*legatus legionis*) whose subordinate officers included 6 military tribunes (*tribuni militum*), the staff officers of the day, and a camp prefect (*praefectus castrorum*) whose duties lay with the camp in which the legion was permanetly quartered. The discipline of the legion and its efficiency as a fighting force rested mainly upon the centurions of whom there were 60 in each legion, all of them men appointed to their office on qualities acquired by long and hard experience. Within their own grade there was a recognised course of promotion from one cohort to another. The commander of the first cohort, the *primus pilus* or *centurio primi pili*, was the senior among them, a position which entitled him to more elaborate living quarters within the legionary base.

A legion was an infantry body, though a squadron of cavalry, numbering 120 men, was attached to each legion for use as dispatch-riders and for similar purposes. The legionaries whom we see portrayed on Trajan's column in Rome wear as their outer garment a segmental cuirass which reaches from shoulder to hip, and beneath this there hangs a kilted tunic. A short sword (*gladius*) hangs at the right side from a military belt, and in their right hands they once carried javelins, held vertically upright, but all these have now broken away. They march bareheaded, with their battle helmets—plain, serviceable articles, quite unlike the vizor masks found at Newstead, or the similar mask dredged from the river Wensum—hanging from their right shoulders. A large, rectangular shield, markedly convex, hangs from the left shoulder of each man, leaving his hand free to grasp the stout stake which rests upon his left shoulder and supports at its end a variety of kit used for foraging and cooking. This is a portrayal of men marching out to a review by the banks of the Danube, and since they are on display in the heart of imperial Rome itself, no doubt their turn-out had first been subjected to the most searching scrutiny. Perhaps the standard among Agricola's men at Inchtuthil was not quite so high as on the Emperor's column in Rome, but even so the equipment there portrayed represents what was at least in theory the legionary standard: and indeed plenty of military sites in Britain have yielded fragments of it, even down to the hobnailed leather footwear. On the other hand we need not necessarily picture such legionaries humping their great weight of equipment across the Cheviots or through the Welsh mountains. Weapons both for attack and defence needed to be immediately ready to hand, but foraging kit could well go with trenching tools, baskets for carrying earth, ropes, tents and other heavy equipment with the baggage train, either on pack-mules or in carts. The legionaries were not merely fighting troops of the first quality. They also carried out the duties which in modern armies are performed by more specialised bodies. They were themselves their own pioneer corps and their own engineers, building roads and bridges, felling timber and quarrying stone. They themselves built the fortresses in which they were permanently quartered, no less than the marching camps thrown up to give protection for a single night, and they were the men who built the great frontier walls as well as the forts along them.

'Fortress' is the word normally used to translate the Latin *castra* when used of a legionary base. At present the sites of six such fortresses are known in Britain, three of them, those at Lincoln, Gloucester and Inchtuthil, having been occupied only for a short period in the first century. The last of these three lies on ground still open, so that it has been possible to recover its internal plan almost in its entirety, despite the fact that it was occupied for only a very few years and that at the end of the occupation it was systematically dismantled. The other three sites, York, Chester and Caerleon, were occupied for most of the Roman period. At York and Chester the remains of the fortresses lie beneath the heart of the medieval and modern cities, so that they can be excavated only when

Roman Britain

opportunity is presented by the demolition of old buildings lying above them. At Caerleon, on the other hand, although part of the site is built over, there are considerable areas of the fortress still lying beneath open fields.

By giving careful attention to the design of the buildings and making the best possible use of the space available, a legion could be housed in an area of approximately 50 acres laid out as an oblong measuring roughly 540 by 450 yards, these being the dimensions of the fortress at Caerleon. The choice of site would be governed by considerations of over-all strategy, ease of supply and local security. The strategical needs of the high command in Britain varied as the frontier rested on a nearer or a more distant line. Lincoln and Gloucester suited the conditions at the middle of the first century, or soon after, but when a more settled state had been reached, York, Chester and Caerleon offered sites which were near enough to the frontier zone to allow the possibility of swift movement to a threatened area, but not so far beyond it as to create a risk of isolation. Moreover, all three sites lay upon waterways whose use will have helped considerably in the difficult problem of supplying such large garrisons not only with their food, but also with the many raw materials necessary for their fighting efficiency. A riverside port lay at Heronbridge on the Dee, where docks and dockside workshops have come to light, and York had direct connections by river and inland waterways with the corn-growing areas of what are now the East Anglian fens.

Local security was achieved by massive defences which had to be strong enough to avert any risk of overthrow from unexpected local attack at a time when most of the legion might be engaged on tasks away from its base. In early days, when this kind of risk was greatest, the defences consisted of a broad and deep ditch, perhaps more than one, enclosing a stockaded embankment built of timber, clay and turf. Resting upon a log corduroy to give it a stable foundation, this embankment would present a near vertical face to the outside, and on the inside, unless that face too was revetted with timber, a steep slope rising to a height of about twenty feet and capped by a rampart walk. At Agricola's fortress at Inchtuthill, exceptionally for its early date, the turf rampart was faced externally with a stone wall five feet thick, but this was probably due to the lack of good clay or turf in the neighbourhood. Here the four sides were each pierced by a gateway with a double carriageway flanked on either side by massive square timber towers. The occupation of the site was short-lived, probably not more than half-a-dozen years, and when it was evacuated its gateways and all its internal buildings, which were also of timber, were carefully and systematically dismantled, as we can well understand if we think for a moment of the immense quantities of seasoned timber required for such a site and of the high value it would have for re-use elsewhere. At York, Chester and Caerleon the earliest timber and clay defences were later replaced by the insertion of stone walls, as well as stone gateways, at the front of the rampart backing. These stone walls underwent successive modifications at York and Chester, those at York still being stout enough to provide a refuge for the invading Danish army during its attack on Northumbria in 866–7. These two northerly fortresses retained their military importance so long as there were Roman troops in Britain, but at Caerleon the site had lost much of its military significance by the end of the second century when the stone rampart was dismantled and what had been a fortress became rather a base depot.

The rampart, offering protection against wind as well as reduced fire risk to other buildings, might be used, as it certainly was at Caerleon, for the legionary cook-houses whose stone hearths were housed in wooden sheds. Elsewhere along the ramparts, as we may judge from the iron bolts found at Caerleon or the double layer of timber strapping to give increased resilience at the south-east corner of Chester, would be mounted the *ballistae* (catapults which threw stones or other missiles) for use in defence of the fortress. There would also be small look-out towers at intervals. The internal buildings of the fortress were so placed in relation to the rampart as to leave a gap—the *intervallum*—some fifty feet wide round the full circuit of the fortress on its inside. Most of these buildings consisted of barrack blocks, workshops and storehouses. The barrack blocks, carefully related in their design to the organisation of the legion as a fighting body, were long narrow buildings which face one another in pairs across a colonnaded street. Each single building (*hemistrigium*) housed a single century with the centurion's quarters at one end and the men's cubicles stretching away to the other. Occupying pride of place at the heart of the fortress, lay the headquarters building (*principia*). Here was a spacious courtyard to which dignity was given by colonnaded ambulatories. Across the full width of the court and beyond it lay an aisled hall used for ceremonial purposes, and ranged round the court were many small rooms each with its own use, whether for staff officers, for armoury, for strong-room or for the legionary standards. Among other buildings placed near the centre of a legionary fortress were the residence of the commanding officer (*praetorium*), the legionary hospital (*valetudinarium*), the drill hall (*basilica exercitatoria*) and the granaries (*horrea*). At Chester water was brought to the fortress from outside by pipe-lines laid in conduits. Elsewhere the water supply might be partly dependent on internal wells and partly on external sources. The needs of sanitation were met by an elaborate system of drains, sewers and culverts which also served for the removal of surface water.

A legionary fortress was so designed that its garrison could in times of need maintain itself entirely within the lines of its own defences, but there were many activities which in normal conditions would be pursued outside the walls. Late in the first century a great stone amphitheatre was built outside the walls at Caerleon. Large enough to house the full complement of the legion, it was probably used for military training and exercises as much as for spectacles of entertainment. Bath buildings lay close beside it. Outside, too, would be the temples and other places of worship for those whose religious needs were not met by the formal cult of emperor-worship. Nor was there room within for the great works depots. At Holt in Denbighshire, twelve miles away from the fortress at Chester, lay the great industrial settlement which provides us with our best example of a legionary manufactory. Here, spread over an area of some twenty acres, were the workshops of the Twentieth Legion where all manner of wall-tiles, flue-tiles, roofing-tiles and water-pipes were produced. Garrisons in all ages have attracted traders and other sorts of people to live beneath their walls, and there is no doubt that, as the occupation proceeded, extensive civil settlements grew up near the legionary fortresses.

The legions provided only a part, and that the smaller part, of the army occupation. When fresh ground had been overrun among the uplands, and their inhabitants brought into temporary unwilling submission, it was only by the visible presence of Roman garrisons among them, able at need to send out a punitive expedition, that continuing restraint could be exercised, and the exercising of this restraint was the task performed by the auxiliary regiments. The auxiliaries were not related in any proportional way to the legions. The number of regiments on duty in Britain will have varied with varying conditions there and in other parts of the Empire, and their distribution within Britain will have been governed by the local needs of the time. They were organised in comparatively small units, the *cohors quingenaria* or *miliaria*, the *ala quingenaria* or *miliaria*, and the *cohors equitata*, according as the unit was one of infantry or cavalry or infantry with a proportion of mounted men and according as its complement was one of about 500 men or one of about 1,000 men. They were of mixed and varied origin, bringing different skills to the tasks which they had to perform. At a time when the Roman Empire was still expanding, the forcible enlistment of newly conquered tribesmen in regiments which were then posted for duty in distant parts was found to be a useful form of insurance against the threat of local insurrection. The rank and file of a Spanish regiment serving in Britain doubtless found it more profitable to accept Roman pay than to join the Brigantes in a rebellion which could not help them back to their Spanish homes however successful it might be.

Information about the very considerable number of auxiliary regiments which served in Britain at one time or another during the occupation is derived largely from inscriptions, often in the form of religious dedications by regimental officers, and from the chance finds of diplomas issued to men who had completed their term of service. The regimental styles give some indication of the diversity of both origin and specialised function among these auxiliary troops. The *Cohors I Hamiorum Sagittariorum*, a regiment of Syrian archers, provided the garrison at Carvoran, one of the forts on the Hadrianic Wall, soon after its completion, and later we find this same regiment serving on the Antonine Wall under the command of Caristanius Justinianus, who was a member of a distinguished family from Antioch in Pisidia. Also serving on the Antonine Wall was a regiment recruited from the opposite end of the Empire, the *Cohors I fida Vardullorum civium Romanorum*, a cavalry regiment 1,000 strong which had been formed in Spain and, after some signal act of distinction while on service, had had Roman citizenship conferred upon its members. Another Spanish regiment was the *Cohors II Asturum* which distinguished itself in action in Britain after earlier service in Germany. Many, and probably the majority, of the auxiliary regiments in Britain came from the neighbouring provinces of Gaul and Belgium, such as the *Cohors IIII Gallorum*, the *Cohors VI Nerviorum* or the *Cohors I Tungrorum miliaria*. The conquest of Britain itself supplied a new source of manpower and within a year of the battle of Mons Graupius the *Cohors I Brittonum* is found on service on the Danube frontier in Pannonia.

The forts (*castella*) in which the auxiliary regiments were housed, resembled in their fundamentals the legionary bases, with the great difference that they were only some three to six acres in size, according to the needs of the garrison to be housed in any particular neighbourhood. As with the legionary fortresses, their outer defences, sometimes enclosed within a series of three or more ditches, were at first of clay and timber, later of stone, but their over-all shape was more pronouncedly oblong, and despite their smaller size, they still had four, and sometimes six, gates. Two streets running across the short axis (*via principalis* and *via quintana*) divided the interior into three sections of which the central third housed the headquarters building, the commandant's house and the granaries. In the remaining two-thirds lay the barrack blocks and the storehouses whose design varied in detail with the nature of the garrison, whether infantry or cavalry or a mixture of both.

Once the frontiers had been marked and garrisoned by auxiliaries, the legions were withdrawn to bases some distance in the rear as a strategic reserve which could be moved swiftly to a point of danger. The first shock of any uprising in the forward areas was taken by the auxiliaries who, although they might also use some Roman equipment, commonly retained their native weapons, such as the bow or the sling. The Syrians, represented in Britain by the cohort of Hamian archers stationed at Carvoran, were renowned as bowmen, and slingstones, sometimes of lead, but more often of stone or clay, are familiar objects on many Romano-British sites. The remains of watch towers along the Cumberland coast and of signalling stations along the road from Strathearn to the Tay are reminders of the way in which, by the blazing log pile at night or the carefully manipulated column of smoke from straw by day, news could be conveyed rapidly from the forward areas to the rear. The legionary bases of Britain, like those of Europe as a whole in the Trajanic age, were all placed near large rivers. Water transport was used both for the carriage of supplies and also on occasion for the conveyance of armies. In later years as the shores of Britain became subject to piratical attacks, the patrols of the *Classis Britannica* played an increasingly important part in the defences of the province.

At the moment of invasion, and during the subsequent advance across the plains and uplands of Britain, the legions were actively engaged in warfare, as well as in the building of roads and fortified positions such as were necessary to secure newly conquered lands. Although small detachments of cavalry were used for reconnaissance and skirmishing, the legion was essentially a body of heavily armed infantry. Their success was due quite simply to their immeasurable superiority over their opponents in discipline, training and equipment. Their main weapon of attack was the javelin (*pillum*), a throwing spear with a tough head and softer shaft of iron which was intended to bend or twist on impact with the enemy's armour or shield and which could not then be easily removed. Encumbered in this way, an opponent was defenceless against an infantry charge in which the short sword was used to somewhat the same effect as the bayonet in more recent times. Artillery, in the form of the catapult (*ballista*) was used for assaulting an enemy stronghold, for defending Roman encampments and also, but more particularly in the fourth century, for the defence of fortified towns.

CHAPTER FOUR

THE NORTHERN FRONTIER FROM AGRICOLA TO THEODOSIUS

Agricola handed over to his successor, says Tacitus, a province which was at peace in itself and secure from danger. Little more than twenty years had passed since the crushing of the one major rebellion against Roman authority by the tribes of lowland Britain, and among the Iceni and the Trinovantes the memory of the price paid would still be very much alive. It was only seven years since Agricola himself had decimated the fighting strength of the tribes in north Wales, and in south Wales the great fortress at Caerleon stood as a visible reminder of the heavy odds against the success of any native uprising. In the far north the tribes of Caledonia had been utterly defeated in pitched battle. Here, it might well seem to Tacitus, was a situation which could give cause for nothing but satisfaction, a new province conquered and brought securely within the Empire, soon to repay the cost of its conquest. Yet Agricola's successors in Britain quickly found that the position was quite otherwise. The province may have been at peace, but, as the event was to show, it was certainly not secure. Continuing advance and static defence are wholly different states which call for differing dispositions of the troops available. Although the Romans knew that Britain was an island, its total conquest lay beyond their grasp, and perhaps it could never be achieved without that much more advanced development of sea-power towards which the Vikings were the first people of north-western Europe to make any real approach.

The danger to Roman Britain at the time of Agricola's recall lay in the absence of any clearly marked frontier. More than 225 miles of difficult country lay between the legions at York and Inchtuthil, country which could be crossed only at marching pace. We do not know exactly how many auxiliary regiments Agricola had under his command, nor do we know how they were deployed, but we know enough to be able to perceive that the occupying armies were very widely dispersed in a way which is likely to have been costly in man-power and which could hardly form a satisfactory basis for the long-term control of the province. Throughout the occupation Britain did in fact remain a frontier province in which there was considerable military activity, but it was not the only frontier province, and herein lay the great difficulty, since the governors of Britain could not expect their military demands to be given precedence over those of other frontier provinces which lay nearer the heart of the Empire. While all seemed to be going well in Britain, danger was threatening on the Danube frontier, and, soon after Agricola had left Britain, one of the four legions was withdrawn. The legion in question was the Second Adjutrix which had been stationed at Lincoln at one time, but was at Chester when the transfer was ordered. Chester could not possibly be left without a garrison and the legion chosen to replace the Second Adjutrix was the Twentieth which may have been in the far north at Inchtuthil.

We know that Inchtuthil was now evacuated, in a peaceful and orderly fashion with the careful and methodical dismantling of its outer defences and its internal buildings. We know also that Fendoch, one of Agricola's regimental forts on the edge of the Grampians, and other forts farther south were similarly dismantled, but until we have learned more about Agricola's *praesida* along the Forth-Clyde isthmus, we shall not be able to say for certain how much of these northern lands was abandoned at the same time. It is, however, sure that parts at least of the southern uplands of Scotland remained firmly in Roman control for some years yet. At Newstead on the Tweed in about the year 86 the fort originally built by Agricola was demolished and replaced by another with more massive defences than its predecessor. This new fort continued in occupation until about the year 100, when it too was abandoned. The abandonment of Newstead may seem to be symptomatic of the evacuation of the southern uplands of Scotland as a whole and of a general withdrawal perhaps beyond the line of the Cheviots. We have no written evidence to guide us and not yet a sufficiency of excavated sites to make good the failure of the written record, but Newstead dominates the Tweed valley, as well as its upper catchment area, and if control of this eastern side was lost it is difficult to see how the western side can have been retained.

The evidence in general seems to point towards a shortening of the long lines resulting from Agricola's forward thrust and towards the consolidation of a military area which might be less exacting in its demands on man-power. From Caerleon, in addition to an inscription recording the completion of an important building, possibly the headquarters building, in the year 100, there is other evidence pointing to a general reconstruction of the whole fortress, beginning in the last years of the first century and extending over the first ten years of the second. A similar process of remodelling was taking place at Chester, the other fortress on the Welsh front, where, probably during the decade 105-15, a stone wall was inserted in front of the old timbered rampart. Here too there are fragments of a Trajanic building inscription which seem to refer to work done during the replacement of internal wooden buildings by others built of stone. Activity of this kind was not confined to the legionary bases, for there is evidence from a number of Welsh sites suggesting similar processes of overhaul and reconstruction. The same tale is told at York where a building inscription records work completed by the Ninth Legion during the year 107-8.

If we are right in regarding the first decade of the second century as one of steady and methodical consolidation, we shall also be right in deducing the conditions of peace and security that made possible the performance of such work. But there are hints, and more than hints, that before the century had advanced many years further there was serious trouble in Britain. One of the hints is provided by the sudden and total disappearance of that same Ninth Legion which had been engaged upon the work of reconstruction at York. Since it no longer figures in the army list, it may be presumed to have been cashiered as the result of some shameful defeat, but unfortunately we have not yet enough evidence to show whether that defeat took place in Britain in some unrecorded disaster or perhaps in some other part of the Empire. Certainly it is not easy wholly to dissociate the disappearance of the Ninth Legion, last recorded at York, from the words of those historians whose record, brief and allusive though it is yet testifies to an uprising in Britain which took place during Hadrian's reign and which cost the Romans heavy losses of men. By 122 another legion, the Sixth, had been sent to York, and in that or the previous year Hadrian himself was in Britain to supervise the early stages in the construction of a new frontier, radically different from anything that had been seen in Britain previously.

A map drawn to a small scale will show that in general the line chosen by Hadrian for the new frontier was that of the Tyne Gap which had already been used by Agricola for the road between Corbridge and Carlisle, but such a map effectively conceals the fundamental differences between the line chosen by Agricola to provide quick and easy communication between east and west, and that chosen by Hadrian to give a strong defensive position for a frontier which was to be permanently manned. Agricola's road took the direct and easy passage through the Gap. Hadrian's line ran a mile or two farther north in order to take advantage of the great natural protection offered against attack from the north by the massive rock outcrop known as the Whin Sill, and also of the distant outlook to the north. This natural formation which presents a steep, though not difficult, slope towards the south, offers a sheer face to the north for many miles together, thus needing very little artificial strengthening to make it virtually impregnable.

The function of the new frontier was to give to the people who lived within it such a measure of security against the ill consequences of continuing tribal warfare that there might be opportunity for the ordered development of economic, social and even intellectual life. A peaceful and prosperous province was likely to be more profitable than one continually exposed to attacks from outsiders, but, as the Anglo-Saxon Church found to its bitter cost late in the eighth and in the ninth centuries, increasing prosperity and a rising standard of living could quickly provoke the envy and hostility of those who did not share them. The prosperity of lowland Britain depended as much during the Roman occupation as it did in the Middle Ages upon the imposition of some restraint upon the borderland between the lowland and upland zones, but what must surely astonish those who come to look carefully and imaginatively at the Hadrianic frontier in Britain for the first time is the immense grandeur of the scale upon which it was conceived and carried into execution. Here was a great fortified belt more than seventy miles long from end to end, skilfully engineered and powerfully manned by a large number of troops, some of whom had been brought from distant lands. Strength and the appearance of permanence are its most striking characteristics, and at no time in the later history of Britain, not even in the twentieth century, can we find a defensive frontier constructed on such a scale. Perhaps the nearest approach, and it is not indeed a very near one, lies in the great dyke by which Offa, king of Mercia, defined the limits of his kingdom against the Welsh, though this was more of a boundary line than a defensive frontier.

We must not suppose that all this was done simply for the security of Britain. The island had itself been invaded and occupied partly because, as a source of hostile attack, it threatened the security of Gaul. The Hadrianic frontier was only incidentally the frontier of the province of Britain. Fundamentally it was the extreme north-western sector of a frontier which cuts across Europe from the Black Sea to the Rhine mouths, a frontier which took varying forms dictated by local geographical conditions and changing ideas on military strategy. Hadrian, himself an engineer and architect, knew this frontier from end to end, in a way that is given to few of us to know it nowadays. As a young officer he had fought on the Danube front where he surely saw the works constructed by Domitian across the Romanian plain between the lower Danube and the Black Sea. He had also seen active service higher up the Danube in the province of Pannonia. At the time of Trajan's death, Hadrian was governor of Syria where he was responsible for a long stretch of the eastern frontier. Added to all this, he brought with him to Britain further experience gained from a prolonged visit to the Rhineland frontier where a complete reorganisation was carried out under his direction. The scale and solidity of the frontier in Britain becomes intelligible only if we try to see it as Hadrian himself saw it. In relation to the imperial frontier as a whole it was very short, but it was vitally important. In western Spain and Gaul the Romans had reached the ends of the world as they knew it, but in Britain much of Scotland and, as they well knew, the whole of Ireland, lay outside their grasp, doubtless because these lands seemed not to offer an adequate return on the resources that would need to be spent on their conquest. Moreover, those parts of Britain which had been conquered comprised by far the largest island possession of the Empire, and for a people whose seafaring experience was limited to the Mediterranean, this would give added reason for ensuring that its defences should be made as strong as the whole resources of the Empire could make them.

The work of construction was put in hand in 122 or 123,

when Aulus Platorius Nepos was governor of Britain. Building continued for some ten years during which there were various modifications of plan, some being matters of minor detail, others of greater military importance. In its final form the frontier emerged as a continuous stone wall with many buildings spaced along it for the accommodation of its garrison. In the east the Wall ended, at a place which is still called Wallsend, upon the northern bank of the Tyne where an open reach gave a good view down the widening estuary, though not quite to the open sea. The lie of the coast towards the north, receding slightly westwards, rendered it unnecessary to take any precautions against an outflanking movement on this side. In the west, the deep indentation of the Solway Firth presented a very different situation, and though the sands were treacherous enough to strangers, no doubt there were as many who could find their way across in Roman times as there were in the days of Nanty Ewart and Redgauntlet. Here the Wall was carried on some miles beyond Carlisle along the southern shore of the Solway to terminate at Bowness. Even so the flank lay wide open to the Novantae of south-western Scotland, and to meet this threat a series of small look-out posts was continued some thirty miles down the Cumberland coast in order that continuous watch could be kept over the wider parts of the Solway which could be crossed easily enough by boat.

The Wall itself was in its first state built of stone only in its eastern half. It was first designed to be 10 feet thick, although in many places it was not built to a thickness of more than 8 feet. Conjectures about its height have varied and there are some who think it to have been about 16 feet high to the rampart walk, with some additional breastwork on its outer edge. Bede says that it was standing 12 feet high in his day, and he was a careful man who had surely been to look for himself, yet that was some three centuries after it had ceased to be a frontier. The western half of the Wall, for 31 miles from the river Irthing to Bowness, was built of turf or clay fashioned into a rampart about 20 feet wide at the base and about 12 feet high. The reason for this change of materials lies in the differing geological conditions prevailing on either side of the river Irthing. To the east there was an abundance of lime for providing the mortar necessary for the stone structure, but there was none readily available to the west. The turf Wall had only a short life. Once the frontier reorganisation had proceeded far enough to ensure military security it was dismantled and replaced by a stone wall similar to that in the eastern half. Over much of its length the Wall was protected on its northern side by a ditch of standard military design, having an average width at the top of about 27 feet and depth of about 9, but where, as along much of the central sector, there was a sheer face to the north, no ditch was necessary.

Wall and ditch together provided a barrier formidable enough to those who had no more than primitive means of assault, but it was not intended to be either a fighting platform or a total barrier between those who lived on its northern and southern sides. Incorporated in its design from the very first was a large number of regularly spaced buildings to house a patrolling garrison. These buildings consisted of fortlets placed at a distance of one Roman mile from each other, whence they are now called milecastles, and square turrets so placed that two turrets lay in between each two milecastles. Each milecastle had two wide gates, one to the south and the other to the north. Such gates could be, and no doubt often were, securely closed, but perhaps they may allow us to think of this frontier as performing some of the functions of dykes built to defend low-lying land against the tides of the sea, with frequent sluices and culverts which in quiet seasons can be left open to direct the ebb and flow of the waters into the proper channels, but which in times of storm and stress need to be completely shut.

The most important military modification of the original design took the form of the addition to the frontier itself of a series of permanent forts for the housing of regiments of auxiliaries, some of them cavalry, some of them infantry. There were sixteen of these forts, varying somewhat in size and not showing that regularity of spacing which is characteristic of the milecastles and turrets. At some of the chosen sites, the lie of the ground dictated the relationship of the fort to the Wall itself, as at Housesteads, where the long axis lay east and west with the frontier Wall itself forming the north wall of the fort. But where the lie of the ground permitted, as at Rudchester and Chesters, the forts lay athwart the Wall, so that three gates gave access to its northern side. The designs of these Wall forts did not differ in their essentials from the auxiliary forts of the times of Agricola or Trajan, save that timber gave way to stone.

One further element completes this complex of frontier

works. Lying always to the south of the Wall and its forts, but not keeping at any constant distance from it, there was dug a great running earthwork which is now known as the Vallum. Though still to be seen plainly enough in its stride across the country, wind and weather, as well as the plough, have caused so much erosion that its formidable nature can now be fully appreciated only when it is seen in section as it was when originally dug. Its central feature was a great flat-bottomed ditch, 20 feet across at the top, 8 across at the bottom and about 10 feet deep. The upcast from this ditch was placed in two mounds set so far back from the lips of the ditch itself that the complete work spanned about 120 feet from side to side. The only lawful means of crossing this work was by way of the causeways which were built opposite the forts and which involved a passage through strong gates under the control of the fort garrisons. The importance which was attached to the Vallum is sufficiently indicated by the determination of its builders not to allow themselves to be turned aside from their purpose, even though its passage might at one time lead them through a belt of solid rock and at another time across a water-logged morass. The Vallum was undoubtedly a formidable obstacle which by its presence gave plain notice to all who approached that it was not meant to be crossed save at the proper times and in the proper places. Though not in itself a military work, it was subject to patrols carried out by military garrisons. It served in fact as the southern boundary of the great military zone which cut across the country from sea to sea, a zone to which there was to be no admission save by authorised persons.

The construction of this great fortified frontier was an immense undertaking which required many years, as well as almost the whole of the army in Britain, for its completion. Although native labour is likely to have been used for the heavy work involved in the digging of ditches and the carrying of materials, the actual building of Wall, turrets, milecastles and forts was carried out by the legions, assisted by some auxiliary regiments. The Wall itself was constructed in a series of independent lengths allotted to the three legions who worked in leap-frog fashion. Within the legionary length, the work was organised by cohorts and within the cohorts by centuries, leading eventually to a small unit of about 45 yards in length to be constructed by each century. The completion of each such unit bore the signature of its builders in the form of a small inscription inserted in the Wall at the appropriate place.

Work on the frontier, still the greatest monument to Roman achievement in Britain, was completed in about 133, surely bringing as one of it immediate consequences a marked easement of the problems facing the high command in Britain. The abandonment of all the lands north of the Tyne-Solway line, save for a relatively small area at the head of the Solway Firth, which was guarded by outpost forts at Bewcastle, Netherby and Birrens, will itself have resulted in considerable economy of man-power and supply, but this was not the only area from which garrisons were withdrawn at about this time. The situation in Wales, now effectively pacified and not as yet subject to any external threats, was secure enough to allow a substantial reduction in the numbers of its occupying troops. Some of the auxiliary forts were wholly evacuated and even the fortresses at Chester and Caerleon were held by greatly reduced numbers, at least for as long as their two legions were largely engaged in the construction of the northern frontier itself, and perhaps for longer. As a result of this great reorganisation, the heavily occupied military area of Britain was limited to the line of Hadrian's frontier and the Pennine hinterland, a reduction of half or perhaps even two-thirds in the area previously so held. All this surely meant that fewer men were needed and that, being more concentrated, those that remained could be more easily supplied. And yet something went wrong. For all its apparent permanence, the great Wall of Hadrian had been a frontier for less than twenty years when a further radical revision of frontier policy was put in hand, a revision which amounted to the reoccupation of lowland Scotland up to the line which had previously been held by Agricola.

There is no detailed narrative of the march of events in Britain for the later years of the reign of Hadrian nor for the reign of his successor, Antoninus Pius, so that the grounds upon which this change of frontier policy was based must remain largely a matter of speculation, aided by a study of the new frontier in comparison with the one which it displaced. It may be that the seizure of the Tyne Gap, an age-old line of communication between east and west, and its conversion into a forbidden military zone, had unforeseen local consequences, especially if, as seems possible, this military zone cut transversely across the lands of the Brigantes, always the most formidable enemies of Roman authority in Britain. It is significant that the boundary between England and Scotland was eventually established along the mountain line, the Cheviot watershed, and not along the river valleys, thereby leaving the Tyne valley to one side and almost the whole of the Tweed valley to the other, both of them potentially rich agricultural areas. Perhaps, too, the very concentration of strength, though giving added security to the individual auxiliary garrisons who thereby became less isolated from one another, was in itself a source of danger, since it so greatly increased the area over which there could be no effective supervision. It was one matter for Agricola to march into Caledonia and win a great battle, but it was another matter to leave Caledonia to her own scheming in the hope that a stone wall might be strong enough to uphold any assault that might issue from her mountains. Perhaps the cost of its garrisoning and maintenance had proved greater than expected. Perhaps there were men who thought that the Forth-Clyde line might be less expensive to maintain, and perhaps there were even those, pursuing a policy of change for change's sake, who thought that the garrisons might become less efficient unless they were more actively engaged. But one point seems clear enough—if the change seemed a big one from an insular point of view, it would have looked small enough from Rome.

Antoninus Pius succeeded Hadrian in 138, and his biographer tells us that at the beginning of his reign there were insurrections in Britain as well as in other parts of the Empire. The restoration of order in Britain and the great change of frontier policy were put in hand by his governor, Lollius Urbicus, who was at work at Corbridge in 139 after service in Germany, Pannonia and Palestine. His campaigns in Britain seem to have been designed to relieve pressure on the Hadrianic frontier by driving many of the inhabitants of southern Scotland into the more northerly parts of their country, perhaps beyond the Forth and the Clyde—if, that is, we are entitled so to interpret the two tantalising words *summotis barbaris* by which these campaigns are described. There are others who have thought that the movements which he inflicted on the barbarians were of a more drastic kind and resulted in the transplantation of many of them to the German frontier as forced levies in the Roman army.

The new Wall which Lollius Urbicus then proceeded to build ran from Bridgeness on the south shore of the Firth of Forth to Old Kilpatrick on the north shore of the Clyde, the distance, a little over 37 miles, being almost exactly half the length of Hadrian's Wall. Its superstructure which was built mostly of turf, rested upon a foundation consisting of a compact mass of undressed rubble contained within two continuous lines of kerb stones laid so as to give a base width of 14 feet. It seems likely that its height would have been about 10 feet, with the sides sloped at an angle to give a width of about 6 feet at the top, but it does not now survive anywhere to a height sufficient to allow us to say whether or not it was crowned with a defensive palisade. Along its northern side and separated from it by a berm or ledge of appropriate width there ran a V-shaped ditch which was of substantially larger dimension than that in front of Hadrian's Wall. There were 19 forts spaced at fairly regular intervals along its 37 miles, but if this figure is to be compared with the 16 forts along the 76 miles of Hadrian's Wall, it should be remembered that the Antonine forts were very much smaller than their Hadrianic counterparts, the smallest of them being no more than half an acre in size. At two or three sites small enclosures have been located in between neighbouring forts and it may be that there was a regular series of such enclosures intended, like the milecastles on Hadrian's Wall, to house patrol units, but there was nothing on this Antonine frontier comparable with the Hadrianic Vallum.

If we look at this new Wall built by Lollius Urbicus for Antoninus Pius in isolation we see at once that it was dangerously exposed to outflanking attack at both its eastern and western ends, and also that behind it there lay a broad belt of potentially menacing upland country, yet an appraisal of its military value in these terms would be gravely at fault since it was not, and was never intended to be, an isolated work. The danger of outflanking from the east across the Firth of Forth was met by the reoccupation and garrisoning of the Agricolan road along the edge of the Highland massif as far as the Tay. The encirclement of Fife in this way forestalled the kind of threat which resulted in the disastrous defeat of the Northumbrian army, led by Ecgfrith, beyond the Tay, late in the seventh century. At its western end the Wall terminated on the north bank of the Clyde. Some little distance farther to the west, and on the south side of the Clyde, a cavalry regiment was stationed in a five-acre fort at Whitemoss. There is a little evidence to suggest that a system of signal stations was in operation down the Ayrshire coast. Away to the south. Hadrian's Wall now ceased to be a barrier to traffic passing between north and south. The patrolling system was abandoned, the gateways of the milecastles left dismantled and unguarded. At frequent intervals along the Vallum gaps were dug through the mounds and the spoil from them tipped back into the ditch so as to make level passages across, perhaps more as an indication that this was no longer a forbidden zone, than with any eye for the convenience of those who lived near by. Yet the Wall was not wholly abandoned since garrisons remained in some at least of the forts. Between the two Walls, regiments were stationed at widely spaced intervals not only along the more easterly road followed by Agricola between Corbridge and Inveresk, but also in Nithsdale, Annandale and upper Clydesdale. Indeed the western side seems to have been rather more heavily garrisoned than the eastern. Among the minor, but functionally very important, structures forming a part of the Antonine Wall were several large turf foundations which served as stances for beacons and enabled the Wall garrisons to maintain touch with both their forward and their rearward areas. Meanwhile much farther south among the Brigantes, many of the forts in the Pennines were evacuated. Thus the general outcome of the new frontier policy carried out by Lollius Urbicus was a pronounced northerly shift of the area of Britain subjected to direct military government.

The new disposition of military forces did not succeed in bringing a prolonged period of stability to the frontier areas. Shortly after the middle of the second century, during the period 155–8, there is evidence of a widespread revolt which led not only to material destruction, but also to human casualties heavy enough to make it necessary for reinforcements to be drafted from the German provinces for all three of the legions then on service in Britain. Under the Antonine settlement there were still parts of south-western Scotland, notably in the shires of Wigtown and Ayr, which, so far as we yet know, were fairly remote from direct control, and perhaps it was from this area that the assault came. Certainly Birrens in Dumfriesshire and Netherby in Cumberland are among the sites which have yielded inscriptions recording rebuilding after the suppresson of the revolt during the governorship of Julius Verus. A similar inscription from Brough in Derbyshire may at least point to local unrest in that area as well. Whatever the epicentre of the rebellion, there was sufficient force behind it to have caused the abandonment of the Antonine Wall a bare ten years after its completion, as well as of the Antonine forts lying in the more southerly parts of Scotland. It is not yet clear whether this withdrawal was carried out in the face of a vigorous frontal attack, or whether the evidence obtained from one of the Antonine Wall forts, pointing to the peaceful and orderly evacuation of a site which was then deliberately destroyed by its garrison, is due to some strictly local condition or is to be regarded as representative of similar action over a wider area.

Orderly withdrawal was not in any case likely to have been put in hand except in conditions which seemed to threaten the isolation of the garrisons concerned, but whatever we have yet to learn about the detailed course of the rebellion, there is sufficient evidence to show that the loss of southern Scotland was only temporary. After only a short break Newstead was reoccupied, this time by a cavalry regiment one thousand strong. The break in the occupation of Mumrills, one of the forts near the eastern end of the Antonine Wall, was similarly short, and from other sites, both along the Antonine Wall and in its rear, there are enough indications of reoccupation at about this time to point to a restoration of the position which had been established by Lollius Urbicus some fifteen years earlier. The governor responsible for these dispositions, Calpurnius Agricola, was also active farther south. He is named on two inscriptions from Corbridge which belong to *c.* 161–2 and which refer to the presence there of detachments of both the Sixth and the Twentieth Legions. These inscriptions form part of the evidence which testifies to a complete rebuilding of Corbridge at this time; similar rebuilding was taking place at the same time at nearby Chesterholm and also farther away, at Ribchester and Hardknott, the one in Lancashire and the other in Cumberland.

All this activity ranging over such a wide area is at once an indication of the price the Romans were prepared to pay in order to maintain the security of lowland Britain and a hint that the resources which they were able to bring to the task, against the competing demands of the Danube frontier, were scarcely adequate for its performance. If they consolidated on the line of the Tyne Gap, too much of Britain lay beyond any kind of military control, and when they moved up to the more northerly line, there was danger of unrest, and perhaps serious rebellion in their rear. Periods of peace were short-lived on this active frontier and there was little respite for its garrisons. Trouble broke out again early in the reign of Commodus (180–92). There is a hint of legionary disaffection in an alleged attempt in Britain to set up a rival emperor, forerunner of a move which not long afterwards brought great disaster to the province, but the immediate danger came from another native uprising, this time outside the frontiers to the north. The uprising led, we are told, to far the greatest of the wars in which Commodus was involved. The northern tribes crossed the Wall which separated them from the Roman encampments, slew a Roman general who was leading his men in the field and caused widespread destruction.

The author of this account of the war does not state which of the two Walls was involved, but since there are no signs on the Hadrianic frontier of any widespread devastation at this period, we must suppose that it was the Antonine Wall to which he was referring. Yet the archaeological evidence, while confirming the written account up to a point, suggests that the assault and subsequent break-through may have been limited to a narrow front, since there seems not to have been any break in the occupation of parts at least of the eastern end of the Antonine Wall at this date. The failure of such an attack was almost inevitable, and no less inevitable was the punitive campaign which followed it and which was driven home with exceptional vigour by Ulpius Marcellus, a hard man whose reputation for sparing neither himself nor the men under his command suggests that he is not likely to have shown any mercy towards his enemies. And at this point the further history of the Antonine frontier is lost to sight, and must remain so until further excavation has yielded more evidence. It may have been reoccupied for a brief period by Ulpius Marcellus, and then abandoned, or it may have been held until destruction overtook it in the very last years of the second century.

The victories won by Ulpius Marcellus were commemorated on coins issued in 184 and 185. Less than ten years later there befell an event—the assassination of the emperor Commodus in 192—whose consequences may have led those tribes of Britain who had never reconciled themselves to Roman domination to think that there was the opportunity to throw off the yoke against which they had been struggling for more than a hundred years. In different parts of the Empire three men emerged each seeking to win the prize for himself. One of them was Septimius Severus, the governor of Moesia, the second was Pescennius Niger, the governor of Syria, and the third was the governor of Britain himself, Clodius Albinus. Severus defeated Pescennius Niger, and in 196 Albinus crossed to Gaul, taking with him most of the Roman army in Britain. There, in the spring of 197 he confronted Severus, and after coming near to victory was in the end totally defeated, himself committing suicide. The northern tribes of Britain, now confronted only by walls and fortifications which had been wholly abandoned or else were held only by greatly weakened garrisons, broke through the frontier and spread destruction all over the northern part of the province. From a military point of view the extent of the disaster was immense. Hadrian's Wall was overthrown so completely that in many places, when the time come for restoration, it had to be rebuilt from its foundations, so that there was some justification for the biographers of Severus when they claimed that he had in fact built the Wall and not merely repaired it. Forts, milecastles, turrets—all show abundant traces of destruction at this time. Southwards from the frontier the network of forts covering Brigantian territory tells the same tale, even as far as York.

Although the work of repair was put in hand with great speed as soon as Severus had secured his own position, it was almost ten years before it was complete. The Romans, like Alfred the Great under similar conditions of military stress, bought peace from their northern enemies while they began the work of restoration farther south. York was rebuilt, probably under the direction of Virius Lupus whose work at Ilkley and Bowes is attested by inscriptions dating from 197. With the legionary base established again and the Brigantes brought under control, active measures could be started to repair the frontier itself. The forts at Chesters, Housesteads and Birdoswald have all yielded inscriptions recording work done under the governorship of Alfenius Senecio during the years 205–8, and his presence is also attested farther north. When the frontier had been put back into a good state of repair and the forts in both the forward and rearward areas again made serviceable, Severus himself came to Britain to lead an assault deep into the territory of those who had been responsible for the greatest disaster that had yet befallen on the Romans in Britain.

Severus arrived in 208 and, in company with Caracalla, immediately began his preparations for vigorous northern campaigns. The conversion of the fort at South Shields, on the south bank at the mouth of the Tyne, into a supply base capable of housing large quantities of stores in transit, signs of similar activity at Cramond on the Firth of Forth, and the building of a 30-acre fortress at Carpow on the south bank of the Tay near Abernethy to house a large detachment of the Sixth Legion—all these emphasise both the scale of the Severan campaigns and also the part allotted to sea transport in their execution. The objective of Severus was the same as Agricola's, to bring to battle and defeat the tribes living in the deep north beyond the Firth of Tay, perhaps in the hope that the infliction of heavy casualties might so reduce their fighting strength as to remove any future threat from that area at least for a generation to come. The Caledonians were brought to battle and they were defeated, but although they surrendered unconditionally, further expeditions against continuing revolt were necessary in the following winters, and Severus was making ready to prosecute the war with even greater vigour when he died in York in February of the year 211. The work planned by Severus was continued by Caracalla who conducted a further campaign, and after bringing it to a successful conclusion withdrew to the line of Hadrian's Wall which once again became the northern frontier, though garrisons were stationed at a few points on its northern side to keep a watchful eye on the tribes of the lowlands. Historians have singularly little to say of any military or political events affecting Britain in the third century save at its beginning and end. The frontier now entered upon a longer period of peace than it had ever experienced before, and it was not until influences of quite a different sort began to make themselves felt towards the end of the third century that the peace was once more broken.

Perhaps the best witness to the efficacy of the Severan settlement is that at the end of the third century, one in which the situation for the Romans on the Rhine and Danube frontiers had undergone a marked deterioration, the British frontier still stood where Severus and Caracalla had placed it, seemingly unscarred. Within the province itself, now divided into two for purposes of administration, almost all the towns, even the smaller ones among them, were enclosed within stone walls, many of them completed before the end of the second century. Unless we are being greatly misled by the inadequacies of the written sources, Roman Britain in the third century was experiencing a period of balanced equilibrium similar to that which Bede witnessed in Anglo-Saxon England during the later years of his own life. In both ages there was peace on the frontiers and internal security resting on strong government, but, and the parallel here is a striking one, in neither age had adequate provision been made for defence against the possibility of attacks upon the long, exposed coastlines of the island. The civilisation of both ages was destroyed by barbarian invasion.

Saxon pirates in search of booty first became a serious threat to the security of Britain in the second half of the third century. They could find their loot in the towns and farms of eastern Britain and northern Gaul, just as the Vikings found it five hundred years later in the remote and secluded monasteries which had been built on innumerable island and coastal sites. The Saxons who lived in the low countries between the Rhine mouths and the Elbe will have had even better opportunities than the more distant Vikings for discovering that Britain might offer easy scope for self-enrichment. Some of them were in close contact with the imperial boundary and may have been emboldened by the severe setbacks which the Romans had lately suffered along parts of their frontier lands. Many of the Rhinelanders and some of the Frisians were even on service in Britain itself as garrison troops. Although the economic prosperity of Roman Britain may well have varied from one age to another, the island surely seemed a source of almost unimaginable wealth to those who struggled to win a livelihood in the difficult and dangerous conditions prevailing along much of the eastern shores of the North Sea. Seafaring, on however small a scale, was almost a necessary condition of life in these areas and, if fortified land frontiers could not be overrun, the sea, for the time being at least, was open to any boats which were stout enough to make the crossing to the east coast of Britain.

The first signs of the new dangers which were beginning to threaten the island come from south-eastern Britain. An inscription from Reculver refers to the erection of military buildings there early in the third century. At Richborough the monument erected in commemoration of the conquest of

Britain, was enclosed by defensive ditches and made serviceable as a look-out station which might help the *Classis Britannica* in its task of anticipating piratical attack. The fleet itself was strengthened and placed under the command of Carausius, himself a native of Belgium. No doubt his own personal knowledge of the waters on both sides of the sea in which he had to operate played a large part in the successes which he won against the marauding pirates, but the tactics which he employed led to an accusation being brought against him that he preferred to wait until a raid had been carried out so that he might then catch the raiders when their ships were heavily laden with booty. Such methods might have been justified if he had then handed over the recovered loot to the imperial treasury, but it was alleged, Carausius kept the booty for the enrichment of himself and his crews. When he learned that he was going to be brought to trial he had himself proclaimed emperor and took possession of the Low Countries and Britain as well as the northern parts of Gaul. For six years (287–93) Carausius reigned in Britain, enjoying the recognition granted to him by a central government which had little choice in the matter so long as he held both sides of the Channel and undisputed command of the waters between. In 293, Constantius Chlorus, the Caesar in command of transalpine Gaul, began to encroach on the north Gaulish lands held by Carausius, but although he succeeded in capturing Boulogne, the north Gaulish naval base, he was unable to defeat Carausius at sea. Soon afterwards, however, Carausius was murdered by Allectus, his chief financial officer.

Britain remained outside the Empire for another three years under the rule of Allectus, but during this time Constantius Chlorus was building ships in Gaul in readiness for an invasion and by 296 his preparations were complete. His fleet set sail in two divisions, one from Le Havre and the other from Boulogne. A sudden fog enabled some of his ships to slip unseen past those of Allectus which had been lying in wait off the Isle of Wight, and in the land battle which followed Allectus was totally defeated. A medal struck to commemorate the occasion shows Constantius Chlorus on horseback being received by a kneeling figure at the gates of London. Yet, like Severus before him, he had much to do to make the province once more secure. Allectus had been able to muster an army for his defence only by stripping the northern forts of their garrisons, and the undefended frontier was again overwhelmed as it had been in the days of Clodius Albinus a hundred years earlier. The extent of the disaster in the northern parts of Britain may have been even greater on this than on the previous occasion since there are signs of destruction at Chester as well as at York. Once again the Hadrianic frontier had to be restored and we know that the work was carried out on a thorough scale. At York itself the fortress was completely rebuilt, but fortifications could now no longer be confined to the northern frontier areas.

The threat of attack against the eastern and southern shores of Britain could be met most effectively by naval patrols ready to put out to sea as soon as warning of the approach of raiders had been received, but there was need also of land-based garrisons, infantry or cavalry, that could be used against those bands of raiders who were successful in evading the naval patrols. To meet these needs a number of fortresses were built at various commanding points along the coast between the eastern side of the Wash and the Isle of Wight. In the fourth century they formed a unified command under the Count of the Saxon Shore, but there is still much to be learned about the origin and history of the individual forts. Only one of them, the fort at Richborough, has been extensively excavated, and we can see here that, late in the third century, the site previously occupied by the look-out station was used for a massive six-acre fort characterised by the thickness of its walls as well as by other features designed to make it as nearly impregnable as possible. Similar forts were built at Dover and Lympne and these three, together with a fourth at Reculver, built *c.* 210–20 and slightly different in character, formed a compact group which enabled a watch to be kept upon the narrowest part of the Channel as well as upon the approaches to the Thames estuary.

The east coast rivers which run far into the heart of Essex and Suffolk would have given as ready a means of access to the Saxon raiders in the third century as they did to the Vikings in the ninth if they had not been defended by forts placed to overlook the Blackwater estuary at Bradwell, and the Stour and Orwell estuaries at Walton Castle, a site now lost beneath the encroaching sea. Other forts of similar kind were built farther north, one, now called Burgh Castle, in a commanding position on high ground near the junction of the Yare and the Waveney, and another close by the Wash at Brancaster, this last closely resembling the fort at Reculver and perhaps of similar date. Two of the most important harbours on the south coast, Pevensey and Porchester, were also fortified. Fortresses of this kind, reflecting new conceptions of static defence in which *ballistae* mounted on projecting bastions played an important part, were not confined to Britain's southern and eastern coasts. There is evidence enough of contact between Britain and Ireland during the latter days of the Roman occupation, and although not all of it was warlike, the construction at Lancaster and Cardiff of forts displaying the same prominently defensive features characteristic of the Saxon Shore forts suggests the beginning of raids from across the Irish sea such as that in which, at a later date, Patrick himself was carried off prisoner to Ireland.

Britain was a prosperous country in the fourth century, but a country set in an increasingly hostile sea, and as we look back it is not difficult to perceive in the light of subsequent events that the island could not long have remained securely within the Empire unless there had been a fundamental change in the outlook of those responsible for her military defence. Stone walls had served well enough, but only so long as they were adequately manned and so long also as the only enemy to be feared was one who came down from the northern mountains. It is significant that it was a man such as Carausius, one familiar with the problems of seafaring in waters so very different from the Mediterranean, who seems to have been the first to understand that in these changing circumstances the security of Britain could be achieved only by winning dominion over the seas across which her enemies might come, but significant also is the fact that the security which he brought to the island was accompanied by his own rebellion against a central authority which found itself powerless to overcome him. The Roman military tradition, based as it was primarily upon the use of highly trained foot soldiers, had no experience upon which it could draw to meet a situation in which many hundreds of miles of coastland lay open to attack from east, west and even south. The Wall, restored by Constantius Chlorus, could keep out the northern enemies, and the Saxon Shore forts no doubt gave a considerable measure of protection to the south-eastern parts of Britain, but complete and lasting security would have demanded a much more highly developed naval organisation, with large battle fleets, as well as fast naval patrols, stationed at ports from which all the seas surrounding Britain could have been effectively brought and kept under control, naval bases so fulfilling the role in defence which had formerly been played by the legionary fortresses. Without some such far-reaching changes as these, Britain would escape disaster only for as long as the attacks continued to be the work of small bands acting in isolation and therefore able to do only small, local injury.

The concerted action which disclosed the real weakness of Britain's defences came in 367 when a combined assault was made upon the province by Picts from the distant north, by Scots and by Saxons. In the north the Wall and its forts were again overthrown, a disaster for which the treachery of frontier scouts was in part at least responsible. The Scots assaulted the western side of the country while Saxons, supported by Franks, came to land in the south and east, simultaneously with an attack upon northern Gaul. Of the two chief military officers in Britain, the Count of the Saxon Shore and the Duke of the Britains, the former was killed and the latter isolated in ambush. The impact of the attack was so great that some of the defending forces were brought near to a state of disintegration and there were many cases of desertion. News of the disaster reached the emperor Valentinian as he was campaigning in Gaul. It was some time before he was able to take effective measures, but eventually he dispatched Count Theodosius, a distinguished soldier of Spanish origin, with a force adequate to deal with the situation. Landing at Richborough Theodosius made his way with some difficulty to London which he found to be in a state of siege. Armed bands were swarming over the country driving away cattle and prisoners. Ammianus Marcellinus, our authority for these disastrous happenings, presents us with a picture of a province in which there had been a total collapse of both civil and military government, yet perhaps we can be too easily led by him into overestimating the magnitude of the disaster. There were certainly some parts of the province which escaped unscathed, and recovery, even far away on the northern frontier, was swifter and more complete than might have been expected. The storm was locally violent while it lasted, but it passed swiftly away and there are many signs that Britain was no less prosperous at the end of the century than in the decades nearer to its beginning.

The onslaught that took place in 367 may well have been on a scale even greater than the great Danish invasion of almost exactly five hundred years later, yet the outcome was very different. The Roman arm was still powerful in this fourth century and its reach was long. Within three years peace had been restored to Britain, the Hadrianic Wall repaired and fresh dispositions made against any recurrence of such a disaster. There are signs that Theodosius recognised the changed conditions which demanded measures markedly different from those which had been adopted with success by Severus and Constantius Chlorus. Although Hadrian's Wall was rebuilt for the third time, we seem now to lose sight of the garrisons of regular troops by which it had previously been held and find instead that the forts and the civil settlements which had grown up outside their walls have in some fashion coalesced so as to form small fortified townlets, with a mixed community of men, women and children living within their defences.

So fundamental a change in the nature of this northern frontier might well seem to have been inviting just such another disaster as the dispositions now being adopted by Theodosius were surely designed to avoid, yet, so far as we can see, no such disaster befell. The long history of this great frontier work ends in no blaze of glory. There are no skeletons of massacred garrisons, no heaps of burnt ash from fiery destruction. The truth seems rather to be that, like the proverbial old soldier, it simply faded away, and the explanation of such an unexpectedly peaceful end may well be that Theodosius, seeing that the Wall could no longer be profitably manned as in earlier days, adopted other means of bringing security to the northern parts of Britain. We cannot trace the details of the process, neither can we be sure of the part played by Theodosius, but we can at least see that during the century which followed the work of restoration which he directed, the Tyne Gap wholly ceased to serve as any kind of military or political boundary and that, bestriding it to both north and south, and reaching up to the line of the old Antonine Wall, a series of self-governing independent British kingdoms came into existence under Roman protection. The real northern boundary then lay along the Forth-Clyde line, separating the British on the one side from the Picts and the Scots on the other. It may well have been Theodosius who initiated in this northern area the policy of creating treaty states whose own prosperity, and indeed very existence, depended upon their being able to defend themselves against external attack. But this is to anticipate the course of events.

CHAPTER FIVE

PROVINCIAL GOVERNMENT AND TOWN LIFE

Britain's position as the north-western frontier province of the Roman Empire, acting as a protective breakwater to both Gaul and Belgium, compelled the establishment there of a large permanent army of occupation. The episode of Clodius Albinus does not lack parallels in later times when men holding high office in Britain saw that the army might be used to further their own ambitions. It was mainly to guard against such dangers that those provinces of the Empire in which large bodies of troops were stationed were kept under the direct control of the emperor himself, forming the so-called imperial provinces, in contrast with the senatorial provinces which continued, after the settlement achieved by Augustus, to be governed by men of consular or praetorian rank. In law, then, the governor of Britain was the emperor himself, and it was as governor and supreme commander-in-chief that Claudius, Hadrian and Septimius Severus came to visit their province. In practice, however, the emperor's authority in Britain was exercised through a subordinate who remained directly responsible to him. The full title of this officer, the effective governor of the province, was *legatus Augusti pro praetore*; and that is how we find him entitled on an inscription from the Antonine Wall recording work done there *sub Quinto Lollio Urbico Legato Augusti pro praetore*, or on another, from Corbridge, recording a religious dedication *sub cura Sexti Calpurnii Agricolae Legati Augusti pro praetore*. Owing obedience to this governor, but not always paying it, were the commanders of the legions (*legati legionum*) and of the auxiliary units (*praefecti*). And upon him there rested not merely the military command of the forces within his province, but also the administration of law and justice throughout its civilian areas. For this latter purpose the governors had, on some occasions at least, the assistance of a *legatus juridicus*; five such *legati* are known to have functioned in Britain at different dates between the beginning of Agricola's governorship and the early years of the third century.

Britain was regarded as one of the most important of the

imperial provinces and appointment to office as its governor was a high distinction. There was, however, one respect, and a very important one, in which the governor's authority was not absolute within his province. The general oversight of all that had to do with the imperial revenue from Britain was entrusted to an official who was entitled *procurator Augusti* and who was responsible directly to the emperor. This sharp division between civil and military government on the one hand and financial organisation on the other may remind us that the justification for heavy military expenditure was a sound economic return. The procurator was concerned with all imperial property in Britain, such as large agricultural estates, lead and copper mines and other industrial establishments, as well as with ensuring that taxes, both in money and in kind, reached the departments to which they were due. The land-tax, the poll-tax, the corn-tax, the customs duties on goods crossing the imperial frontier—these and other taxes amounted to a heavy burden upon the population generally. The welfare of the province might depend to a very large extent upon the attitude adopted by the procurator towards his financial duties, and also upon the relations between himself and the governor. The office of the procurator was in London, and in London still is the tombstone erected by the wife of one of them, Alpinus Classicianus, styled thereon *procurator provinciae Britanniae*. He was successor to Decianus Catus whose harsh exactions from the recently conquered tribes of lowland Britain had been one of the important factors leading to the rebellion of the Iceni and the Trinovantes under Boudicca in 60–61.

During the first century and a half of the occupation Britain remained a single province, but the reorganisation carried out by Septimius Severus affected the civil area of the province no less than the frontier zone. Perhaps with an eye to lessening the danger that some other governor might seek to exploit the forces at his command to further his own ends, Severus divided the country into two separate provinces which were known as Britannia Superior and Britannia Inferior. We know from inscriptions that the two western legionary bases, Chester and Caerleon, were in Britannia Superior, and that the third, York, together with Lincoln, was in Britannia Inferior. We do not know where the boundary ran between the two provinces, but the arrangement seems to hint at divided military controls as being one of the motives by which the change was prompted.

At the end of the third century Britain was affected by the great imperial reforms which were introduced by Diocletian. The Empire became a tetrarchy, with two Emperors and two Caesars, and the expectation that each of the Caesars would in time succeed to the position of Augustus. In its civil aspect Britain now ranked as a diocese under the government of a *vicarius*, forming one of twelve similar units embracing the Empire as a whole. The *vicarius* of the diocese of Britain was not responsible directly to the emperor of the west, but to a praetorian prefect whose headquarters were at Trier and who had the whole of transalpine Gaul and Spain, as well as Britain, under his surveillance. As a diocese, Britain was subdivided into four provinces entitled Britannia Prima and Britannia Secunda, Maxima Caesariensis and Flavia Caesariensis. At the end of the fourth century, after the restoration following the great Picts War of 367–70, there was a fifth province with the name Valentia. Nothing is known about the boundaries of any of these provinces, and next to nothing even of their general whereabouts. Cirencester seems to have been in Britannia Prima, and it is possible that London was the centre of Flavia Caesariensis. It is a safe conjecture, not wholly without some supporting evidence, that London, by now much the most important city of Roman Britain, was the seat of government of the *vicarius*.

It is a commonplace that the Romans gave to Britain a system of communications which, taking account of the needs that it was designed to serve, has never been surpassed. These needs were threefold—military, administrative and commercial. Troops disembarking at Richborough or some other Channel port had before them a march of about three hundred and fifty miles if they were destined for Hadrian's Wall, and we are not likely to be mistaken in thinking that many of the major roads were built in the early stages of the conquest—the Kentish network linking the south-eastern harbours at Lympne, Dover, Richborough and Reculver with Canterbury, and running directly thence to the fords across the Thames where London soon began to grow; the great northern road running along the western edge of the Fens to Lincoln and then on to York; the midland route to Wroxeter and Chester; the western route to Silchester, Old Sarum and Dorchester; the Fosse Way from Lincoln to the Devon coast; and of course the networks in Wales, Brigantia and southern Scotland where the roads are likely to have had little else but a military function.

The administrative functions of this road system became obvious when we notice how several of the tribal centres lie as the hub of radiating spokes. Five roads converge upon Silchester (*Calleva Atrebatum*). Winchester (*Venta Belgarum*), Cirencester (*Corinium Dobunnorum*) and Wroxeter (*Viroconium Cornoviorum*) are similarly well served. Such roads as these opened up the tribal areas and enabled contact to be maintained between their capitals and their lesser administrative centres. They were a means towards assisting the local magistrates to carry out their judicial duties and towards easing the task of fiscal officers responsible for the collection of taxes. The upkeep of such roads would fall upon the local community. A courier service provided the only means whereby the central government could convey to the regional centres decisions on matters affecting the government of the province as a whole, and also the only means of keeping itself well informed about local political or economic conditions. For this purpose a government postal service was maintained along certain routes. A document of the third century, the *Antonine Itinerary*, gives details of sixteen routes along which such a service was maintained and which would accordingly be equipped with rest-houses and posting stations where horses could be changed by those engaged in the imperial service.

Although built primarily to meet military and administrative needs, these roads would also meet various local needs as well, especially in the transport of agricultural produce. There are, however, some roads whose course seems to suggest that they were built primarily for commercial purposes. Particularly striking is the series which runs southwards from London towards the Sussex coast at Chichester, Brighton and Lewes. A lateral route running east and west along the northern edge of the Sussex Downs forms an interconnecting link between these three roads near their southern ends and shows clearly enough that, except perhaps in the case of the road to Chichester, and then only for secondary reasons, these three roads were not built primarily in order to establish connections between London and the south coast itself. Their course lies through the Weald which was one of the major centres of the iron industry in Roman Britain, and is clearly aimed at the Sussex Downs, an important corn-growing area. Farther to the east a branch road was driven southwards from the London–Canterbury road at Rochester to the area of extensive iron working inland from Hastings. The Weald itself, in Roman no less than in Anglo-Saxon times, offered unlimited swine pasture, and there can be no doubt that these roads of Weald and Downs were built to bring their varied and valuable products the more easily to the London markets. Another group of roads strongly suggestive of commercial uses is that which converges upon Water Newton (*Durobrivae*) in the east midlands. This site, enjoying in the early days of the occupation some military importance as a station on the road between London and Lincoln, later became the centre of a highly organised pottery industry which was spread out along the banks of the Nene and distributed its products widely over the country.

The building of the roads themselves would be done by local labour gangs under the direction of Roman engineers to whose outstanding skill in surveying a chosen course abundant testimony survives to this day. Straightness, the most familiar characteristic of a Roman road, was achieved by setting out alignments from one high point to another. This seeming straightness is sometimes more apparent than real. Whereas the modern motorway makes use of slow swinging curves in order to change direction, thereby seeking to secure the safety of high-speed travel and at the same time to avoid monotony, the Roman engineer, who was bound by neither of these considerations, made his changes of direction by turning at the necessary angle on the high point itself, whence a sight could be taken for the next alignment. Thus, while there are some instances of direct alignment over long distances, as in the twenty-five miles between Rochester and Canterbury which show virtually no change of direction at all, it is rather more usual for a road to be laid out in a series of straight, short lengths. Steep gradients giving direct approach to the objective were generally preferred to the easier slope which would have involved a longer way round, although it was found necessary to make a zig-zag approach for heavy traffic coming down the steep approach to Chew Green in Northumberland from the south, and carefully graded roads are sometimes found on the steep escarpments of downland areas.

The first step in the construction of a road after the survey work had been completed was to build a broad mound, the *agger*. This mound, which was made from material scooped from the sides, thus leaving either two running ditches or else a series of pits, formed a well-drained base upon which the road itself could then be laid. The materials used were naturally those which were most readily available in the area, and they were laid in a series of superimposed layers giving a compact surface of gravel, flints or small stones. There was great variation in the width of roads, twenty-four feet being common on the more important, and fifteen to eighteen on the lesser. Unusual local conditions might give rise to exceptional methods of construction, as in the use of iron slag for metalling on parts of the road between London and Lewes, and in the remarkable paved surface of the road up the steep slope of Blackstone edge in the southern Pennines.

The road system provided the links between the different units which formed the basis of local administration in Roman Britain. The *colonia*, of which there were four in Britain—Colchester, Gloucester, Lincoln and York—and the *municipium*, the status which is believed to have been held by Verulamium, both consisted of communities of Roman citizens living under constitutions based upon that of Rome itself. There was a local senate (*ordo*) comprising, nominally at least, a body of a hundred men who were called decurions and most of whom had been magistrates. The magistrates were elected annually, one pair (*duoviri jure dicundo*) being responsible for judicial matters, and the other pair (*duoviri aediles*) for public buildings and finance. In addition there was a body of men called *seviri Augustales* whose responsibilities lay in the maintenance of the emperer-worship. A *colonia* was normally a new settlement of veteran legionaries whose service had been completed, whereas the status of *municipium* was conferred by charter conveying special privileges to some already existing community. The basic difference between these two on the one hand and the *civitates* on the other was that the inhabitants of the former enjoyed rights of Roman citizenship, whereas those of the latter did not. *Colonia*, *municipium*, *civitas*—all alike comprised a substantial area of land as well as the urban centre which formed the focal point of each. The *civitates* too had their own senate and their own magistrates, though we should remember that these people, beneath the guise of such civilised terms as *ordo* and *decurio*, were in fact the local tribal aristocracy.

Administratively below the level of the *civitas* were two

other units, the *vicus* and the *pagus*. The status of *vicus* was that normally acquired by the settlements of civilians that grew up outside the walls of military sites, such as those identified at Housesteads and elsewhere along the Hadrianic frontier. An inscription set up by the *vicani* of *Veluniate*, that is, Carriden, the eastern terminal fort of the Antonine Wall, demonstrates that this status might be achieved by people living in remote areas where no marked degree of Romanisation was to be expected. The inhabitants of *Petuaria*, Brough-on-Humber, one of the chief towns of the Parisi, were also *vicani* in this technical sense. In Gaul the *pagus* was a subdivision of the *civitas* and it seemed likely that it served this same function in Britain even though there is no direct evidence.

Overriding these different local units, but with rather limited functions, was the *concilium provinciae* to whose annual meeting first held at the temple of Claudius of Colchester the *civitates* sent their representatives. The prime concern of the *concilium provinciae* was to supervise the maintenance of the state religion, the worship of the emperor, which may have served in some slight degree as an unifying bond between the different parts of the country, although the existence of such a wide variety of religious cults made its influence in this respect very much less than that of the Christian Church in Anglo-Saxon England. Beyond the religious aspects of its duties, the *concilium provinciae* was the means whereby a direct approach could be made to the emperor without going intermediately through the governor, and it was therefore a means by which even the governor himself could be criticised. Despite the various changes of machinery introduced by Severus and later through the reforms of Diocletian, the local government of Roman Britain remained essentially unchanged throughout the occupation. St Patrick's father, living late in the fourth century and perhaps into the fifth, was a decurion and the *civitates* were in communication with the emperor in the early years of the fifth century when the central organs of government had ceased to function.

Britain formed a geographical unit by her own nature and it was only in the north that failure to reach the sea imposed the necessity of creating an external boundary, but internal administrative unity, though ultimately dependent upon the security arising from a strongly held frontier, was an end which could be achieved only by skilfully organised means. Intruders had to be kept out, and local divisions, at least in so far as they might give rise to warring factions, had to be overridden within. The Roman army was responsible for the first of these tasks, the Roman road system played an important part in achieving the second. Organised force, a highly efficient system of communications and accumulated experience in methods of government were able to bring to Britain within less than a generation of the invasion, a degree of administrative unity such as the Anglo-Saxons were able to achieve only after being settled in the country for the best part of five hundred years. But no Anglo-Saxon king ever had at his command the resources that were available to any of the governors of Roman Britain. It was an external force of a very different kind, the Christian religion, that first provided the means of a slow return towards unity in this later age, partly because of what it taught and partly because it gave Britain fresh opportunity for drawing upon inherited imperial experience.

Bede described London in the eighth century as the market-place of many people who came to it by sea and land. The conditions which made it so already prevailed in the days of Tacitus who used much the same words when he was writing of London as it was in the year 60, before it had been laid waste in the great rebellion. The origin of the city was determined by those who had both the wit to perceive and the means to exploit the peculiar advantages which might be enjoyed by a trading community established on the two low, yet commanding, hills which were divided from one another by the shallow valley of the Walbrook and which are now crowned by Leadenhall Market to the east and St Paul's Cathedral to the west. These two hills lay near to the tidal limits of the Thames estuary, but, and this was of even greater importance, they also lay at a point where the near approach of firm gravel to both banks of the river made the work of bridging the river itself a matter of no great difficulty, not at least to the Roman engineers who were the first to accomplish it. Here was the natural meeting-place between merchants who travelled by road within Britain itself and those who came from overseas and who, whether they had sailed from nearby Gaul or from more distant Mediterranean ports, would find that the Thames estuary offered an approach slightly less hazardous than was involved in negotiating the many treacherous sandbanks which lay athwart the route to Colchester, the most prominent city of south-eastern Britain before the Roman conquest.

The first Roman settlement was on the more easterly of the two hills, but it spread rapidly across the Walbrook to the west and when its stone walls were built in the second century they enclosed an area of some 325 acres, larger by one-third than Cirencester, the second largest city of Roman Britain. Although we lack proof that London enjoyed a titular dignity such as might have been conferred upon it by the style *colonia*, *municipium* or *civitas*, yet there is no doubt of its commercial pre-eminence among all the cities of Roman Britain, and even if we lack documentary proof that it came to be recognised as the provincial capital at a fairly early date in the occupation, at least it may be said that no other city in Britain has yielded evidence of a stronger claim to that distinction. At the beginning of the second century, or perhaps even earlier, at a time when the military tide had swept far away to the north, a fort was built in the area where now lies Cripplegate, some little way back from the wharves lining the water front. Memories of what had happened in London, no less than in Colchester, in 60 may have suggested that it would be wise to take precautions against any repetition of such a disaster. Much evidence has come to light that the city was again swept by a fire in the time of Hadrian, but fire has always been a common hazard among closely packed, wooden buildings and we need look no further for explanation. The placing of a garrison in the Cripplegate fort suggests not only the need to provide some security for valuable goods housed in vulnerable warehouses, but also the desire to give at least a token display of the military strength upon which the government of the province ultimately rested. Fragmentary inscriptions of not wholly certain interpretation hint that London became the provincial centre of emperor-worship and also the meeting-place of the provincial council. The buildings housing the financial administration, whose presence in London has been argued from many tile stamps referring to the chief customs officers of the province, will have needed at least that measure of protection afforded to the Bank of England in modern times. The financial importance of London in the fourth century is placed beyond all doubt by the reference to a *praepositus thesaurorum* there and there alone in the whole of Britain, and early in this century the distinguished title *Augusta* was conferred upon the city.

The city wall, now shown to have been built not earlier than *c.* 190, followed an almost semi-circular course from the Tower in the east, northwards to a point near Finsbury Circus and then back to the river south of Ludgate Hill. The nature of the site makes it impossible to learn much in detail about the plan of the city, but the aftermath of bombing has given fresh opportunity for excavation of which the most outstanding results have been the discovery of the Cripplegate fort whose northern and western walls were later incorporated in the city wall itself, and of the temple of Mithras by the banks of the Walbrook. The flagon which came from the temple of Isis and the ritual implement used in the cult of Cybele are other witnesses to the influences of the East among the merchants who transacted their business in the great basilica or commercial hall which crowned the more easterly of the two hills and which was twice rebuilt within the Roman period.

The greatness of Roman London rested upon its commercial prosperity, upon the particular conditions of locality no less than time which made it a market-place for traders from many different nations. Although London had no commercial rival in Roman Britain, the conditions prevailing at York were highly favourable for the development of a thriving mercantile community, for here was a site enjoying the strongest military protection, served by a river port, linked for a time at least by inland waterways with East Anglia and the southern midlands, and enjoying what was surely the almost insatiable market provided by the regiments garrisoning the military zone of the province. York lacked the peculiar advantage which was conferred upon London by the shortness of its sea communications with Gaul, but it may be significant that a few years before 600, when Pope Gregory in Rome was looking towards Britain as a lost province to be recovered for the Church, his choice fell upon London and York as the seats for the two archbishops he envisaged when the conversion of the English should be complete and the new Church established.

York, unlike London, is known to have enjoyed the highest grade of civic dignity which could be bestowed by Rome, that of a *colonia*. The very earliest Roman *coloniae*, those founded within Italy itself, were established primarily for strategic purposes, the protection of the Italian coastline in general. In later times, and within Britain itself, although some element of that primary purpose still remained, they met both the need to make some provision for legionaries who had completed their term of service and the desire to establish a highly Romanised form of life which might influence and later even coalesce with local native communities. York was one of four *coloniae* in Britain. It is first mentioned as such in an inscription of A.D. 237 but we do not know the date of its foundation nor have we yet been able to identify the circuit of its defences. It lay on the opposite bank of the Ouse from the fortress and, unlike the other three *coloniae,* it was not the successor to an evacuated military site, but the companion of one which continued to be garrisoned by legionaries. The richly varied collection of remains which have been recovered from its site witnesses the high degree of civilisation enjoyed by its inhabitants, but we cannot say whether, like the other three, it was a new foundation established as a *colonia* from the beginning, or whether what seem to be distinctive features in its history suggest that the grant of status came in recognition of growth and dignity already achieved.

The first *colonia* to be established in Britain was at Colchester where it was founded in the year 49 by Ostorius Scapula and given the title *Colonia Victricensis,* although the native name *Camulodunum* remained. The circumstances of the time reveal very clearly that the object of the foundation, apart from making provision for veterans, was to create a community which was expected both to act as a focus of loyalty among the recently conquered tribes of East Anglia and Essex, and also to serve as an example of Roman civilisation to those who lived in the nearby native capital. The consequences of its early failure to achieve either of these aims have been told elsewhere. Senate, temple and theatre all perished in the destruction of 60, but a new *colonia* was built literally upon the ashes of the old. It was planned in the customary Roman style with numerous streets intersecting one another at right angles and subdividing the whole area into a number of separate *insulae,* about forty in all. Save for the great temple of Claudius whose supporting platform was used by the builders of the Norman castle, little is known about the internal buildings, whether public or private, of either the first or the second *colonia.* Despite the disaster of 60, the rebuilt *colonia* was not provided with any walls, and it is an indication of both the vigour with which the revolt was suppressed and of the security later prevailing in this part of the country that no walls were built before the second century, and even then probably not before its second half. When they were built they had a circumference of 1¾ miles, enclosing an oblong area of about 108 acres, and so solid was their construction that they still remain standing today, in some places almost to their original height. No less impressive are the remains of the great West or Balkerne Gate which formed the main entry into the town and which, with its four portals, two of them over 17 feet wide, and its flanking towers, once displayed a majestic and monumental splendour unparalleled elsewhere in Britain. Through this gate passed the road to London along whose sides lay the chief cemeteries of the *colonia*. Two notable tombstones, one of Favonius Facilis, a centurion of the Twentieth Legion, and the other of Longinus, a trooper in a regiment of Thracian cavalry, are surviving monuments of the earliest military occupation of the site. Both were thrown down in the rebellion of 60. Later suburban development outside the walls of the *colonia* was also mainly in a westerly direction where there is evidence for the manufacture of pottery on a large scale, including Samian ware. Temples and smaller relics suggestive of religious activities, and also a theatre, have been found on several sites within two or three miles of the *colonia*, notably at Gosbecks towards the south-west. The many mosaic pavements discovered within the walls, the sculptures, including a famous representation of a Sphinx, and the rich tombs, some of them furnished with inscriptions cut in Purbeck marble, all testify to a wealthy community possessing a high degree of Romanisation.

The other two *coloniae*, those at Lincoln and Gloucester, followed the rather formal, semi-military pattern to be seen at Colchester, though both were later foundations and originally no more than half its size. Lincoln, *Lindum Colonia*—its name scarcely changed at all—was founded in the nineties and occupied the hill-top site which had been evacuated when the legionary base was moved forward to York. It was from the first a walled town because the old legionary defences were still there and could readily be adapted to suit the needs of the new *colonia*. The great timbers of the east gate which had formed the main entrance to the legionary fortress, seem to have remained serviceable until well into the second century. In its early days the area of the *colonia*, about fifty acres, coincided exactly with that of the fortress, but vigorous suburban growth down the southern slope of the hill led, at a date which has yet to be determined, to an extension of the walls southwards almost to the banks of the Witham and thereby to the doubling of the enclosed area. Gloucester—*Colonia Nervia Glevensium*—was founded a year or two later. It too was the successor of a legionary fortress, abandoned when the legions moved westwards to Caerleon, but there is no sign that Gloucester ever expanded beyond its original walls, not at least to an extent that required the enlargement of the area at first enclosed.

The *coloniae*, with their remains buried deeply beneath medieval and modern buildings, all lie on sites which are difficult to excavate in more than a piecemeal fashion. The same is true of most other Romano-British towns; and of the few which remain still easily accessible beneath open fields only one—Silchester (*Calleva Atrebatum*) has been fully excavated. Although it is easy to find fault with the manner in which these excavations were carried out, their results did produce a picture of a Romano-British town as it was during the third and fourth centuries, a picture moreover which may be held as representative of a tribal capital of that age. In size Silchester was much the same as Colchester, 100 acres against 108, but its shape, an irregular polygon, contrasts sharply with the military appearance of Colchester, Lincoln and Gloucester. Lying at its centre and occupying nearly two acres of ground was the chief of its public buildings, the forum, which was designed to serve both as a civic centre and as a market-place for traders. *Mutatis mutandis*, the modern Guildhall of Cambridge and the open market which lies before it offer an instructive parallel to the kind of activities which took place in the forum of a Romano-British town—and Cambridge is by no means the only modern English town to retain this juxtaposition of civic and mercantile interests.

The Silchester forum, surrounded on all sides by a colonnade whose pillars of Bath stone supported a penthouse roof, was entered from the east through a monumental gateway over which was placed an inscription whose letters, each cut eleven inches high, were displayed on polished slabs of Purbeck marble. Only a few fragments now survive from what must have been an impressive example of Roman monumental lettering. Remains of similar dedicatory inscriptions have been recovered from near the forum at St. Albans and also at Wroxeter.

Within the gateway was a large gravelled courtyard, open to the sky and surrounded on three sides by colonnaded porticoes beyond which lay a number of rooms, of which some will have been used as shops for traders, others as offices for government officials. Along the full width of the fourth side and opposite the main entrance lay the great basilica. More than 230 feet from end to end and almost 50 feet wide, it was divided lengthwise into a central nave and two side aisles. Although it was not constructed on such a massive scale and was neither so broad nor so lofty, the Silchester basilica was longer than the Norman nave of Ely Cathedral. At either end in apsidal recesses were the raised platforms, *tribunalia*, upon which rested the seats of magistrates. Beyond the basilica was a further range of rooms with the *curia*, the meeting-place of the cantonal senate, centrally placed. The floors of the basilica were of red tesserae set in cement, its walls were frescoed and its columns were made of Bath stone with Corinthian capitals. Part at least of the *curia* was lined with white Italian marble and much Purbeck marble was used in other parts of the building. Among its statuary were a stone image, twice life-size, of the guardian deity or *tutela* of the Atrebates, a bronze representation of an emperor, also more than life-size, and a bronze eagle with wings outstretched for flight, the latter perhaps no more than a fragment of some larger composition. No building on such a scale as this had been seen in Britain before the Romans came and it can hardly have failed to impress the Atrebates with the qualities of Roman civilisation.

The other public buildings included temples, a bath-house and a large *mansio*, or hotel, in which official visitors and those using the Imperial Post were accommodated. The religious activities of the town were mainly concentrated near the east gate where two temples of the characteristic Romano-Celtic style were housed within a sacred enclosure of three acres in extent. In medieval times a church and a cemetery came to overlie part of this sacred enclosure. A third temple of similar form and a fourth, circular within and polygonal without, lay nearer the centre of the town to the south of the forum. Much nearer to the forum and lying within the same central *insula* was a small apsidal building not erected before 360 and presenting many features characteristic of a Christian church. Although no specifically Christian object was found within this building, a few objects bearing Christian imagery upon them have been found in other parts of the town. At the lower end of the declivity which was crowned by the temple enclosure lay the public bath-house, conforming in type to the establishments which are familiar from a large number of civilian as well as military sites throughout the province. In such a building provision was made for gymnastic exercise, as well as for the full ritual of the Roman bath taken by methodical progress through a series of interconnected rooms heated to varying degrees. The heat was produced in a furnace whence it was carried beneath the floors by a hypocaust system, and upwards through the walls in box-shaped flue tiles which were embedded therein.

The town bath-house was an important centre of social life. One or two of the larger private houses at Silchester had their own private bath-houses and there was also a separate establishment for the use of guests who were accommodated in the *mansio*. This was a large building placed near the south gate and designed in the form of three wings placed symmetrically round a courtyard whose fourth side was enclosed by a stone wall. In its general plan the *mansio,* substantially larger than the largest of the private houses, resembles the guest house of the temple settlement at Lydney. No theatre such as has been discovered at Canterbury and at St Albans has been found within the walls, but outside, near the east gate, lay an amphitheatre, so far unexcavated. The density of the population within the town is difficult to estimate. The streets near the centre are quite thickly lined with buildings which served as shops, warehouses and workshops, many of them planned as simple rectangles with a narrow open front facing the street. There is also a considerable number of larger buildings, perhaps fifty or so, some of the biggest being built round courtyards, others L-shaped or of simple corridor plan. These were the private houses in which lived the local aristocracy and the more prosperous among the merchants. Some were heated by hypocausts, some had mosaic floors and some may have been of two storeys. The site yielded a plentiful supply of water which was drawn from numerous wells, usually lined with oak boards, sunk within the area of the town itself. The plan which resulted from the excavations carried out mainly between 1890 and 1910 shows many areas wholly free from buildings, not merely among the *insulae* which lay on its outer fringes near the walls, but also in some of those more centrally placed. Yet the impression of an open town of almost rural appearance may well be deceptive, for we do not know how many timber buildings might have been discovered through the application of more exacting methods of excavation.

The Silchester which we can envisage from the plan of its streets, buildings and encircling walls is somewhat artificial, partly because the picture is a composite one drawing its different elements from different periods in its long history, and partly because the town itself was largely a product of forced and unnatural development. It did not grow like London, neither was it created like Colchester, as a habitation for men already imbued with the ways of Roman civilisation. Its forum and its public baths represent the products of very heavy capital expenditure, yet those who later laid out its street grid did not trouble to align it exactly with the forum, nor did it matter to them if the colonnaded portico of the bath-house happened to project five feet across the line of one of their streets. The offending columns could be removed and their stumps buried beneath the metalling of the road. There is more than a suggestion here of the hand of authority and external planning. More recent but limited excavations on selected parts of the site, helped by illuminating results obtained by aerial photography in a season when parched ground displayed underlying foundations with particular clarity, have done something to place the Silchester buildings within a context of historical change.

We now know that the site of the town was already a centre of habitation before it was Romanised and that the stone wall by which it was encircled during the last two centuries of its existence represents a comparatively late phase in a complex history of change and development. The earliest defences which enclosed an area partly inside and partly outside the existing walls, were of earthen construction, and so also were the defences by which they were superseded in the Flavian period when the town embraced an area of 200 acres with streets laid out in the grid characteristic of Roman town planning. In the Antonine period, *c.* 145, the area of the town was reduced to 100 acres so that in some places the earlier street grid protruded beyond the new defences which were still of earthen construction. Near the end of the second century a stone wall was built upon the same line as the earthen defences of the Antonine period.

Leicester (*Ratae Coritanorum*) is another of the tribal capitals built upon a site already previously occupied, in contrast with Exeter (*Isca Dumnoniorum*) where the Roman town was built upon a virgin site. These three were all much of a size and there are a number of other Romano-British towns approximating to 100 acres. In appearance, however, Leicester is strikingly different from Silchester, its sharply rectangular plan seeming to hint at military influences early in the Roman occupation, influences which are not unexpected in a town sited on the Fosse Way. At Leicester, too, we have remains of a commercial hall and of a suite of public baths comparable with those at Silchester, and if the road builders at Silchester sliced off the elegant front of its bath-house, the surveyors at Leicester contrived to lead their aqueduct to the wrong point.

The development of St Albans (*Verulamium*), which ultimately covered an area of 200 acres and so became the third city of Roman Britain in point of size, presents an even more complex picture, with many problems still waiting solution. The area of Roman occupation was near, but not directly upon, a Belgic *oppidum* which is thought to have been built in the time of Tasciovanus *c.* 15 B.C., and which lay upon a low plateau overlooking the valley of the river Ver from the west. The abandonment of the 'upland' site at the time of the Roman occupation was prompted by the passage of Watling Street along the floor of the valley, as it followed its north-westerly course from London to Chester, and by its junction near to St Michael's ford with the road from Braughing and Colchester, both of them Roman towns with a pre-Roman history. In its passage towards the ford, Watling Street runs obliquely across the Flavian street grid of the town in a manner which suggests that the road is earlier. Traces of an earthwork of Claudian date have been found near the river but it remains as yet uncertain whether these represent part of a military or of a civic defensive system.

Like Colchester and London, St Albans was sacked at the time of the Boudiccan rebellion. In describing this disaster Tacitus uses the word *municipium* which, like the modern 'city', had both a general and a technical sense. If, as seems most probable, Tacitus intended the word to be understood here in its technical sense, then it is to be inferred that at an early date St Albans acquired the status of a chartered town, with important consequences both for its own constitution and for the inhabitants of the neighbouring countryside. Tacitus also tells us, though not with specific reference to St Albans, that Agricola gave both private encouragement and public assistance in the building of temples, public squares and private mansions, as a means of introducing the people to such delights of civilisation as might divert them from their warlike habits, even though such amenities might in reality be no more than a further measure of enslavement to Rome. We can now discern something of the impact of this policy upon St Albans. Excavation has recovered some fragments of an inscription bearing Agricola's name, dated exactly to the second half of the year 79 and coming from a monumental gateway leading into a forum such as adorned the centre of Silchester. This Agricolan forum, with a temple enclosure a little to its western side, stood at the centre of a street grid laid out along the southern bank of the river and all enclosed within a defence work comprising an earthen bank and ditch embracing about 150 acres. The date of these defence works is yet uncertain, but the ditch was being abandoned and allowed to silt up towards the end of the first century. A later stage in the development of the town is represented by the building during the Hadrianic age of an amenity such as Tacitus might have regarded as one of those which make vice agreeable. It took the form of a theatre built on a site adjacent to the temple and so designed that it could provide both for stage performances and for the less instructive, but perhaps more frequent, spectacles of bear-baiting, cock-fighting and the like.

There are some indications of a westerly extension of the area of the town before it was finally enclosed within stone walls which are believed to have been built late in the second century and which embraced some 200 acres. These stone defences consisted in their outer element of a massive ditch some 80 feet across and 20 feet in vertical depth. Separated from the ditch by a wide berm was a stone wall 8 feet thick and not less than 12 feet high with a solid earthen bank abutting against its inner face. The passage of Watling Street through the walls was marked by two monumental gateways, the 'London' and the 'Chester' gates, both of them with double roadways flanked by footways and great projecting drum towers. These defences seem to mark the end of what might be called the monumental stage in the growth of St Albans which had begun a century earlier with the building of

Agricola's forum. There are no signs of public works in the city during the third century. Before the end of the fourth century the theatre had fallen into disuse save as a rubbish pit, and at least in places the defences had been allowed to fall into a state of decay. Yet it would be wrong to conclude, solely because some of the public buildings of the town were being neglected, that a state of decay was general throughout its whole area. In modern times abandoned theatres, and even abandoned city churches, have been the companions, and perhaps even the symptoms, of a high degree of commercial prosperity. There were certainly some parts of the city in which new buildings were being erected during the first half of the fifth century.

In their material aspect, particularly in their planning and their public buildings, many of the towns of Roman Britain seem to look very much like one another, but this superficial appearance of uniformity does not provide adequate ground for supposing that those towns by which it is displayed experienced similar trends of economic fortune. There is no single town whose history can be told in terms of its commercial life, and we need to exercise great care before we form opinions about the history of a town of some 200 acres if the evidence for those opinions is derived from only a very small number of its buildings. And it will be even more dangerous to transfer opinions so formed to other towns and make them of general application throughout the province as a whole. At St Albans the new town replaced an earlier site which had lain on higher ground, and there was a similar shift into the valley from Maiden Castle in Dorset to Dorchester. It seems very probable that several other tribal capitals were, like Leicester (*Ratae Coritanorum*) of military origin, among them Cirencester (*Corinium Dobunnorum*), whose remains suggest that outside London it was the most prosperous city in the province, Aldborough (*Isurium Brigantum*) whose smaller size reflects the hardier world in which it lay, and Wroxeter (*Viroconium Cornoviorum*). The forum at Wroxeter was constructed on a scale even more massive than that at Silchester, but its dedicatory inscription shows that it was built during the reign of Hadrian in the years 129–30, and therefore some fifty years later than the Agricolan forum at St Albans. Wroxeter was in a more exposed position than St Albans and more likely to have suffered through any breakdown of the frontier defences. Its forum was burnt down later in the second century and again at the end of the third, after which it was not rebuilt.

At Caerwent (*Venta Silurum*) we find the same regularity of outline seen at Leicester, as well as forum, temple and baths such as are found at Silchester, yet it was a mere 44 acres in size which is considerably less than a quarter the size of St Albans and less even than the 50 acres normally required for a legionary fortress. In its size Caerwent closely resembles an East Anglian tribal capital, Caister-by-Norwich (*Venta Icenorum*). Yet these two are exceptionally small for tribal capitals and the explanation may lie in the vigorous opposition which was offered to the Romans both by the Iceni and by the Silures. More representative are Winchester (*Venta Belgarum*) and Canterbury (*Durovernum Cantiacorum*), both of them upwards of 100 acres within the circuit of their walls. Canterbury was built on the site of an extensive Belgic settlement. Fragments of marble and other polished stones from Egypt, Algeria, Asia Minor, Greece and Italy hint at the former splendour of its basilica whose site can now be deduced only from the remains of the gravelled courtyard of the forum. We do not know when this basilica was built, but we know that there was already a theatre in the city before the end of the first century, some thirty years or so before the theatre at St Albans was built, and that at about the end of the second century it was rebuilt on a much more massive scale suggestive of great prosperity among the citizens of the town at that time. Canterbury lay in a peculiarly favoured position. The roads from the south-eastern ports converged upon it and it was far from even the nearest areas of military occupation. Because of the security of its situation it was able to remain an open town, unprotected by either earthen bank or stone wall, for much longer than most other towns in the province. It was not until 270 or later, when the threat of Saxon piracy was growing and when the stone walls of St Albans were already falling into decay, that it was eventually enclosed.

The development of the cantonal capitals on a scale such as we see at St Albans, Silchester or Wroxeter required large sums of money, as well as the skills of surveyors and stonemasons. Lately we have become aware of an increasingly large number of small towns, if such a word may be used of the modest enclosures sometimes of no more than a few acres. There were many separate factors which might have acted individually or together towards the growth of such small urban centres. A military garrison tended to attract a civilian population, and although such a settlement growing up outside the walls of a fort might cover only a small area, it could be formally recognised as a *vicus* and its inhabitants, the *vicani*, thereby enjoy some powers of government. Such was the *vicus* at Housesteads on the Hadrianic Wall, a straggling collection of poorly built shops and houses whose inhabitants would find pleasures therein of a different order from those to be enjoyed at Canterbury or St Albans. And such also we may suppose to have been the *vicus* at *Veluniate* on the Antonine Wall. Yet the status of *vicus* might imply a much greater degree of civic dignity, for this was the status of Brough-on-Humber (*Petuaria*) which was one of the chief towns of the *Parisi* and which, like Canterbury, had its own theatre. Brough offers a particularly good example of a civilian town emerging from what had been a wholly military site, a process which was perhaps more frequent near the military areas of northern Britain than it was in the south. Brough had the advantage of its site by the Humber crossing, and Corbridge too was well favoured, since it lay not only by the crossing of the Tyne, but also almost within the military zone itself, so that it could serve partly as a military supply base and partly as a civilian town. Farther west Carlisle, originally military, grew into a civilian town of some importance.

Other factors were at work in the lowland areas. There were the little towns which lay on the routes served by the Imperial Post and which met some of the needs of local administration as well as those of travellers. Such was Kenchester (*Magnis*) on the route between such important places as Caerleon, Wroxeter and Chester. Such also was Mildenhall (*Cunetio*) in Wiltshire, no more than 15 acres in size. Even smaller, only 8 acres, was the fortified site at the head of Southampton Water, *Clausentum*. Braughing, in Hertfordshire, formerly a Belgic centre, developed into a Roman town and became the hub of roads converging upon it from several different directions. Water Newton (*Durobrivae*) in Huntingdonshire had the advantage of lying on Ermine Street, the main road to the north, but although it may have had a military origin, its importance was due rather to its proximity to the great centres of pottery production in the east midlands. Farther north, in Lincolnshire, there were other small towns at Ancaster, Horncastle and Caistor. Many more names could be added to this list and others surely await discovery.

The evidence derived from securely dated buildings at Canterbury, Colchester, St Albans and Wroxeter, coupled with the remarks made by Tacitus about the policy pursued by Agricola, cannot leave us in any doubt that from *c.* 75 until at least *c.* 130 a great deal of money was being spent in the province on the provision of at least the public amenities of town life—market-places, temples, theatres, bath-houses and the like. Whether the impetus continued into the age of the Antonines now seems uncertain in view of recently accumulated evidence which suggests that the enclosing of these new towns within stone walls took place much later than was formerly supposed. The great walls and gates at St Albans had seemed to be securely dated by careful excavation to the period 125–50, but further work has shown that they can hardly be earlier than *c.* 180–90, and this too seems to mark approximately the earliest date for the stone walls of a number of other towns. Considering the problem in a historical context, it might seem that the overthrow of the Hadrianic frontier in the time of Clodius Albinus would have provided an occasion revealing the dangerously exposed position of unwalled towns, and we might well feel tempted to regard the St Albans walls, the London walls and many others, as representing the civilian counterpart of the great work of military restoration which was carried out by Severus and brought to completion by Caracalla. But we have yet to learn whether archaeological evidence will allow us to date these walls as late as the early years of the third century.

This was certainly an age of general security within the province, at least until its later decades, and perhaps the neglect of the St Albans walls, and of the guard chambers by the south gate at Caister-by-Norwich, may be symptomatic of such security. But they may also be symptomatic of changes which were overtaking the Empire as a whole and by which Britain cannot have been wholly untouched. By the end of the second century the long process of imperial expansion had ceased. New sources of wealth were no longer being acquired and much of the old wealth was squandered in the long and costly civil wars which marked imperial history in the third and fourth centuries. Economic decline had begun. As yet we have hardly sufficient evidence to show in detail how the towns of Britain were affected by these changes. Whatever may be the significance of the seeming decay of public buildings at some sites, there is certainly no sign of any general trend leading to the eventual abandonment of towns in the fourth century. At about the middle of that century the defences of several towns were reorganised by the addition to their outer faces of a number of bastions, variously shaped and designed to serve as platforms upon which *ballistae* or spring guns could be mounted. This change was accompanied by the excavation of a wide and rather shallow ditch placed at such a distance from the bastions that any marauders who sought to approach the walls across the ditch would find themselves directly exposed to the missiles fired by the *ballistae*. It has now been established that the town defences were reorganised in this fashion at places so widely separated from one another as Aldborough and Brough in the north, Kenchester in Herefordshire, Caerwent in Monmouthshire, Great Casterton in Rutland and Chichester in Sussex. Similar reorganisation is suspected at many other sites, including London, so much so that the change appears to be characteristic of the country as a whole. If it is a reflection of the less secure conditions of the fourth century and the increasing risk of attack by marauding bands, it is no less an indication that the towns themselves, so far from being neglected and half deserted, were very much alive and thought to be well worth the trouble and expense of defending.

CHAPTER SIX

THE COUNTRYSIDE IN ROMAN BRITAIN

A generation ago the population of Roman Britain, other than the army, was envisaged as living in three different kinds of settlement—towns, villas and villages. The towns were held to represent the means by which an attempt was made to convey the privileges of Roman civilisation to the native population, an attempt whose failure, incipient in the third century, was thought to have become total in the fourth. Villa and village were seen as reflecting two types of settlement which were in fundamental contrast with one another. The villa had almost taken on the appearance of a 'gentleman's country residence', standing isolated in its own grounds, remote from the dwellings of the lower orders and enjoying all the conveniences of Roman civilisation in its material aspect. The villages were seen as rather squalid groups of huts whose inhabitants had been barely touched by Roman civilisation. It was realised, however, that the relationship between villa and village could not be analogous with that between medieval manor and its nearby cottages, since it was known that villas were found only in certain parts of the country where there were no villages, and villages in other parts where there were no villas.

Whether or not we are any wiser in our own generation than were our fathers, we now believe that there was still a vigorous life in the towns in the fourth century, and we have learned by fresh discovery that there were many more small towns than had formerly been supposed. A later generation than ours may perhaps question the use of the word 'town' in relation to settlements which were often very much smaller than many of today's villages, though the usage may be justified by the fact that most, if not all, of such urban centres came to be enclosed within stone walls. If the towns have increased both in absolute number and in the tenacity of their life, the villages, as formerly conceived, have dwindled in number as we have come to understand that much of what had been interpreted as evidence of village life was no more than the accumulated debris arising from the continuing occupation of a farm over several centuries.

The village, as we imagine it to have been during the Middle Ages and as we can still see it in some of the remoter rural areas now, had only a small place in the Romano-British scene. There have been similarly important changes of opinion about the nature of the economy represented by the villas. As knowledge grows, whether of town, villa or so-called village, the picture becomes increasingly complex.

Towards the end of Aristotle's life, or perhaps shortly after his death, a Greek navigator called Pytheas who lived in Marseilles, carried out a voyage of exploration which took him through the straits of Gibraltar and northwards along the Atlantic coasts of Spain and Gaul as far as Britain, and farther. The work in which he recorded what he saw on his travels has not survived and we know it only as we find it embedded in the works of later writers, some of whom were hostile to him and disbelieved much of what he said. He made his voyage about three centuries before the Romans invaded Britain, but because of the extremely conservative tendencies of agricultural practice his observations about the economy of southern Britain in what was then the Iron Age are relevant to Romano-British times. Approaching the south-western peninsula of Britain he saw something of the export trade of British tin to Gaul from the emporium which is generally believed to have been at St Michael's Mount. Farther east he noted that the population was large and that corn was produced in abundance, but owing to the dampness of the climate it had sometimes to be threshed under the cover of barns, while the grain itself was stored beneath the ground. The people, who were generally peaceable, lived in simple dwellings made of wood and thatch, and some of them brewed a drink which was made from grain and honey.

This slight but valuable sketch of the economy of part of southern Britain in the Iron Age has lately been amplified by excavations of which the most important originated from a chance photograph taken by a pilot officer of some crop markings which he observed as he was flying a mile or so to the south-west of Salisbury. No sign of habitation was visible on the ground, nor was the place even known by name, but it has since become famous at Little Woodbury. The chalk upon which the site lay was particularly favourable to excavation since it was in such good condition that the least disturbance of its surface could be clearly seen and recorded. The settlement was found to have been upon an area of rather more than three acres which were enclosed within a wooden palisade, not of a strongly defensive kind, but of the sort that would give protection against the depredations of animals. A more formidable ditch was begun, as if to meet dangers arising from more disturbed conditions, but it was never completed. Within this enclosure were two circular dwelling-houses of which the larger was some 50 feet in diameter, the smaller rather more than 30. The framework of the houses consisted of massive upright timbers. The precise nature of the infilling of the side walls is uncertain. It was not of clay or cob, but may have been of planks, wattle-work or straw of which the last was used for the roof. In the remainder of the enclosure there were large numbers of pits dug into the chalk, post-holes, shallow depressions, primitive ovens made of cob and quantities of burnt flints and ash.

Minutely careful investigations of the several different ways in which the surface of the chalk had been changed by human activities shed much light upon the methods of husbandry followed by the farmers who occupied this site without any perceptible break for some three hundred years from *c.* 300 B.C. When the harvest had been completed the heads of corn were hung out to dry on racks such as remain in use today in many countries where the climate is damp. Part of the grain was then set aside for seed and was stored above ground in small granaries raised on posts where it could be protected against vermin as well as against damp. The remainder, which was to be used for food, was first parched in ovens made of cob and was then poured for storage into suitably lined pits, many of them being dug into the chalk to a depth of six feet or more. When the grain was needed for use it was winnowed in shallow depressions in the chalk and then ground.

Not the least important result of the Little Woodbury excavations is that they have provided the means of reinterpreting the evidence won from earlier excavations at sites of a similar character in other parts of southern England. In particular, the recognition of the pits as storehouses in which grain could be kept underground, in the fashion noted by Pytheas, removes once and for all the notion that these were underground dwellings inhabited by the men of the Iron Age. Although it is easy to calculate the cubic capacity of one such storage pit, further calculations aimed at discovering the total annual grain consumption of a community such as that which lived at Little Woodbury, and the total acreage tilled by it, are subject to several uncertainties. The pits themselves vary greatly in size; we do not know how long each pit would remain fit for use, and we cannot be certain how many pits were in use at any one time. Making allowances for these uncertainties, it has been reckoned that something like 74 bushels of grain were harvested each year, with one-third of this total being kept as seed corn, and that, allowing for fields lying fallow for two years, some 15 to 20 acres of land would have been needed in the conditions of the age to produce a crop of this order. In addition to their arable land, the Little Woodbury community—and it needs to be stressed that this was a single farm and in no sense a village—would be able to pasture sheep on the downland grass and also a small herd of cattle. The site also yielded the bones of pig, horse and dog, but the lack of any nearby water-supply suggests that cattle played the lesser part in the economy of this farm. Pottery making and some cloth weaving were done upon the site. We know from other sites showing similar characteristics that the fields of a farm like that at Little Woodbury were laid out in small plots, usually of a rather square shape, seldom larger than two acres and often much smaller. Many fields of a similar kind have left their traces on the chalk uplands of Dorset, Wiltshire and Sussex.

Little Woodbury may be regarded as representative of a large number of similar farms on the chalklands of southern Britain during the Iron Age. The farm, and not the village, was the characteristic habitation in this age. Yet Little Woodbury itself is believed to have been abandoned in the first century B.C. after an occupation of some three centuries. And we must not forget that, while its inhabitants were living there in conditions which required no more protection than was given by a light stockade, other parts of the Wessex landscape were beginning to be dominated by the great hill forts whose immense ditches and ramparts testify to conditions of a very different kind. Nor must we forget that the evidence for this kind of community comes from southern Britain and more particularly from its chalklands. We do not know what sort of farms Pytheas would have found on the heavier, richer lands of the east midlands, though we have some ground for believing that if he had visited the north he would have found very little indication of the practice of agriculture save on the smallest scale. The mainstay in the rural economy of northern Britain was not in corn growing but in cattle raising.

If the discovery of fresh evidence and the reinterpretation of the old have seemed to require several major changes of opinion about the rural economy of Roman Britain, there is one aspect of the earlier view which has not yet required modification. The 1956 edition of the Ordnance Survey *Map of Roman Britain* shows even more strikingly than did its predecessor of 1928 that while there is a marked preponderance of villas in some parts of the country, farms of the more primitive type represented by Little Woodbury are noticeably predominant in others. Many areas of the country have yielded evidence for the survival of earlier farming practices during the Roman occupation on sites which were affected only in the most superficial way by Roman civilising influences. One such site, characteristic of others in its neighbourhood, is at Woodcuts in Cranborne Chase, about twelve miles to the south-east of Little Woodbury. The settlement here, which covered about 4 acres, began in the period A.D. 10–25, approximately a generation before the Roman armies reached this part of the country. It lay mainly within a roughly circular enclosure about 300 feet in diameter and its inhabitants pursued the same methods of farming as had been practised by those who had formerly lived at Little Woodbury. The occupation continued through the age of the Roman invasion without any noticeable interruption, save for a suggestion that the inhabitants had now to submit to an annual requisition of grain which may have amounted to between three-fifths and one-half of their total harvest. At about the middle of the second century some additions were made to the original enclosure: one of them, in which a deep well was sunk, was probably for cattle or sheep, and in another there were ovens for parching corn. This phase of the occupation continued until about the year 300 or a little longer and was followed by a third phase which is again marked by substantial alterations in the general plan of the settlement, and which seems to have continued until after the middle of the fourth century.

The farmers of Woodcuts were evidently living much the same kind of life in about A.D. 350 as had been lived by their predecessors at Little Woodbury in 300 B.C. The advent of the Romans had meant a heavy burden of taxation and later in the Roman period there may have been a forced shift under

Roman pressure from corn growing towards a pastoral economy, but they certainly knew nothing of the delights of civilisation which had been given to those who lived at Silchester or Cirencester. A small amount of coined money had come into their hands, their pottery was of better quality and they had some little wealth in jewellery, but certainly no theatre in which it might be displayed. The squarish fields, often called 'Celtic' fields—though the term 'Celtic' when used in this connection has no more meaning than the term 'druid' when applied to circles of standing stones—which are associated with this kind of farming have survived most commonly in Wiltshire, Dorset, Hampshire and Sussex, but we ought not to regard this pattern as representing the original distribution since we can recognise such fields now only in the areas, mostly but not all chalkland, which have not been heavily or continuously ploughed since Roman times. Other and smaller patches are known on the North Downs, in Wales and along the Welsh border, and in Yorkshire, particularly on the limestone of upper Wharfedale in the neighbourhood of Grassington.

In all these areas we seem to be looking at the survival into Roman times of Iron Age agricultural practices which are reflected in the fields as well as in the homes of the farmers, but there is one other area in Britain in which this same pattern first took shape within the Roman period itself, namely in the Fens of East Anglia. Relics dating from the Iron Age in this part of the country are found only round the fringes and not within the Fens themselves, a pattern of distribution similar to that shown by the cemeteries of the Anglo-Saxon period. At an early date in the Roman occupation there took place a movement of population into the Fens, and more particularly into the relatively higher silt lands, on such a large scale as to leave little room for doubt that it was directed by the government. The Romans had experience enough to realise the potential wealth that might be reaped from land of this kind, and they took measures to improve both drainage and communications by the building of roads and the digging of canals, of which the most ambitious, the Car Dyke of Cambridgeshire and Lincolnshire, stretched for some seventy miles from near Cambridge to join the Witham at Lincoln. A further extension, the Foss Dyke which joined the Witham to the Trent, provided a route by inland waterway from Cambridge to York. It may be that the defeated Iceni were drafted as forced labour for the construction of these great works and subsequently settled on the land when it had been brought to a state fit for production. Whatever the source of labour, the labourers themselves were left to follow their own ways of farming, living in simple buildings of wood and thatch, and growing their corn in small fields which now reveal to aerial photography a pattern much the same as that to be seen on the chalklands of southern England.

Much has yet to be learned about the history of this fenland colonisation and the way in which it could be affected by changing demands for its products as well as by natural catastrophe. Evidence of one such catastrophe comes from a small group of huts which have been excavated in the Welney Washes. Here, a period of occupation which began in the first century came to an end in the third when a belt of tidal silt six feet thick was deposited in the bed of the stream by which they stood. A further occupation began late in the third century and continued into the fourth, although it was then proving necessary for the farmers to embank their fields, as if to give protection against incursions of water. This was probably the beginning of the process which by the fifth century, if not earlier, had turned the whole of the Fens into a watery waste fit only for those who sought to earn a living by fishing or fowling, or for such as Guthlac, the eighth-century hermit, who sought there a proving ground for his sanctity. Certain similarities between the farms of the East Anglian Fens and those of the Wessex chalklands, as well as the absence from both areas of towns, villas and other indications of the more sophisticated kind of life to be observed in other parts of the country, have led to the suggestion that both regions may have been imperial estates whose products were intended to meet the needs of military areas, those of the fenland going north by barge to York, and those of Wessex to the Welsh command based on Caerleon.

However much the working lives of the farmers who lived at Woodcuts in Dorset or at Welney in the Fens were subject to control and exploitation by provincial or local government officials, the homes in which they lived remained virtually untouched by those Roman civilising influences which are one of the most characteristic features of the settlements which we call 'villas'. There are more than 600 sites at which Romano-British villas or farms have been identified with certainty, and more than 100 others at which remains suggestive of villas have been found. The most northerly villa so far discovered lies not far from Durham but, although there are a few in Yorkshire and a few along the eastern borders of Wales, the great majority lie south of the Humber and east of the Severn, with strong concentrations in particular areas. They are numerous in the more westerly parts of Kent and in Surrey, but they are strikingly absent from the Weald. They are found in western Sussex, and there are many of them in a wide area round Winchester, southwards to Chichester and the Isle of Wight, where there are several, and northwards to Silchester and the Wilshire Mildenhall, but there are none in the New Forest. They are very rare, but not wholly unknown, on the Wiltshire and Dorset chalklands, but farther west they are thickly grouped near Ilchester, near Bath and on the Cotswold plateau near Cirencester, whence a line of them extends in a north-easterly direction along the oolite ridge through Northamptonshire to Lincolnshire. They are also found along almost the whole of the Icknield Way from the eastern side of the Wash near Brancaster, skirting the eastern and southern sides of the Fens and leading on by the Chilterns to the upper Thames. There are some in Essex, particularly to the west of Colchester, but the numbers known in Norfolk and Suffolk are smaller than might have been expected, save along the line of the Icknield Way. The relative paucity of villas in these two counties, as well as the slight scale of urban development in the same area, may seem to be a consequence of the disastrous conflict between the Romans and the Iceni in 61. Villas are absent from the Essex side of the Thames estuary, and also from the area north and west of London. The villas did not spread into the north-west midlands, and save for the Welsh outliers and a few in Shropshire there are virtually none west of a line joining York, Leicester and Gloucester. This north-west midland area which belonged mostly to the *Cornovii* remains a puzzling blank on the map of Roman Britain, showing scarcely any relics of either military or civilian occupation.

We have long been familiar with the plans of a considerable number of Romano-British villas, as well as with some of those features of their construction which the term 'villa' itself most readily evokes—the mosaic pavements, the hypocausts, the patterned wall plaster and similar amenities of the kind which were not known in Britain before the Roman conquest. But the sort of digging which laid bare the plan of a villa and revealed its mosaics to the gaze of those with a taste for classical culture, while failing either to relate the different parts of the structure to one another or to relate the varied assortment of debris to the ruins of the building within which it was found to be lying, had the effect of producing an antiquity in somewhat the same way as a conjuror's hat may be made to produce a rabbit. The villa was presented to the spectator not as the material remains of many generations of men and women who had experienced changing conditions of fortune during the successive centuries in which they had lived upon the site, but as a static antiquity which at one moment lay buried beneath the ground, and at another stood fully revealed. It is largely for this reason, that, although we know a great deal about some aspects of villas, we do not yet know nearly enough to be able to draw many general conclusions about the part which they played in the rural economy of Roman Britain.

Some of the villas were large and luxurious establishments whose owners were wealthy men employing labour, not by any means all of it paid, on a very considerable scale, establishments whose associated acres of land could have been reckoned in thousands rather than in hundreds, while others could not unjustly be described as squalid. In between these extremes there were many houses which offered their owners, mostly native landowners of moderate substance, a degree of comfort greater by far than that which had been experienced by their pre-Roman ancestors or was still being experienced by their contemporaries in Cranborne Chase or the East Anglian fenland. The number of villas whose history can be traced in detail throughout the period of their occupation is still exceedingly small, but among them there are two which lay not far from one another in the territory of the Catuvellauni. One of them, Park Street, lay a little more than two miles south of St Albans on a gravel terrace overlying the chalk and within sight of Watling Street as it approached the London gate of St Albans. The other, Lockleys (see plan), lay at Welwyn, rather less than ten miles to the north-east of St Albans and close by the road from Colchester. Here too the site, known in modern times as some of the richest barley land in Hertfordshire, was chalk with superficial deposits of clay and gravel.

The settlements at Park Street and Lockleys experienced a closely similar history, as we might have expected from their proximity to one another. In both places occupation had already begun before the Roman conquest. Park Street yielded fragments of pottery from the Bronze Age and also from the early Iron Age, though no structures were found in association with them. Three separate structural stages could be distinguished in the first century A.D., all of them Belgic rather than Romano-British in character, the buildings being simply made of timber and the floors of clay or rammed chalk. The third of these three Belgic phases is thought to have been brought to an end by a destructive fire which can probably be associated with the events of 60 when the nearby St Albans was also burnt. The discovery at Park Street of an iron slave-chain with an attached manacle, in circumstances which indicate that it was not a Roman import but had been in use before the Roman conquest, suggests that these Belgic farmers were men of greater substance than we might have inferred from the slight and unimpressive remains of their buildings. That they continued to prosper, despite the indications of fire, is shown by the complete rebuilding of their house according to Roman standards in about the year 65, a time at which we think of them as Romano-Britons rather than Catuvellauni, even though we have no reason at all for thinking that the change in the appearance of the house denotes an equally radical change in its occupants. The new house was built above the earlier huts to a simple rectangular plan with five rooms and a cellar. Its lower courses were constructed of flint bedded in mortar of excellent quality and its quoins were of brick. It is probable that the upper parts of its walls were mainly of timber, but its roof was certainly tiled. Its windows were glazed, its inside walls were covered with brightly decorated plaster, and Purbeck and Sussex marble was used for some of its fittings. In matters touching their personal comfort the lives of the Park Street household had certainly been transformed, though not, it may be noted, until more than twenty years after the invasion.

The history of the settlement at Lockleys, some twelve miles away to the north-east, followed an almost identical course, although there was no trace here of any occupation during the Bronze or early Iron Ages. The first settlement on the site is represented by the remains of a circular hut which was in

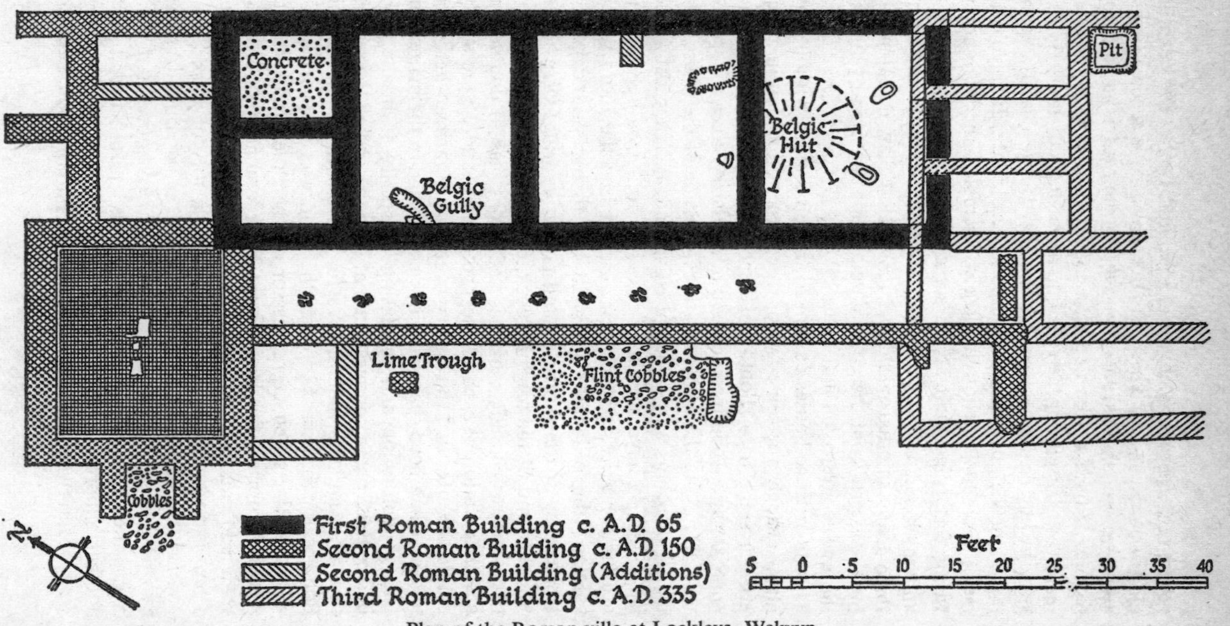

Plan of the Roman villa at Lockleys, Welwyn

occupation approximately during the first twenty-five years of the first century A.D. This was superseded by a second Belgic house whose plan is uncertain but which was inhabited for some time both before and after the Roman invasion. Neither the invasion itself nor the rebellion of the Iceni under Boudicca left any discernible traces. During the decade 60–70 a completely new house was built upon the old site. In plan and method of construction it closely resembled the new house which was being built at the same period at Park Street—a long rectangle divided into five rooms, with flint for the lower courses and internal plastering. It had no cellar, but along its south-western front there was a verandah supported by timber posts which rested on flint bases.

Both of these houses continued to be occupied without any major changes for some two or three generations, but in about 150—and the date should not be regarded as more than an approximation—both were rebuilt. At Park Street a corridor was built along the whole length of one side of the house, and blocks of rooms were added at either end. A hypocaust which is thought to have been used for corn drying, rather than as heating for a living-room, was inserted into the room which adjoined the cellar. At Lockleys the timber verandah was replaced by a stone corridor, and projecting wings were added at either end of the original block. One of these wings was of two storeys. The effect of these additions was to double the accommodation at each of the two houses, and we are surely entitled to infer that the history of these two farms, whether or not there had been changes of ownership, had in the main been one of continuing and increasing prosperity from the days before the Roman conquest until at least the end of the second century. And such indeed, save for the greater impact of the Boudiccan rebellion, had been the history of the nearby St Albans with its Belgic predecessor on the Prae Wood site, its Agricolan forum, its Hadrianic theatre and its monumental walls and gateways built near the end of the second century. There is a continuing similarity in the history of Park Street and Lockleys later in the Roman period, even though it is less easy to see how they fared. The Lockleys house, first built *c.* 65, then refashioned *c.* 150, continued in use for at least another hundred years, but there came a time when the upper floor of the two-storeyed wing collapsed into the room beneath and a time also when there was heavy damage by fire to some of the other rooms. These troubles had occurred before *c.* 340 when there was a final rebuilding which did not, however, include the restoration of the two-storeyed wing whose collapsed floor was found by the excavators just as it had fallen. The occupation of the Park Street house likewise continued for a century or so after the rebuilding of *c.* 150, but towards the end of the third century there was so much decay in parts of the building as to suggest that it may have been totally abandoned for a time. Yet this was not the end of its history, since there was a further rebuilding early in the fourth century.

The historical sequence disclosed at Lockleys and Park Street seems likely to be fairly representative at least for the lands of the Catuvellauni, but we do not know, nor will it be easy to learn, how many other Romano-British villas were built on sites which were already the dwelling-places of Belgic farmers, and how many, by their location on virgin sites, suggest the breaking of fresh ground. If this difficult problem awaits a solution and if there are other and no less difficult problems concerning the end of life in the villas, yet there are some signs that much of lowland Britain shared in a general growth of prosperity during the first and second centuries, in the manner typified by the successive new stone houses built at Lockleys and Park Street, and shared also some measure of decline in the third century. What is beyond all doubt is that these houses, as they were after the middle of the second century, are of a type which is exceedingly common not only in Britain, but also in Germany, Belgium and northern France. The type known as the 'winged corridor' plan, consists simply of a range of rooms planned as a long and rather narrow rectangle, with a corridor along the length of one side and projecting wings at either end. To choose examples from widely separated areas, we can see it in a simple form at Mansfield Woodhouse in Nottinghamshire or at Frilford in Berkshire, and in rather more elaborate forms at Brislington near Bristol, at Newport in the Isle of Wight and at Folkestone in Kent. We can also see it in exceptional circumstances, strikingly revealed by aerial photography and later excavated, at Ditchley in Oxfordshire, exceptional because the farmhouse itself is here seen in relation to its farmyard and other farm buildings. The house at

Ditchley lay towards the back of a rectangular enclosure surrounded at first by an earthen bank which may have been topped by a fence, and later by a stone wall. Across the end of the enclosure farthest from the house, and covering a substantially larger area than did the house itself, was a range of buildings whose plan suggests that here lay the barns and storehouses used for the general purposes of the farm, the places in which were kept its stock and its tools. Some part of this area may also have provided accommodation for labourers. There was a granary in this part of the enclosure and elsewhere there was a well and a threshing-floor. It has been calculated that the Ditchley villa, the whole carefully designed with an eye to social distinctions between its owners and those who worked for them, was related to an estate of scarcely less than five hundred acres.

There is no need to emphasise the contrast between the living conditions endured at Woodcuts and enjoyed at Lockleys, yet the characteristic Romanised farmhouse of the second century, if we are not overbold in so regarding Park Street and Lockleys, was not a luxurious establishment. It had no bathhouse, none but the most rudimentary form of mosaic floor, and, if it had any heating system, the purpose of it was to dry the corn rather than to warm the rooms which were occupied by the farmer's household. The villa at Lullingstone in Kent shares some of the characteristics of this kind of country dwelling. It occupied a pleasant site in the valley of the Darent where there was good farming land which was already being cultivated before the Roman invasion, and it came to form one of a small group of villas lying along the valley bottom at intervals of three or four miles from one another. The replacement of the native farm by a building of flint and mortar in the second half of the first century and its continuing occupation for a hundred years or so conforms with the pattern seen elsewhere. Late in the second century the old house was remodelled by the addition at one end of a large suite of baths and by other refinements which suggest that it had passed into the hands of an owner with a taste for luxury and the means to indulge it. Two handsome busts of Greek marble, recovered from what had been the cellar of the first house, adorned the villa at this or some later stage of its history, but the hint of departure from the normal run of development was not fulfilled. The new splendour was short-lived and by *c.* 200 the house had been deserted, remaining so for much of the third century until its reoccupation *c.* 280 by a new owner who repaired the tumbled bath-house and built a massive barn with a raised floor beneath which air could circulate freely in the manner seen at granaries of military forts. The history of Lullingstone in the fourth century is one of continuing prosperity. A further remodelling which took place *c.* 330 gave part of the house something of what in present parlance is called 'the open plan', with an apsidal dining-room raised upon a dais and opening from one side of a large central room in which many guests could have been accommodated with comfort. These two conjoined rooms were floored with an elaborate mosaic pavement of which the larger part showed Bellerophon killing the Chimaera, while the smaller part in the dining apse portrayed the abduction of Europa by Jupiter in the guise of a white bull, with a Latin couplet alluding to the first book of the *Aeneid.* A visitor to Lullingstone in the fourth century could have looked forward to a good table and enlightened conversation, as well as to a luxurious bath.

Lullingstone was certainly the property of a wealthy man. It was also at some stage in the fourth century the property of a Christian who decorated the walls in one part of the house with the Christian monogram and with human figures shown in the attitude normally adopted by the early Christians while at prayer. The work of skill, patience and perseverance which led to the reconstruction of these Christian figures from the many thousand fragments of painted plaster into which they had been broken when the room which they had adorned collapsed into the room beneath, has given Lullingstone a unique interest among the villas of Roman Britain, though it may also have provoked fruitless reflections upon what similar evidence may have been overlooked in the past by less careful excavators. Although we have at present no parallel from Britain to these Christian wall frescoes, the greater luxury revealed at Lullingstone in the bath-house and in the elaboration of its mosaic floors finds its counterpart at many other villas in different parts of the country. Scenes from Virgil have been recovered on wall plaster at Otford, another of the Kentish villas, and on a pavement at Low Ham in Somerset. Racing in chariots and on horseback is portrayed on a pavement at Horkstow in Lincolnshire, and farther north, at Aldborough in Yorkshire, a semicircular dining-room, much like that at Lullingstone, included among its mosaics representations of the nine Muses, with an accompanying inscription in Greek. What purports to be the figure of Venus adorns a pavement at Rudston, another of the Yorkshire villas, though the workman who laid it would scarcely have won by his efforts the favour of the goddess whom he sought to portray. Even the most northerly of the villas, that at Old Durham, had its bath-house, built in the fourth century.

Lullingstone in the fourth century was comfortable and even luxurious, but in some parts of the country, villas were being built or enlarged to an altogether grander scale whose plan might evoke comparison with some of the houses erected by the nobility in Elizabethan or Jacobean times were it not necessary to remember that most villas, however spreading might be their ground plan, were not normally built to a height of more than one storey. One such lay at Brading on the Isle of Wight where a house of the winged corridor type, with pavements showing scenes from the Eleusinian mysteries, stood at one side of a large square courtyard with other buildings grouped about it. A similar plan is to be seen at North Leigh in Oxfordshire where after a long history of growth from quite small beginnings, the establishment eventually assumed the shape of a great courtyard with the main house ranged along the side farthest from the entrance, long ranges of many rooms forming two other sides of the rectangle, and the fourth cut off from the outer world by a wall through which access was gained to the courtyard by a gateway beside which stood a janitor's lodge. Such houses as these, like the similar establishments at Bignor in Sussex and at Woodchester in the Cotswolds, were of vast size in themselves and can only be regarded as the centres of equally vast estates which were worked by the labour of slaves or serfs. Woodchester and Woodcuts are the two extremes of Romano-British farming economy in the southern part of the country, Lockleys and Park Street the mediocrity.

Most of the population of Roman Britain, from the owners of big estates at one end of the scale to the slaves by whom the estates were worked at the other, was engaged in the production of food. Corn was a staple article of diet, the hides of cattle were scarcely less valuable than their flesh or their milk, and sheep were needed for their wool as well as for their mutton. In all these aspects Britain was able to produce enough, and a little more than enough, to meet her own requirements. Corn was being exported to the Rhineland in the fourth century, although we do not know whether this was always a regular feature of Romano-British economy. The demands of the army are not likely to have left a very large surplus beyond the needs of the civilian population. British cloth enjoyed during the Roman occupation a European reputation for good quality which it still retained in the Anglo-Saxon period, and it seems certain that many of the country establishments were engaged in the different processes of wool production, more particularly in the Cotswolds. We know little of the way in which cloth was produced, but there is record of a state weaving mill at Winchester. Spindle whorls and loom weights are of course common objects on dwelling sites, but the spindles and looms to which they belonged would have been used mostly to meet domestic requirements.

Britain was regarded as a fertile island whose crops, because of the dampness of the climate, were, as Tacitus records, quick to grow even if they were slow to ripen, yet it was his belief that the reward of conquest for Rome would not lie in Britain's agricultural produce, but in her mineral wealth, particularly in her gold and silver. Bede makes no mention of gold among Britain's minerals, but he specifies copper, iron, silver and lead, and also plentiful supplies of jet. All these natural resources were exploited by the Romans, although they were disappointed if they had been expecting a large yield of gold from Britain. So far as we know, the only British gold mine which was worked by the Romans lay at Dolaucothi in Carmarthenshire. Mining seems to have begun here before the end of the first century and to have continued for a hundred years or more. There are extensive remains, not only of opencast workings, but also of adits and galleries in the auriferous rock. The ore itself was treated in the immediate neighbourhood of the mine, being first pounded on stone blocks and then milled in rotary querns. Water for washing the dust, as well as for general use, was brought a distance of eight miles along a carefully engineered leet to discharge into settling tanks and thence into a small reservoir. Other signs of the use of the most advanced mining techniques known to Roman engineers suggest that the Dolaucothi mine was run under at least some degree of state control.

Lead was by far the most important of Britain's minerals to be worked by the Romans. It was doubly valuable, both for its own uses and for the silver which was extracted from it by the process of cupellation. Its importance to the Romans is apparent from the speed with which the lead mines were brought into production. The Mendip lead in Somerset, perhaps already being extracted on a small scale before the Roman conquest, was being worked under Roman control by A.D. 49, only six years after the invasion. Direct government control is witnessed by a number of lead pigs bearing imperial stamps, the names of the emperors concerned ranging from Claudius to Marcus Aurelius and Lucius Verus (164–9). The distribution of some of these pigs suggests that lead was being exported from the Mendip area during the first and second centuries. One of Nero's reign was found at the mouth of the Somme and two of Vespasian's at *Clausentum,* the Roman port at the head of Southampton Water. Three other pigs of Vespasian's reign come from Charterhouse which served as the administrative centre of the Mendip mines. In Flintshire a mining community was established by *c.* 70, very soon after the area had been pacified, at Pentre Ffwrddan from where the lead deposits in the Halkyn Mountain were worked. Some of the pigs from this area bear the name of the tribe in whose area the mines lay, the Deceangli, a name which still survives as Tegeingl. The Derbyshire lead deposits were worked extensively around Matlock and at a number of subsidiary sites. Some degree of imperial control during the part of the second century is indicated by the stamping of Hadrian's name on one of the Derbyshire pigs, but several others bear the names of private individuals which give no evidence of date. The centre of the mine-field, or possibly the whole of the mine-field itself, Flintshire and Derbyshire—were the principal centres of lead mining in Roman Britain, but the industry was also carried on in Shropshire in the Hadrianic period, as well as in the Yorkshire dales and at Alston in Cumberland.

One of the most widely used metals in Romano-British, as also in Anglo-Saxon, times, was bronze, which had a long hard-wearing life, but which could be worked by different techniques into patterns of great intricacy. Britain possessed deposits of each of its two principal elements, copper and tin. The Cornish export trade in tin which flourished greatly in the first century B.C. was largely eclipsed in the Augustan age when the Romans gained possession of the Spanish tin mines and so were able to undersell the British products in the Mediterranean market. Although tin mining in Cornwall may not have stopped completely, there is little sign of much activity there during the first and second centuries. Shortly after 250 the Spanish mines were closed, and renewed prosperity came to the Cornish trade for the third and fourth centuries. Tin was still being exported from Cornwall in the sixth century. Spain was also the principal Roman source of copper, but the metal was mined at a small number of sites in Britain. In Shropshire the deposits at Llanymynech Hill were worked by miners who seem to have lived in a cave from which galleries were cut deep into the rock. Copper was also mined in Carnarvonshire at Great Orme's Head, and at a number of sites on Anglesey, principally at Parys Mountain near Amlwch.

Among Britain's other natural resources iron was too widely and plentifully distributed in the Roman Empire to give the British deposits any particular value as an export, but there was plenty of need for the metal within Britain itself. The Weald and the Forest of Dean were the two chief centres of iron working, but there is plenty of evidence to show that deposits of iron were being exploited in other parts of the country, notably in Northamptonshire and Lincolnshire, as well as in Yorkshire and farther north. Surface deposits of coal were widely used, but there was abundance of wood for fuel, and coal mining was never developed on an industrial scale. Among Britain's minor natural resources the jet of Whitby was the raw material for an extensive trade in *bijouterie* and it was still being used for the manufacture of necklaces after the foundation of Hild's monastery there in the seventh century. Kimmeridge shale was also used for ornaments, as well as for dishes and even furniture. Purbeck marble formed a valued base for monumental inscriptions and also provided a hard surface suitable for mortars.

The manufacture of pottery was an important domestic industry. Large numbers of kilns have been found widely distributed over the country, though none has yet been discovered in the areas most closely associated with pottery manufacture in modern times. The great legionary kilns at Holt near Chester were solidly built, permanent structures not unlike modern brick ovens, but the normal Romano-British pottery kiln, whether it was producing to meet only local needs or whether its wares enjoyed a wider market, was of much simpler type, consisting only of stoke hole, flue, furnace and oven floor so designed as to give an updraught, though kilns with a horizontal draught have been found at Farnham. When a load of pottery was ready for baking it was laid on the oven floor which was then covered with a dome-shaped superstructure of branches which supported turves, straw or clay. This covering served for only one firing and would have to be renewed each time the oven was used. The familiar red glazed Samian ware was a luxury product which was in common use only in the military areas of the province, and mainly in the second century, but it was almost all imported from those parts of Gaul which yielded the special clay required in its manufacture. Attempts were made to establish the production of Samian ware in Britain, but it was only at Colchester that they met with even limited success.

Although some other kinds of pottery were imported during the earlier part of the Roman occupation, notably the *mortaria* with their hard gritted surfaces specially designed for the pulverising of food, it was the native potters who met the common needs of both the civilian and the military areas of the province, and they soon acquired the skills which enabled them to meet all the demands which were made upon them. Water Newton on the Nene lay at the centre of one of the most important areas of pottery manufacture. From the kilns here and in nearby parts of Northamptonshire and Huntingdonshire, came Castor ware, a thin hard ware with a rather dark lustrous glaze and characteristically taking the form of drinking cups decorated in barbotine with conventional scrolls of ivy leaves or with scenes portraying animals or humans variously engaged. Production had begun here before the end of the second century and continued well into the fourth, the output achieving a very wide distribution in the military as well as in the civil areas. The New Forest potteries which were active mainly in the third and fourth centuries had a wider range of products but with more restraint in decoration and a more limited distribution of their wares which never extended much outside southern Britain. Other centres of manufacture on a scale seemingly greater than was needed for merely local needs lay in Surrey, the more northerly parts of Suffolk, Lincolnshire and the East Riding of Yorkshire. The discovery of previously unknown kilns, sometimes as many as thirty in a single field, is still of common occurrence and there is much yet to be learned about the manufacture and distribution of pottery in Roman Britain, especially in the lowland areas.

CHAPTER SEVEN

RELIGIOUS BELIEFS IN ROMAN BRITAIN

Inscribed altars are the principal source of information about the pagan religious cults of Roman Britain. Carved from a single stone and varying in height from a few inches to several feet, as the importance of the occasion might demand or the resources of the devotees allow, such altars were the means by which the worshippers conveyed their gifts to the gods of their choice. The choice which they made, according to the favours they had received in the past or were looking for in the future, could be exercised over an immensely wide range of gods and goddesses, some of them possessing followers in the most distant parts of the Empire, some of them enjoying only a very local reputation.

An altar constructed on a vastly greater scale than any of those now to be seen in museums, stood in a prominent position, supported by statues on either hand, in a forecourt which formed the southern approach to the great temple of Claudius at Colchester. This temple, with a deep colonnaded portico and colonnades running along each side, was built *c.* A.D. 50 to serve as the centre in Britain of the official religion, the worship of the emperor. Its superstructure has all perished, but the vaults, originally filled with rammed earth, which served as its supporting podium, still survive beneath the Norman castle as an impressive relic of what was probably the earliest and certainly one of the largest stone buildings of Roman Britain. The maintenance of the state religion, with its costly priesthood and its calendar of feasts and festivals throughout the year, proved to be a burden so heavy that the Colchester temple became to the British a symbol of their subjection to everlasting tyranny, and the hatred which it inspired was one among the factors leading to the revolt of the Iceni in 60 under Boudicca. Colchester had been thought a suitable site to serve as the provincial centre of the emperor-worship because of its prominence as a pre-Roman town and because of the establishment of a *colonia* there at an early date during the occupation. These factors were highly relevant to a religion whose main purpose, for all its initial failure to achieve that purpose, was to encourage loyalty to the imperial house. Although we have no proof, it is thought that the provincial centre of the cult had been moved to London by the end of the first century.

The worship of the emperor was a necessary part of the religious life of the *coloniae*, of the army and of government officials, yet there are not many monuments dedicated exclusively to the imperial house. An expression of loyalty to the *numina Augustorum* was in no way diminished, perhaps it was even enhanced, by associating the imperial house with some other gods or goddesses in the same act of devotion. A temple built in the early days of the occupation at Chichester by a guild of smiths was dedicated not only to the deities of sea and handicrafts, Neptune and Minerva, but also, and by the express authority of Cogidubnus, the loyal ruler of the *Regnenses* of whose kingdom Chichester was the capital, to the welfare of the divine house—*pro salute domus divinae*. Neptune and Minerva were two of the many state deities of Rome who came to Britain with the Romans and who left again when they withdrew, without seeming ever to have taken a very firm hold upon the beliefs of the native population, although they had their devotees among the citizens of the *coloniae* and may have gained more adherents when the privileges of Roman citizenship were more widely extended near the beginning of the third century. An altar from Lympne was appropriately dedicated to Neptune by the commander of the British fleet. Others among the classical deities commemorated in Britain are Jupiter himself, commonly represented simply by the letters I O M for *Iovi Optimo Maximo*, as well as Mars, Apollo, Juno, Mercury and several more. There is plenty of evidence too for the worship of such personified powers as the *Genius* or *Tutela* of a particular place, and others such as *Fortuna, Discipulina,* and *Victoria*.

Just as the gods and goddesses of Greece came to be correlated with those of Rome, so did the Roman deities in Britain frequently become identified with others of Celtic or Germanic origin. If it is unusual to find evidence for the pursuit of a wholly unadulterated Roman cult in Britain, save within official spheres, whether military or civilian, it is exceedingly common to find classical gods closely associated by name, and therefore in worship, with native deities. Perhaps the best known instance is that of the goddess Sulis who was identified as Minerva and presided over the hot spring at Bath. The gorgon's head from the pediment of her temple at Bath is one of the most familiar Romano-British antiquities. Mars, because of his associations with war, proved to be much the most easily assimilated of the Roman pantheon. We find him associated with a great many different names: Mars Camulos, the Celtic war god after whom the Catuvellauni called their chief city Camulodunum; Mars Toutates who was also known among the Catuvellauni and had probably been brought by them also from north-eastern Gaul; Mars Cocidius who enjoyed a strong following in Cumberland; Mars Leucetius, a Rhineland deity who was worshipped at Bath, and several more, not all of them of exclusively warlike interests. In the same way Apollo was identified with a northern British god of youth and music, Maponus, whose sanctuary lay at Clochmabonstane, a megalithic circle of high antiquity on the northern shore of the Solway Firth.

The goddess Brigantia whose worship is attested in south-western Yorkshire and also in the neighbourhood of the Hadrianic Wall, offers a striking example of that syncretism which is characteristic of many of the cults practised in Roman Britain. Early in the third century M. Cocceius Nigrinus who was at the time holder of one of the most important offices in the province, that of *procurator Augusti*, made a dedication in which he styled her 'nymph', a designation which, though suggestive of associations with water and healing, seems but ill-suited to the awesome and embattled figure of Brigantia which we find represented on a relief from Birrens in Dumfriesshire. Whatever may have been Brigantia's origin, she rose far above her barbaric station in life through being associated with some of the most distinguished occupants of the imperial heavens. A centurion of the Sixth Legion at Corbridge dedicated an altar upon which he not only associated Brigantia with Jupiter Dolichenus, whose cult was centred in Syria and who was himself equated with Jupiter Optimus Maximus, the supreme protector of the Roman state, but also bestowed upon Brigantia herself the title Caelestis, thereby suggesting identification with Dea Caelestis, the Romanised equivalent of the chief goddess of North Africa.

As we see her portrayed in the relief from Birrens, Brigantia is a winged figure, with wings also upon her head which is surrounded by a mural crown. She is armed and protected with spear and shield, she carries a globe in one hand and upon her breast hangs a medallion with a gorgon's head. In short she has borrowed something from Minerva, Victory and Fortune to make her fit company for Jupiter Dolichenus, and the motive for this flattering attention seems not far to seek. There were good political grounds for promoting Brigantia to the status of a provincial goddess in the best of divine company at the time when the Severan restoration was being brought to completion by Caracalla after the *débâcle* of 196.

Within her northern province, Brigantia was able to accommodate a seemingly endless throng of gods, goddesses and godlings, many of them brought by the soldiery from foreign lands, some of them native to the countryside. At Birrens itself Brigantia found room to accommodate the Tungrian goddesses, Viradecthis and Harimella. The Syrian archers at Carvoran brought with them their goddess Hamia. Not far away, at Carrawburgh, the nymph Coventina reclined upon her water-borne leaf by the clear spring which bubbled up within her shrine. A little farther south the goddess Garmangabis had travelled to Lanchester in company with its Suebian garrison. At Benwell, in a small rectangular building with an apsidal bay, a centurion of the Twentieth Legion dedicated an altar to Antenociticus and the *numina Augustorum*, and a prefect of cavalry dedicated another in the same temple to Anociticus. One of the buildings clustered outside the fort at Housesteads contained a small semicircular shrine built to house a triad of unnamed deities, hooded and enveloped in long cloaks. Another building yielded a crudely carved altar dedicated to the *Veteres*, a cult which is widely attested in the north and which seems to have had for its object the worship not of the 'old ones', but of one whose name, perhaps Hvitir, led to easy confusion with the Latin adjective. A little farther away a statue of Mercury has been found. The names of several other deities could be added in demonstration of the wide variety of cults which were practised within a relatively small area of military and civilian occupation. Although several of these deities may not have been held in more than local esteem, there were some whose worship is attested in the civil no less than in the military areas of Britain. At Benwell, where Antenociticus and his companion had their shrine, there was also a temple to the *Matres Campestres*, one of the many guises of the Celtic trio of Mother goddesses whose cult was probably introduced into Britain from Gaul where it was widespread. Dedications to the Mothers are known also from Corbridge, York, Chester, Winchester and London. In a famous sculptured group from Cirencester they sit side by side with heavily laden baskets on their knees.

The temple of Claudius at Colchester, built on such a scale that it invited even Roman ridicule upon the head of its founder, was constructed in the classical style familiar in the Mediterranean world. Sulis Minerva at Bath was honoured in a building of similar character, and far away at Corbridge was a small group of temples which, though altogether more modest in scale and cruder in execution, were yet basically of the same plan. These, however, were not typical of the ordinary Romano-British temple which was normally a much simpler building closely resembling in its plan the groups of temples found in Gaul along the valley of the lower Seine, particularly near Rouen, and other groups of the same kind in the Moselle valley around Trier. The continental distribution of the type, some of whose examples lie farther south in Gaul, but none approaching its Mediterranean shores, suggests that it was of Celtic origin and that it was introduced into Britain from the neighbourhood of Rouen. It consisted normally of a square building, rather small, but lofty, lit internally by clerestory windows and surrounded externally by a verandah or colonnaded portico. The walls were usually covered internally, and perhaps also externally, with painted plaster and the floor was commonly tessellated, perhaps, as at Great Chesterford in Essex, with a mosaic panel. Within this sanctuary, too small to admit any congregation, was housed the deity to whom it was dedicated. Those who came to take part in the ceremonies would find room in the enclosures, sometimes of considerable size, which commonly surrounded temples of this kind and which were themselves cut off from the outer world by an encircling wall or ditch or sometimes a combination of both.

Many of these Romano-Celtic temples lie in the countryside away from the principal centres of population in places whose natural features might offer congenial surroundings for the home of a god. One was built late in the fourth century within the ramparts of Maiden Castle after the fortress had lain deserted for more than three centuries, and close beside it there was a two-roomed dwelling for its priest. Another, likewise encircled by a prehistoric earthwork, lay on the hill top at Chanctonbury Ring in Sussex, and a third was built on an eminence rising above surrounding marshland at Harlow in Essex. But the distribution of this kind of temple is by no means exclusively rural. Examples are known from Silchester and Caerwent, and what seems to have been the most important temple at St. Albans was of the same general plan. The site at St. Albans occupied a complete *insula* of the town, adjacent to the theatre and not far removed from the forum. As originally constructed, the temple consisted of the familiar square *cella* surrounded by an external verandah. The enclosure measuring 300 by 160 feet, within which the temple stood, was from the first isolated from the traffic which passed along the streets by a stone wall with buttresses spaced at regular intervals along its outer face. Both the temple itself and its enclosing wall were twice modified by successive reconstructions, the second occasion being at the very end of the fourth century when the neighbouring theatre had long since fallen into disuse.

The juxtaposition of theatre and temple at St. Albans is parallel on a site of exceptional interest not far from Colchester. Traces of several religious sanctuaries have been found in this neighbourhood, apart from the great temple of Claudius within the *colonia* itself. About two miles to the south-west of the town, on Gosbecks Farm, are the remains of a temple standing within a very large enclosure which was divided into two parts. Of the temple building very little remains, but the great, and indeed unique, interest of the place arises in part from the twofold division of the enclosure within which the temple stood, as though to suggest a graduated approach to the heart of a sacred mystery, from the existence of a large boundary ditch which had already surrounded the same rectangular area before the Roman occupation, and from the theatre which lay only a little way to the south of the temple enclosure. Among the antiquities which have been recovered from the area is a notable bronze statuette of Mercury, the god of trade. Evidence such as this can leave us in no doubt that the site at Gosbecks was one upon which great crowds periodically assembled in Roman and also in pre-Roman times to engage in trade, in worship and in what we may call all the fun of the fair. In its day it will have attracted visitors from far and wide, an early predecessor of some of the great fair-grounds of medieval England, such as that at Stourbridge near Cambridge where the fair was likewise held under religious patronage.

The site at Gosbecks had a long history, though perhaps not as long as that of Clochmabonstane, the holy place of Maponus, which was still a recognised gathering-place in the Middle Ages. We may yet discover other temples, like that at what is now Heathrow airport, where the Roman occupation brought changes in material structure, and perhaps also in the deity worshipped, to a place which had already been used as a religious centre in the Iron Age. There is little indication of any pronounced weakening in either the variety or the strength of pagan religious beliefs in Britain as the occupation proceeded. The reconstruction of temples at St. Albans late in the fourth century and the building of the new temple at about the same time in the deserted fortress at Maiden Castle are part of a considerable body of evidence pointing to a recrudescence of pagan beliefs in the later years of the fourth century. Many of the Romano-Celtic temples have yielded evidence in the form of coins and other votive offerings which show that they were still in use at the end of the Roman occupation, and it was a governor of the fourth century who restored the great column which was dedicated to Jupiter at Cirencester.

A hill top overlooking the Severn estuary at Lydney in Gloucestershire provides us with what is perhaps the most striking evidence of a persistently vigorous pagan faith in the very latest days of the Roman occupation. Already occupied, though not so far as we know for religious purposes, before the Roman invasion, it became in the second and third centuries the dwelling-place of a small group of people who were engaged in working a local deposit of iron. Shortly after 364 the site received upon it a remarkable group of buildings whose nature, further illuminated by the very large number of small finds associated with them, indicates that it suddenly became an important centre of pilgrimage. Occupying a prominent position and standing free from the other buildings, there stood a large temple of unusual design, its nave and surrounding ambulatory, with several side chapels, suggesting that it was extended to house a congregation which was expected to take part in some communal act of worship. The plan itself would not have been ill suited to that of a Christian church, but whether or not the design had been subjected to some Christian influence, the cult whose centre it formed, that of the god Nodens, was pagan. Nodens whose affinities lay westwards with Ireland, was a god of hunting and healing. Close beside his temple was a long narrow building divided into a number of small cells in which it is thought that suppliants slept, hoping that they might be visited in their dreams by the god whose help they sought. There was also a large guest-house with numerous rooms arranged round a courtyard and near by was a bath-house of the familiar Romano-British type. Some years after the completion of this group of buildings the whole site was enclosed within a precinct wall.

Few, if any, Romano-British sites of comparable size have yielded evidence so richly varied in its kind and so often unexpectedly informative in its nature as the temple settlement at Lydney. The buildings themselves show by their careful planning, their separate functions and the quality of their execution, which is exceptionally good for their period, that they were designed to be patronised by people of wealth and substance, such as might be found not only on the same side of the river at Caerwent and Caerleon, but also at Gloucester and among the rich towns and farmlands of the Cotswolds on the opposite side of the river. Nodens may well have proved a rival to Sulis Minerva at Bath. Among the subscribers to the building of the temple itself was the officer commanding a supply depot for a fleet based upon the Severn estuary, his contribution taking the form of a mosaic pavement with a frieze of dolphins and fishes and an inscription commemorating the gift. Less exalted in rank, but a witness of military patronage, was Flavius Blandinus, a drill instructor, who recorded the payment of his vow to Nodens on a bronze plaque. It was surely a wealthy patron who gave the bronze image of a young Irish wolfhound, resting with forepaws outstretched and head turned back in eager expectancy of the chase, itself a masterpiece in miniature. Less generous, at least to his enemies, was Silvianus who gave to Nodens half the value of a lost ring and begged that ill health might pursue all who bore the name of Senicianius, until the ring itself was brought back to the temple. The numbers of brooches, bracelets, bronze trinkets, pins and coins recovered from different parts of the site amount to many thousands and are striking testimony to the great popularity of the cult, as well as to the security, on what we might have thought to be an exposed position, of a settlement whose end did not come in any sudden conflagration, but in slow decay and perhaps not before the fifth century was well advanced.

The worship of Nodens was, so far as we know, confined to Lydney where it was established not many years before the birth of St Patrick whose father was a deacon of the Christian Church, and if the evidence has been rightly interpreted, the last days of the sanctuary at Lydney coincided with the building of what has all the appearance of a Christian church at Caerwent, some twelve miles farther down the Severn estuary. Another, perhaps stronger and certainly more hated, rival of Christianity was the cult of Mithras which prospered in Britain mainly in the third century and the earlier part of the fourth. The worship of Mithras, an Eastern deity in origin, first became prominent in the Roman Empire during the age of the Flavians, its chief propagators being the army and travelling merchants from the East. Characteristically, traces of Mithraism in Britain are confined mainly to the northern military areas, though found also at Caerleon, and to London, a seaport frequented by Eastern merchants.

The worship of Mithras was conducted usually in artificial caves, symbolic of the rock from which, according to the legend, Mithras himself had been miraculously born. Four such buildings have been discovered in Britain, three of them on the Hadrianic Wall—at Housesteads, Carrawburgh (see plan) and Rudchester—and one in London on the banks of the Walbrook. They are small buildings designed to hold perhaps no more than a score of worshippers at one time, but long in proportion to their width, and in their internal plan they conform closely with examples known from other parts of the Empire. A single door, placed in one of the narrow ends, gave access to an ante-room which was separated by a screen from the nave in which the worshippers were accommodated on wide, shallow benches attached to the side walls of the building. Beyond, at the innermost end, lay the sanctuary of the god himself with, as its most characteristic feature, a great sculptured relief commemorating the exploit of Mithras when he captured and slew a wild bull through whose death all manner of blessings were released upon the earth. Accompanying Mithras in his temple were the two torch-bearers, Cautes and Cautopates, and in conditions of semi-darkness, with dramatic effect heightened by the skilful use of illumination in the sanctuary, by the sacred fires burning upon the altars and by the pungent aroma of smouldering pine cones, the followers of Mithras ate their ritual meal and endured those processes of gradual initiation by which they were admitted to the several degrees of their cult.

The manner in which the mithraeum at Carrawburgh was desecrated some years before the middle of the fourth century, and the measures which were taken for the deliberate concealment of some of the pagan sculptures associated with the Walbrook mithraeum in London suggested to the excavators of these two sites the iconoclastic activities of Christian believers whose hostility towards the cult of Mithras in other parts of the Empire is known to have been particularly bitter. The seeming virility of pagan beliefs in third- and fourth-century Britain is not counterbalanced by any corresponding body of archaeological evidence which might suggest the activities of equally vigorous Christian communities. In addition to the supposedly Christian church at Silchester and the undoubtedly Christian wall paintings at Lullingstone, the Christian monogram has been found on a mosaic pavement at Frampton in Dorset and on a stone slab by the edge of a well at Chedworth in Gloucestershire. To these may be added a number of other objects, some of them a fair size, such as tombstones, or the leaden tanks used for baptismal rites, and some of them quite small, such as spoons, brooches, rings, pewter vessels and suchlike—but all of them bearing distinctively Christian symbols. Yet the sum total, perhaps no more than fifty objects in all, is not impressive when we compare it with the known relics of Mithraism, only one of the very many pagan cults practised in Roman Britain. But we should be wise to hesitate before concluding that Christianity was an insignificant force in Roman Britain, and to remember that the Christian religion did not demand the manufacture and dedication of cult objects such as formed an essential part of worship at the shrine of Nodens or of other pagan deities, and such as left a rich harvest for archaeologists of later ages. The vigour of the Christian Church in England in the seventh century is attested by historical records and ecclesiastical buildings, but scarcely at all by small objects belonging to its lay members.

When we take into account the written evidence about Christianity in Britain during and shortly after the Roman occupation, we are likely to gain a different impression. Tertullian, an African whose life was spent mainly in Carthage,

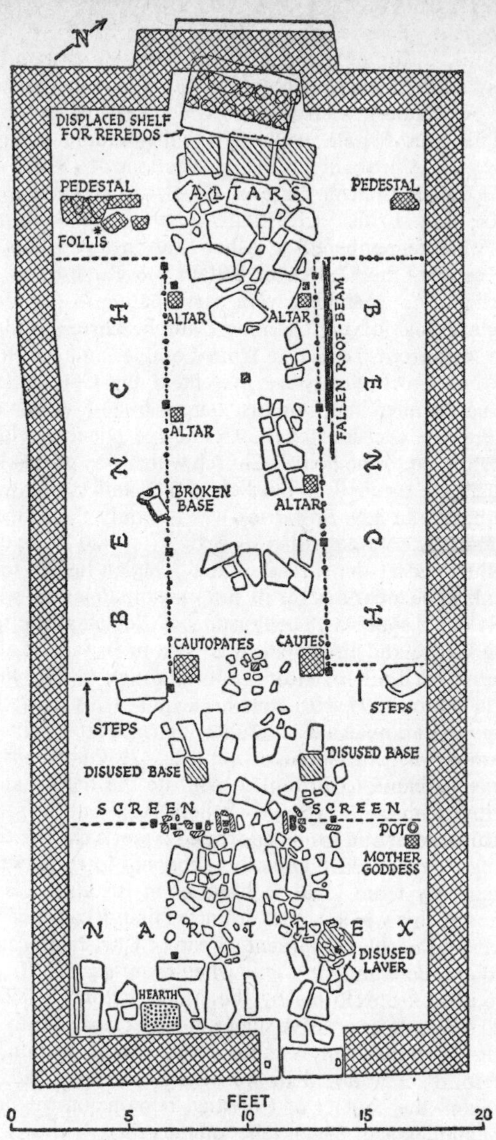

Plan of the mithraeum at Carrawburgh

and Origen, an Alexandrian who later settled at Caesarea, both allude to the preaching of Christianity in Britain in terms which, despite their viewpoint as Christian apologists in an age of persecution, testify to the widespread dissemination of Christianity in Britain well before the middle of the third century. It was probably in the persecutions of Decius (reigned 249–51), rather than in those of Diocletian (reigned 284–305), that the first British Christians suffered martyrdom. Their names were remembered as Alban, Aaron and Julius. By the fourth century the Church in Britain possessed an established hierarchy whose members were participating in the great conciliar gatherings of the Catholic Church. Three bishops from Britain, one from York, one from London, and the third possibly from Colchester, were present at the Council of Arles which condemned the Donatist heresy in 314. Athanasius records that the decisions of the Council of Nicaea, held in 325, were conveyed to the British Church which was probably represented at the Council of Sardica in 347 and certainly at that of Ariminum in 359. St Patrick was not only the son, but also the grandson, of a Christian. Shortly after 420 Pope Celestine was concerned at the spread of the Pelagian heresy to Britain and took some measures for its suppression. Pelagius, who came into violent dispute with Augustine on doctrinal matters concerning Grace and Free Will, was born in Britain at about the middle of the fourth century, and although it was during his years in Rome (394–410) that he acquired his great learning and his reputation as a teacher, his doctrines later gained a firm hold among British Christians, and in 429 Germanus, bishop of Auxerre, came to Britain to confute the heresy and recall the British Church to orthodox beliefs. At about the same date, or a little earlier, Fastidius addressed a work *On the Christian Life* to a British widow, and other works of learning were making their way from Gaul to libraries in Britain. It is in such evidence as this which comes from the first decades of the fifth century, and in the subsequent spread of Christianity to Wales, Ireland and Scotland, at a time when south-eastern Britain was itself cut off from Rome by the Anglo-Saxon invasions, that we find the most impressive suggestion that Christianity had become much more firmly established in Roman Britain, at least in the fourth century, than we might have been led to infer either from the paucity of Christian remains on the one hand or the abundance of pagan relics on the other.

CHAPTER EIGHT

THE AGE OF INVASION

Before we turned to look at some of the characteristics of Romano-British life in the towns and in the farms of the countryside, we had followed the narrative of events as far as the restoration of the frontier by Theodosius after the great onslaught made by Scots, Picts and Saxons in 367. Although this assault was violent, its effects passed quickly away and Britain once again became a prosperous country enjoying the benefits of a strong central government and the protection of a trained army. The breakdown of the former and the withdrawal of the latter were the dominant factors tending towards the chaos and confusion which are the most characteristic features of the age of Anglo-Saxon invasion, chaos which seems the more pronounced by its contrast with the orderly ways imposed upon Britain by Rome during more than three centuries of imperial government. When repeated appeals for aid from Rome went unanswered, only self-help remained as the means of survival. As we look back upon these centuries of turmoil, there is a temptation (against which perhaps even the orderly mind of Bede was not wholly proof) to impose order upon the sequence of events where no order can have been discernible to those who experienced them.

If we stand aside to take a distant view of the years which passed between the restoration of the Hadrianic frontier by Theodosius *c.* 370 until the day when Augustine and his companions settled in Canterbury in 597, we can see in broad outline what had happened in the interval, even though we may find it surpassingly difficult to discern in detail the series of events which had issued in the result that we can see. How far, during these years, had Britain, a diocese within the prefecture of Gaul, moved away from the late classical world into what we call the European Middle Ages? The whole of Ireland and large parts of Scotland had always lain outside the Roman frontiers, and for them the change was chiefly that the barriers which had isolated them from the remainder of Britain had been destroyed. As they had lain beyond the reach of Rome, so also they lay even farther beyond the reach of the Anglo-Saxons. Yet there was one great change which had come to these remote areas of Britain, even though it was not one which at once profoundly affected their political or social organisation. It was the arrival of Christianity spreading outwards from Britain and finding security in the geographical remoteness of its new setting. The year of Augustine's arrival in Canterbury was also the year of Columba's death in Iona.

Perhaps yielding, like Bede, to the temptation to reduce chaos to a deceptive semblance of order, we can observe Britain, a wealthy province still inhabited by men who regarded themselves as 'citizens' (*cives*) and their enemies as 'barbarians', undergoing a process of dismemberment through strains imposed by four conflicting forces. First, there were those inhabitants of Britain who had always lived outside the frontiers of the Roman province. These included the *Scoti,* the name used by Latin writers for inhabitants of Ireland who attacked the province of Britain from the west, and the *Picti,* a name whose origin is unknown, though it was perhaps no more than soldiers' slang, but which was used by Latin writers to refer to the peoples who lived in the far north of Britain beyond the Firth of Forth. Secondly, there were those others who had lived outside the frontiers of the Roman Empire, not in Britain, but on the mainland of Europe, people whose homes lay along the eastern littoral of the North Sea from the Jutland peninsula to the Rhine mouths and beyond. These were the people known to Latin writers as *Saxones*. One group of them, calling themselves *Engle,* gave their name to the country which they invaded. Thirdly, there were the citizens of Roman Britain itself, now, after relying for centuries upon the protection of the Roman army, left to their own devices. And finally, for so long as Britain was even nominally a part of the Roman Empire, there was a fourth factor—the exposure of its inhabitants to the consequences of being involved by their governors or their military leaders in the affairs of the Empire itself. It was indeed this factor which initially proved the most destructive to the security of the province.

When Augustine and his companions reached Canterbury in 597 and began to hold Christian services in a church which reputedly had been built by the Romans, the strains produced by these conflicting forces had completely destroyed Roman

Britain. The old frontiers had vanished, but the new boundaries were not yet established. By this date a group of the *Scoti* who had kinsmen in north-eastern Ireland, had been established for several generations in Argyllshire and the neighbouring islands, but in 597 both Picts and Scots were still independent of one another, and it was not until the middle of the ninth century that the two were amalgamated to form a single kingdom. Moreover, in this year 597, neither the Scots nor the Picts held any lands south of the old Antonine frontier between the Forth and the Clyde. The lowlands of Scotland and the north of England, as far south as the estuaries of the Humber and the Dee, were still very largely in British possession save for some areas in eastern Northumberland and eastern Yorkshire which had fallen into the hands of Saxon invaders from the east. South of the Humber and the Dee, most of the lowland plain of England, that is to say the land which lay to the south and east of the Trent and the Severn had been overrun by the Saxons. West of the Severn, the British remained in possession of what was becoming Wales, though it still comprised a number of distinct kingdoms, and in possession also of the south-western peninsula. When Offa, king of Mercia, died in 796, the boundary between England and Wales had been drawn much where it still runs. The British had lost the greater part, but not all, of lowland Scotland to the English. In the far north the Pictish and Scottish kingdoms were to remain independent of one another until the reign of Kenneth MacAlpin (843-58) when the succession of Pictish kings came to an end. In the far south-west of Britain, the British of Cornwall had lately come under English domination for the first time.

Leaving our distant viewpoint to take a closer look, we can find at least one factor unchanged from Romano-British into Anglo-Saxon times—the physical environment within which the civilisation of these two very different ages developed. The abandonment of military frontiers and the breakdown of political boundaries did not alter the fundamental geographical frontiers and boundaries of the country itself. The broad division of Roman Britain into civil and military areas was not the outcome of Roman imperial policy, but the inevitable consequence of geographical influences. The country which the Anglo-Saxons invaded was still a country basically divided into a Lowland Zone lying exposed to attack from the east, and a Highland Zone whose inhabitants could find a greater degree of security within their moor and mountain fastnesses. An invader with marked military superiority, such as the Romans possessed over the British, could overrun the Lowland Zone within two or three years, but although they could conquer much of the Highland Zone, they could hold it only so long as they could subject it to continuing military government. The Anglo-Saxons had no such military superiority over their opponents and in consequence several generations passed before they were fully in possession of the Lowland Zone. The domination which they won over parts of the Highland Zone was essentially a military domination which they, like the Romans, could retain only so long as they could defeat their enemies in battle. Bede realised this clearly enough when he lamented the excessively large numbers of young men who were betaking themselves to a kind of spurious monastic life, instead of carrying out their military obligations to their kingdom. In political terms this boundary is reflected in Anglo-Saxon times in the division between the kingdoms of the northern English and those of the southern English. It was marked on the eastern side of the Pennines by the Humber and on the western side by the Ribble or the Mersey. We may then expect to find that, in these fluid centuries which lie between the end of Roman Britain and the emergence of the new Anglo-Saxon kingdoms, there will be certain fundamental differences between the northern and the southern sides of this boundary.

However much of the north may have been handed over to native rulers in 370, it is clear that Theodosius had no intention of abandoning what had been in effect the military capital of Britain, namely York itself. Traces of his work are to be found here, as well as elsewhere in Yorkshire, notably at Piercebridge and Malton. And along the Yorkshire coast he erected a number of well-defended signal towers designed to give warning of the approach of sea raiders. The purpose of such warning was presumably to allow naval operations to be set in train as much as to alert the land defences. These signal stations were still in use during the very last years of the fourth century, though at one at least of them the occupation came to a sudden and violent end. By a curious twist of fortune this northern area, after being subjected to direct military government for some three centuries, appears now to have entered upon a period of relatively peaceful development just as the citizens of lowland Britain were finding themselves faced with the grim struggle against the Anglo-Saxon invaders.

We must not be misled by occasional references to *vicani* or to magistrates into supposing that the machinery of local government had developed to the same extent among the northern tribes as it had among the more highly Romanised southerners. The army and not the *civitas* was here the real basis of authority, a situation which may have led the more easily to the growth of independent kingdoms as the authority of the army weakened and finally failed. There is much to suggest that it was a deliberate part of Roman policy to encourage, and perhaps even to create, such kingdoms as a means of establishing a degree of political stability and military security such as the Roman army could not itself impose in the conditions prevailing in the fourth century. Two of the northern British kingdoms, Strathclyde and Manau Gododdin, were ruled in the fifth century by kings whose genealogies show clear signs of Roman influence in nomenclature and titles. The former of the two, with its capital upon the rock at Dumbarton on the northern shore of the Clyde, was heir to the lands of the Damnonii. The kingdom of Strathclyde maintained its independence until the eleventh century and although it was at times hard pressed, it was never completely conquered by the English. The latter of the two, lying southwards from the shores of the Firth of Forth, long preserved in such forms as *Guotodin* or *Gododdin* a living memory of its descent from the people known in earlier times as *Votadini*. It had a shorter history than the kingdom of Strathclyde, partly because it was more directly exposed to attack by the English, and partly because it may have been weakened by the migration of some of its people to north-west Wales, for the purpose of evicting from that area settlers who had come from Ireland. These two kingdoms lay at the northern limit of British lands. Other independent British kingdoms came into being farther south. Among them was the kingdom of Rheged, comprising parts of south-western Scotland and probably parts of Cumberland as well. Farther south still, in part of what became the West Riding of Yorkshire, was the kingdom of Elmet which was not conquered by the English until the early seventh century. Boundaries cannot be accurately drawn, neither is it possible to trace the succession of kings in detail, yet the general picture is of a powerful and unexpected British resurgence in these northern parts of the country, and the replacement of Roman military government by a number of small British kingdoms whose strength proved adequate not only to contain the Picts and Scots in the north, but also to offer prolonged, stubborn, and at times successful resistance to the English attack when it came.

The process of fragmentation which was already beginning in the late fourth century with the establishment of client kingdoms and the reorganisation of the Roman civil administration into five provinces, was accompanied by a steady weakening, and the eventual rupture, of the bonds by which Britain was held within the Empire. In 383, whether furthering his own ambitions or merely acting as a focus for discontented legions, Magnus Maximus, a Spaniard who was then holding high military office in Britain, made a bid for the western empire, and so became the first of a succession of usurpers from Britain with a similar aim. He crossed the Channel and met the emperor Gratian's army near Paris. After some preliminary skirmishing, Gratian's troops began to desert to the other side, and finally Gratian himself took flight, to be murdered soon afterwards at Lyons. For some years the great Empire of Rome was now divided between three men—Theodosius the Great in the east at Constantinople, Valentinian II, Gratian's brother, in Italy, and Magnus Maximus who held Gaul, Spain and Britain, but who was able to do so only by removing troops from Britain to support his position in Gaul. In 387 Magnus Maximus invaded Italy, but in July 388 he was killed fighting against Theodosius. For a short period the Empire was re-united under the government of Theodosius, but on his death in 395 it again broke in half, and there began in the west the long, and from the Roman point of view, disastrous reign of Honorius who, at his accession in 395, was no more than a boy. Before the end of his reign, in 423, Britain had been lost to the Empire, though it had not yet been won by the Anglo-Saxons.

Towards the end of the fourth century Stilicho, a distinguished soldier who had been acting as regent in the west during the minority of the Emperor, is believed to have taken some measures for the defence of Britain. The court poet who sang of Stilicho's achievements on Britain's behalf seems to imply that these measures were successful in their aim, but we have no knowledge of their particular nature. At the opening of the new century, when Rome itself was in danger, Stilicho had to withdraw more troops from Britain, and what remained of the army in Britain, now alarmed for its own safety and despairing of effective help from Honorius, took steps to secure itself by setting up a series of usurpers. The first two—Marcus and Gratian—quickly came to violent ends. The next, Constantine III, allegedly a Briton of low birth, instead of confining his activities to making Britain secure, followed the example of Magnus Maximus by crossing to Gaul of which large parts were in the hands of barbarian invaders. He met at first with some success, but in 411 he was captured in Arles and taken to Ravenna where he was executed.

Britain was now virtually defenceless. Gaul was suffering under fresh incursions from beyond the Rhine. Rome was in no position to send help to either. All three were driven to take what measures they could to secure their own safety without regard to the others. In Britain, now abandoned by the *Vicarius* and the whole of his civilian administrative staff, as well as by the *Comes Britanniarum* and his field army, it fell to the *civitates,* the cantonal capitals in whom authority on matters of local government was vested, to take such action as they could. In 410, the year before the execution of Constantine III, Honorius, the western Emperor, wrote to the *civitates* of Britain enjoining and authorising them to look to their own defences. No doubt Honorius and his advisers regarded this as a temporary expedient to meet a critical situation, with at least the hope, if not the expectation, that Britain would in time be recovered for the Empire. The hope was not fulfilled. Such is the only conclusion that can be drawn from the present state of the evidence.

We cannot do more than guess at the immediate sequel to the letters sent by Honorius in 410. That counsel will have been divided is certain, since there was no central authority by whom a single policy could be imposed. There will have been some who continued to believe that help would yet come from Rome or from Roman forces in Gaul. Such men will have urged that emphasis be sent with reiterated appeals for military assistance. There will have been others to argue that the wisest plan was to follow the policy that had been pursued with good effect in different parts of the Empire, the policy of setting a thief to catch a thief. They would say that the right course was to bring some of the barbarians into Britain and give them land on which to settle in return for their services as fighting men. They could have strengthened their case pointing to the increasingly large Germanic element in the army during the later years of the Roman occupation. But their policy would certainly have roused the violent opposition of those who feared that the visitors might eventually turn against their paymasters and win the whole country for themselves.

Many of the wealthy, not knowing whither they were going, would seek their own personal safety in flight beyond the sea, taking their valuables with them, or burying them in the ground against the hope of the eventual return. During the war against Hitler and the Nazis the plough recovered from the ground a great treasure of silver which had been buried in this way by the edge of the Fens near Mildenhall in Suffolk. Its largest piece, an immense silver dish almost two feet in diameter and more than eighteen pounds in weight, displays a lively representation of the triumph of Bacchus over Hercules, a comforting philosophy for those who could have found little comfort elsewhere, unless, as the spoons marked with the Christian monogram may suggest, the owners were a Christian household. We are heavily indebted to that owner whose precautions, though fruitless for himself, have led to the present-day display of his household silver in the British Museum. Another tale is told by the silver ingots and battered fragments of silver bowls and other objects comprising the hoard of pirates' loot which was buried early in the fifth century at Coleraine in northern Ireland, a tale repeated at Traprain Law, some twenty miles eastward from Edinburgh.

The book written by Gildas is the principal embodiment of a strong tradition that the fall of Britain had been brought about by the policy, catastrophic in its outcome for the British, of inviting Germanic mercenaries to settle within the country, in the hope that they might restore to the island the security which it had enjoyed for centuries through the protection of the Roman army. Gildas was a monk, certainly British by origin and possibly born not far from Glasgow. His book, commonly called the *De Excidio et Conquestu Britanniae*, is generally thought to have been written *c.* 550. He called it 'a little homily' (*admonitiuncula*), and he wrote it for a moral end. His theme was that the miseries of Britain in the past had been due to the wickedness of its inhabitants, and although men were now experiencing a season of peace and prosperity, the old calamities would return if they persisted in their evil ways. We must not at once reject Gildas because he regarded history as a moral teacher. Orosius and Bede did the same, yet it is true that Gildas poured out his words in the trembling cascades of the preacher rather than with the careful precision of a scholar.

Whatever its defects and difficulties, we cannot neglect the story told by Gildas, unless we are prepared to follow those who deny its sixth-century date. His narrative tells of a series of appeals for help addressed to the Romans after the time of Magnus Maximus who left Britain for Gaul in 383. The first two of these appeals were answered, but the third was not, whereupon some of the British surrendered while others continued to fight, eventually inflicting a great defeat upon their enemies. An age of prosperity followed this British victory, but after some time the threat of invasion was renewed. To meet these new dangers 'a proud tyrant' and his councillors decided to call in the Saxons to fight for them. The British gave them lands in the eastern part of the island, and when news of their successes reached their homelands more of their kinsmen crossed the sea to Britain. After a while, a quarrel broke out between the Saxons and the British, and the Saxons rebelled, causing widespread destruction all over the island. A little later some of the Saxons went back to their homes across the sea and the British, led by Aurelianus, won a victory over those that remained. Thereafter there was a period of fluctuating warfare during which sometimes the British and sometimes the Saxons were victorious, but in the end the British won a great victory at Mons Badonicus, and this victory inaugurated a period of peace which was still unbroken when Gildas was writing.

What Gildas seems to be saying in effect is that those who had advocated the policy of setting a thief to catch a thief had carried the day and that they had paid for their folly by losing their country to the Saxons. It is the 'proud tyrant' who is made the scapegoat for this disaster. In its broad outlines the story seems likely enough in the conditions of the age as we know them, even though there are one or two unexpected points about it. It is a little surprising to be told that after the failure of the last appeal for Roman help, the British succeeded by their own efforts in repelling the dangers by which they were threatened. It is even more surprising to be told that after the Saxon revolt, the British were yet strong enough to inflict upon the Saxons a defeat so heavy that it was followed by a prolonged period of peace. The difficulties of the narrative appear only when we begin to ask detailed questions—who was 'the proud tyrant' and when did he live, whereabouts 'in the eastern part' of the country were the first Saxons settled, who was Ambrosius Aurelianus, where was Mons Badonicus, what was the date of the battle fought there and what its outcome, how long-lasting was the age of peace which followed the battle? These are the questions which take us to the heart of the problem, and the fact that we cannot yet answer them with certainly does not seem adequate reason for evading all attempts to give answers based on reasonable conjecture.

One of the major difficulties is that of setting this story within a chronological framework. Bede, with his strong interest in chronology, sought to determine as nearly as he could the date at which the Saxons came to Britain. The *adventus Saxonum* marked for him, in retrospect, the beginning of an era from which he might date such important events in the history of the English as the arrival of Augustine in Canterbury or the conversion of Edwin, first Christian king of Northumbria, or even the ending of his own *History*. Yet on this matter of the *adventus Saxonum* even Bede was never able to achieve precision, and his failure to do so is a strong indication that the *adventus Saxonum* is largely the artificial conception of a scholar writing history, not a specific occasion known to those who had experienced it. So far as we can now see, the Anglo-Saxon invasions were a long, continuing process not marked by any single episode corresponding with the landing of the Roman legions in 43 or with the battle of Hastings in 1066. It was natural enough that historians should seek to determine exactly the beginning of this new era, but their very attempts to do so can now be a cause of difficulty.

The letters sent by Honorius to the *civitates* of Britain in 410, urging them to look to their own defence, seem to mark, as much as any single event can so mark, the end of Roman Britain. The phase of self-help which led to the first stage of prosperity mentioned by Gildas ought thus to fall in the decades following 410. If we are correct in thinking that Gildas was writing at about the middle of the sixth century, the second phase of prosperity which Gildas himself experienced had not yet come to an end by *c.* 550. Between these two limits we must place the settlement of Saxons in eastern Britain by 'the proud tyrant', the Saxon rebellion, and the warfare between the British and the Saxons which culminated in the British victory at Mons Badonicus.

'The proud tyrant' whom Gildas makes the scapegoat for the loss of Britain is known to us from other sources by the name of Vortigern. There was a tradition of British origin that he had begun to reign in 425 and there was an English tradition that he fought against Hengest and Horsa in Kent in 455. An inscribed cross which now stands near the abbey of Valle Crucis not far from Llangollen has been read as meaning that Vortigern was the ancestor from whom the rulers of the Welsh border kingdom of Powys were descended, and that Vortigern himself was the son of a daughter of Magnus Maximus, but the inscription is now mostly defaced and illegible, and we are dependent on a reading made by a Welsh antiquary in the seventeenth century. Other evidence, part literary and part archaeological, begins to suggest that we may envisage Vortigern as a man born in aristocratic surroundings late in the fourth century within the territory of the Cornovii which included both Wroxeter, one of the major cities of Roman Britain, and Chester, one of the legionary bases. In circumstances of which we have no knowledge, he seems to have won for himself a position of authority not unlike that which had been held by the governors of Roman Britain in earlier times, authority which evidently ran over most of the Lowland Zone of Britain, if in fact it reached as far as Kent where he is said to have been fighting against Hengest and Horsa in 455. The years of Vortigern's reign, if the dates are even approximately correct, allow time enough for the first phase of prosperity following upon the abandonment of Britain by Rome to her own devices in 410. Yet Vortigern himself was represented as an evil man who not only lost Britain to the Saxons, but also committed incest with his own daughter. It is possible that the explanation for his bad reputation may be found in an episode which took place in 429, the one episode in these years whose date is securely established.

In this year the Pope in Rome sent a representative to Britain charged with the task of countering certain heretical tendencies by which the Christian Church in Britain was being brought into a state of corruption. These heresies sprang from the doctrines of Pelagius, a Briton by origin who had won for himself great renown in Mediterranean lands by his opposition to the teaching of Augustine. The papal emissary was Germanus, bishop of Auxerre in Gaul. Germanus came to Britain and after overthrowing the heretics by theological argument, he guided the Church in Britain back to the Catholic faith. However surprising it may be to learn that, in a country which might seem to some to have been in a state of dissolution in the face of barbarian attack, there were, nevertheless, men who were able to engage in deep theological argument, the visit of Germanus to Britain in 429 and the circumstances by which the visit was prompted are well authenticated. We may certainly conclude that at this date the Churches of Gaul and Britain were in communication with one another, and that far away in Rome the Pope was well informed about the doctrinal vagaries of the British Church. Whether the synod at which Germanus confounded the Pelagian heretics was held at St. Albans (*Verulamium*), as many believe, seems less certain.

Theological battles and military warfare are distinct and separate activities which ought to be kept apart from one another and not inextricably confused, as they were some fifty years after the event by Constantius who wrote a *Life* of Germanus. In this work, Constantius represents Germanus, after successfully routing his theological enemies, as winning a military victory on Easter Sunday over bands of Picts and Saxons who had disturbed the season of Lent, by the expedient of getting his supporters to shout loud and sudden Alleluias from a hidden ambush. The 'Alleluia Victory', won by Germanus over barbarian invaders of Britain, is surely no more than a tale conceived by someone who had misunderstood the whole situation and supposed that Germanus' victory had been won in a military battle rather than in theological argument. If we think that the reign of Vortigern coincided at least in part with Gildas' first phase of prosperity, we can see how it was that men were able to hold theological discussion in seeming security. And if we may suspect that the great crime of Vortigern was that he himself was a follower of the Pelagian heresy, we can understand why he was represented to posterity as an evil man. Many of his contemporaries would have regarded the act of introducing Saxon settlers into Britain as the normal kind of action to take in the circumstances prevailing at the time.

Yet Vortigern may have been doubly unfortunate—not merely a Pelagian heretic, but also the man in whose reign the British paymasters first began to lose control of their hired mercenaries. The story of the fall of Britain is not so simple as Gildas represents it to have been. The chance survival of certain detailed information associating Vortigern with the settlement of Hengest and Horsa in Kent has given disproportionate prominence to events in one particular part of the country, to the neglect of certain general tendencies whose significance is now becoming clearer. There is good evidence that Frisians were prominent among the settlers in Britain in the fifth and sixth centuries, but Frisians had already been numbered among the garrison of Roman Britain in the fourth century. There was a cohort of them stationed at Rudchester on the Hadrianic frontier where they were in a good position to learn about any weaknesses in the military defences of the province. If Vortigern was well informed about the state of Britain in his father's lifetime he may have known more than we do about the group of Alemanni who were settled in Britain under their king Fraomar shortly after the middle of the fourth century. There was no basic difference between this kind of action and the action taken by Vortigern. Both aimed to employ the same means to the same end, namely the defence of Britain, and both were tending towards the production of a hybrid state which was not Romano-British nor yet Anglo-Saxon, but Romano-Saxon.

This is the name which has been given in recent years to a kind of pottery which is symptomatic of a civilisation which was coming under increasingly strong Germanic, or Saxon, influences at a time when Britain was still a secure part of the Roman Empire. The characteristics of this pottery are that it is made according to the techniques practised in Roman Britain, but yet bears upon it the decorative motifs familiar on the much cruder pottery, not thrown on the wheel, which is characteristic of the Anglo-Saxons. This fusion, in common objects of everyday use, is highly suggestive of the peaceful coexistence of some who, in a later age, might have been called Anglo-Saxons, and others, in an earlier, Romano-Britons. Pottery of this kind was being made in Britain from the closing years of the third century until, and probably beyond, the breakdown of Roman rule. Its distribution is no less significant than its nature. It has been found in some of the forts of the Saxon Shore—Burgh Castle, Bradwell-on-Sea and Richborough; in some eastern seaports—Caister-by-Yarmouth, Felixstowe and London; and in some inland towns on the eastern side of

Britain—Colchester, St. Albans and York. In other words, it is found generally in that 'eastern part' of Britain in which Vortigern is said to have settled the Saxons, but it is proof that this same eastern part of Britain was receiving strong Saxon influences long before the days of Vortigern. The neighbourhood of the Saxon Shore forts and of other eastern seaboard towns would be likely places in which to settle Saxon *foederati* who were intended to secure this same seaboard against further attack.

We have not yet been able to identify any of the settlements alleged by Gildas to have been made by Vortigern, as we should so easily have been able to do if the settlers had lived in newly built, fortified encampments resembling those of the Romano-British army of occupation. They may yet be found in or beside some of the Saxon Shore forts. The remains of some of them may be represented in some of the many cemeteries which have been discovered widely spread over the eastern half of Britain, but it is only in very rare circumstances that even individual burials in such cemeteries yield approximate evidence of date. When we find, as we do at York, one Saxon cemetery adjoining a Roman burial ground about half a mile from one of the gateways of the Roman legionary fortress, and another lying in the midst of a Roman burial ground in which pottery of Romano-Saxon type has been discovered, it is easier to regard these as representing the remains of *foederati* settled near York to strengthen the northern defences, than to suppose them to have been the burial grounds of hostile invaders.

Let us recall the sequel to Vortigern's invitation to the Saxons to settle in Britain. For a while the policy was successful, but later the British and the Saxons quarrelled and there was a widespread Saxon rebellion. Shortly afterwards some of the Saxons went home, but the British found a leader, Ambrosius Aurelianus, who led them to victory over the remaining Saxons. After a time of continuing warfare, with fluctuating fortunes, the British won a great victory at Mons Badonicus and there followed an age of peace which was still unbroken at the time when Gildas was writing. There were different traditions about the date of the *adventus Saxonum*, perhaps because different authorities held different opinions about which episode in the long process of invasion could, in retrospect, be regarded as marking the *adventus* itself. The Saxon rebellion against the British came shortly after the middle of the fifth century and was marked, in Kentish tradition, by a series of battles of which the first was believed to have been fought in 455. After a second battle, attributed to 457, the British 'deserted Kent and fled with great fear to London'. A third battle is ascribed to 465 and a fourth, after which the British 'fled from the English as from fire', to 473. These episodes are recorded in the *Anglo-Saxon Chronicle*, which is to say that they represent English tradition. Anyone reading this *Chronicle* might well conclude that, after the first victory won by Hengest over Vortigern, the Anglo-Saxons proceeded to make a series of fresh conquests which quickly brought the greater part of the country into their possession. There is scarcely a hint in this source of the British recovery recorded by Gildas, yet, for his unexpected statement that after the rebellion some of the Saxons went home, we can find no less unexpected confirmation that the tide of movement in this age was by no means only from the Continent to Britain.

Continental tradition, of which one version was recorded by Rudolf, a monk of Fulda, claimed that the continental Saxons were descended from the *Angli* of Britain. Although the account of the migration from Britain is legendary, it is to be noted that there was a canton called Engilin between the Unstrut and the Saale, and that other place-names in this area compounded with *Engel-* or *Angl-* suggests some sort of contact with the *Engle* or *Angli*. Procopius records that each of the three races who inhabited Britain—the English, the Frisians and the British—were so numerous that every year they sent large numbers of their people to the lands of the Franks who gave them places in which to live. Because of these migrations, the king of the Franks had claimed Britain itself as being within his dominions, and, as proof of his claim, he had included some of the Angles in a recent embassy sent by him to Constantinople. The evidence from Procopius seems also to refer plainly to the movement which we know to have been taking place at this time from south-western Britain into what had formerly been the Roman province of Armorica in Gaul, the movement which in fact turned Armorica into Brittany.

Gildas himself describes the flight of some of the British out of the country before the advancing Saxons, placing it after the Saxon rebellion and before the British recovery initiated by Ambrosius Aurelianus. It has been established partly on historical and partly on linguistic grounds, that there were two waves of migration from Britain into north-western Gaul, of which the first started *c.* 450, that is at about the time of the Saxon rebellion, and originated from the neighbourhood of Hampshire and the adjacent parts of southern Britain. The second wave came from the more westerly parts of southern Britain, mainly Devon and Cornwall, and began after *c.* 575 when the Saxons first began to offer a serious threat to these westerly parts of the country. But the British were not the only people moving into western Gaul from Britain. At Herpes, in the Charente Department of France, almost as far down the western coast as Bordeaux, a cemetery has yielded jewellery which resembles some of the jewellery recovered from graves in Kent so closely as to suggest direct movement from Kent to this part of western Gaul.

Ambrosius Aurelianus, to whom Gildas gives the credit for initiating the British recovery which culminated in the victory at Mons Badonicus, remains something of a puzzle. He is described as the last of the Romans in Britain, born to a family who had worn the purple and having descendants who were still known in the days of Gildas himself, though they had greatly fallen from the former high estate of their ancestors. We cannot connect him securely with any particular localities, nor can we place him in time except to say that he flourished after the Saxon rebellion and before the battle of Mons Badonicus. He ought therefore to belong to the middle or second half of the fifth century, perhaps a generation later than Vortigern. We can only guess that he was a soldier who, by his success in warfare against the Saxons, won for himself much the same kind of position as had formerly been held by Vortigern. His was an age, Gildas would have us believe, of fluctuating fortunes when sometimes the British and sometimes the Saxon were victorious. There may be a reflection of a time of English supremacy in the tradition which made Ælle, an English king who ruled over the South Saxons in the second half of the fifth century, the first of those who were later called Bretwaldas.

The heart of the matter lies in the battle, or, as Gildas himself calls it, the siege of Mons Badonicus—*obsessio Montis Badonici*. Nothing could contribute so greatly to a better understanding of the Anglo-Saxon invasions than exact knowledge about the site, date and consequences of this British victory. But on all three of these points we remain in doubt, despite the many attempts to find answers to at least the first two. Among the many places which have been claimed as the site of the battle, the great Iron Age hill fortress called Badbury Rings, near Wimborne in Dorset, seems the most likely. It has been claimed that the battle was fought in the year 486, though at least one authority places it as late as 516. Perhaps *c.* 490 may be right to within five or ten years. We can see, on the authority of Gildas, that among the consequences of the battle was a period of peace which evidently lasted half a century or more. Since Gildas claims that he himself experienced this age of peace we must, if we are to place any belief in him at all, believe him on this particular point. But where in this age of equilibrium did the boundary between the British and the Saxons run? And when did this age come to an end? The second question is more easily answered than the first.

In 552 the Saxons defeated the British at Old Sarum and in 556 they defeated them again at Barbury near Swindon. In 571 the Saxons defeated the British in a battle which won for them the towns of Limbury in Bedfordshire, Aylesbury in Buckinghamshire, and Benson and Eynsham in Oxfordshire. In 577 the Saxons won a battle against the British at Dyrham in which they gained the towns of Gloucester, Cirencester and Bath. These engagements do not form a series in a concerted plan and they were not the only engagements fought between the Saxons and the British at this time, but they suggest that the final conquest of much of midland and southern England from the British took place during the years between 550 and 600. North of the Humber the British suffered a major defeat by the Saxons at a place which is generally believed to have been Catterick in *c.* 590. In 603 Æthelfrith, king of Northumbria, won a major victory over Aedan, king of the Scots.

Both north and south of the Humber the second half of the sixth century seems to be the age in which the Saxons finally established their domination over the British. Yet we ought to distinguish between battles, as a result of which leadership passed from one side to the other, and the slow, continuing process of migration whereby the land of Britain gradually came into the possession of new owners. A forward glance to a later age of invasion may be helpful. On three separate occasions in the ninth century Danish armies advanced into the heart of Wessex, compelling Alfred on the last of these occasions, in 878, to withdraw for safety to the stronghold at Athelney in the Somerset marshes. Yet Wessex was never settled by the Danes. In the tenth century when Edward the Elder conquered the east midlands from the Danes, this part of the country became part of Edward's kingdom, yet the Danish settlers remained in possession of their farms and towns. The relations between the British and the Saxons in the fifth and sixth centuries may have been in some ways comparable with the relations between the English and the Danes in the ninth and tenth.

CHAPTER NINE

THE SOUTHERN ENGLISH SETTLEMENTS

The name 'Northumbria' derives from Old English *Norð-hymbre,* earlier *Norðanhymbre,* and means 'the people living north of Humber'. Its counterpart, *Suðanhymbre,* which, had it survived, would have yielded a modern Southumbria, was current for a time but never became established in Anglo-Saxon geographical nomenclature. Yet, despite the separate political entities of which they were composed, the English who lived south of the Humber could be designated comprehensively as 'the South English'. Thus, when Æthelbald, king of Mercia, made a grant of land to a nobleman in 736 he styled himself king not only of the Mercians, but also of all the provinces 'which are called by the general name "South English" '—*quae generale nomine Sutangli dicuntur*. By this date the kings of Mercia had achieved supremacy over all the southern English, and many of the smaller kingdoms had become little more than subject provinces of Mercia. Before the establishment of Mercian domination in the eighth century, England south of the Humber and the Ribble and west of the Severn had been divided among a considerable number of independent kingdoms, at one time perhaps as many as ten.

Bede, who was writing in the eighth century, at the time when Æthelbald was reigning in Mercia, thought that the inhabitants of these various kingdoms were descended from three Germanic races whom he called Saxon, Angles and Jutes. From the Saxons were descended the East Saxons, the South Saxons and the West Saxons. From the Angles were descended the East Angles, the Middle Angles and the Mercians, as well as all those who lived north of the Humber. From the Jutes, he wrote, were descended the people who lived in Kent and the Isle of Wight, as well as on the mainland opposite the Isle of Wight. Bede's remark about Jutes settling in part of what is now Hampshire is confirmed by a chronicler of the late eleventh century who records that the New Forest was known to the English as *Ytene,* the genitive plural of a late Old English form *Yte* which corresponds with Bede's Latin form *Iutae.*

Despite this confirmation of Bede in a point of detail, there is about his account a tidy artificiality which, though it may be relevant to the political order prevailing in the seventh and early eighth centuries, had little application to the age of invasion and settlement which preceded the emergence of the several kingdoms.

Both Angle and Saxon are indeed ancient names, the former first recorded by Tacitus in the first century of the Christian era, and the latter by the geographer Ptolemy in the second. Bede called the homeland of the Angles *Angulus*, a name which survives in the provincial name Angeln applied to an area near Slesvig. If the name is related to the Old English *angel*, meaning 'fish-hook', it is possible that there is some topographical reference to the shape of the Jutland peninsula in whose southerly part the Angles lived before migrating to England. The Old English form of Bede's *Saxones* is *Seaxe*. The meaning is not certainly known, but it might be derived from *seax*, the name given to a single-edged weapon which we can regard as knife, dagger or sword according to its length. But whatever may have been the original meanings of these names, they would be susceptible to change over the centuries. Tacitus regarded the *Angli* as a distinct Germanic tribe, but there is no evidence that either the Anglo-Saxon settlements in Britain, or the political geography of Bede's England, were characterised by sharp tribal or racial distinctions. Even where such distinctions may have existed before migration, the process of migration itself will have done much to obliterate them. The boundary between the *East Engle* who gave their name to East Anglia and the *East Seaxe*, their southern neighbours after whom Essex is named, was in Bede's time a political and geographical boundary, not a tribal or racial boundary. The name of the kingdom which dominated Bede's England was not a tribal name in origin, nor was it even an ancient name. The *Mierce*, from which Mercia is named, were the 'borderers', the people of the march, and the name may well not have come into existence before the seventh century.

Apart from Angles, Saxons and Jutes, it is certain that there were numbers of Frisians among the invaders, such men as gave their names to Frieston in Lincolnshire and Friston in Suffolk. There were also some of the Swabians, remembered now in the Swaffhams of Norfolk and Cambridgeshire. The invaders came to Britain from those parts of western Europe along the eastern shores of the North Sea where now lie Denmark, north-western Germany, Holland and Belgium. A few may have come from farther north, from the southern parts of Sweden. Some may have moved gradually south-westwards along the coast until they could make a short crossing to Britain from the neighbourhood of Calais and Boulogne. Others made the longer journey from Holland and Belgium where the pottery called Anglo-Frisian, with its smooth, well-made fabric, quite unlike the gritty inferior pottery found in many Anglo-Saxon cemeteries, seems almost indistinguishable from pottery found at such places as Hough-on-the-Hill and Sleaford in Lincolnshire, at Caister-by-Norwich and North Elmham in Norfolk, or at Northfleet and Sarre in Kent.

We know little about the boats that were being used in the North Sea areas in the fifth and sixth centuries. The Sutton Hoo ship which was buried at about the middle of the seventh century remained only as a ghost ship, to be reconstructed from the pattern left upon the sand by its decayed timbers and clench nails. It was a rowing-boat drawing no more than 2 feet of water when light, and with its prow rising about 12½ feet above the level of the keel-plank amidships. There were 9 strakes on either side of the keel-plank and the inner framework was constructed with 26 transverse ribs. It had seen much service before it was buried, but it had certainly been a fine ship, stable in the waters for which it was built, graceful in its lines, swift and easy to manoeuvre for its 38 oarsmen. But it had no mast nor any other equipment to suggest that it could have been sailed. This Sutton Hoo ship was undoubtedly a better boat than the great open rowing-boat which was found in a bog at Nydam near Schleswig, and therefore in the area from which the Angles are believed to have come to Britain. The Nydam ship, dating from about the end of the fourth century, was slightly shorter than the Sutton Hoo ship, 73 feet compared with 80, but it was markedly narrower in the beam, 10 feet against 14, and it had no keel. The Nydam ship would have served well enough as a warship, provided that it carried enough ballast to offset the instability inherent in its narrow, sharp lines. We may believe that it was such boats as these that brought the Saxons across the sea, first as pirates to attack the eastern and southern shores of Britain in the third and fourth centuries, and later as settlers in a country no longer under Roman protection.

Even though they are not to be compared with the magnificent warships built by the Vikings in later centuries, the Nydam and Sutton Hoo ships were the work of skilled shipwrights, well suited to the waters in which they were to be used. Yet it would be a mistake to suppose that open rowing-boats were the only kind of boat known in northern waters during these centuries, and, in particular, to suppose that the use of sail was unknown. The monks of Iona in the sixth century were using the skin-covered curachs such as are still to be seen in the stormy waters off the western coasts of Ireland, but they were also using heavy long-ships which were built of oak and pine, and which were normally sailed rather than propelled by oars. When Paulinus fled from Northumbria after the death of Edwin in 632 he made the journey to Kent by sea, and surely we do right to imagine him going in a sailing-ship rather than in a rowing-boat. Whether their journeys lay in eastern or in western seas, the men who voyaged in these boats were beset by great perils and hardships. Some of the most vivid passages in Old English poetry are those which tell of the storm-tossed winter seas. A seafarer speaks:

> Many a grievous night-watch befell me at the prow of my ship, as she lay tossing by the cliffs. My feet have been numbed with cold, pinched with the icy grip of frost, while burning sorrows have beset my heart. The man whose lot falls most joyously on land cannot imagine how I, care-worn, have endured the winter in paths of exile on the ice-cold sea, robbed of dear kinsmen, hung with icicles, amid the flurrying showers of hail. There I heard no sound but the roaring of the sea, the icy waves. Sometimes for my delight I had the song of the swan, the cry of the gannet and the call of the curlew, instead of the laughter of men, the song of the gull instead of the drinking of mead. Storms would beat against the cliffs, and the tern with ice-like plumage give answer: time and again, with sea-sprayed feathers, the sea eagle shrieked, nor was there any protecting kinsman to comfort my desolate heart.

The evidence of written traditions, archaeological remains, place-names and geographical situation leaves no room for doubt that Kent was an area of early and concentrated settlement, even though there are difficult problems about the origin and identity of the settlers whom Bede called Jutes, as well as about their relationship to Hengest, the traditional founder of the Kentish kingdom. The defence of this exposed corner of Britain was an obviously pressing necessity if south-eastern Britain as a whole was not to be overrun, and it seems very likely that Vortigern sought to provide for it by settling within it bands of fighting men. Hengest and Horsa were believed to have come to Kent during the reign of the emperors Martianus and Valentinus, that is between 450 and 455. A person called Hengest is known to us from Germanic literature and the probability is that the two are the same. Yet we are not bound to suppose that he and his warriors were the first comers in Kent. There may have been others before him and there were certainly others after him. According to English tradition, Hengest turned against Vortigern in 455, and two years later he had taken possession of the whole of Kent, driving the British in flight to London. The date of Hengest's death is not recorded, but the *Anglo-Saxon Chronicle* places the accession of his son under the year 488, assigning him a reign of 24 years. After the death of Hengest's son *c.* 512 we have no information about the succession of kings in Kent until the reign of Æthelbert *c.* 560-616, but this is no ground for thinking that the succession was broken or that the British ever recovered control of Kent.

No other part of the country surpasses Kent in the wealth of grave-goods associated with the Anglo-Saxon settlements. Large numbers of cemeteries have been found, many of them lying east of a line drawn from Reculver, at the northern end of the Wantsum Channel, passing through Canterbury and onwards to Lympne on the south coast. Other cemeteries lie in the northern part of the country along the Roman road from Canterbury to Rochester, but west of the Medway there is a notable decrease in their frequency. The earliest of the Germanic cemeteries in Kent may well date from the first half of the fifth century, and it is not to be supposed that the practice of interring weapons, jewellery and other personal belongings with the dead ceased at once upon the arrival of Christianity. There was a relapse to paganism after the death of Æthelbert *c.* 616 when the Kentish Christian mission came near to extinction. Moreover Bede tells us that the first English king to order the abandonment and destruction of idols throughout his kingdom was Erconberht who reigned in Kent from 640 to

664. Sutton Hoo, by far the richest of all Anglo-Saxon burial deposits, is thought to date from the middle of the seventh century and the presence in it of silver spoons bearing Christian symbols suggests that the deposit may have been a monument to a Christian rather than to a pagan. What can be somewhat loosely called 'pagan Saxon cemeteries' may in fact contain material ranging in date from as early as *c.* 400 until as late as *c.* 700, or perhaps even later in some parts of the country. It is this wide temporal range, combined with the lack of such datable objects as coins, that makes it impossible to use archaeological evidence to reconstruct a chronological account of the invasion in Kent, or in any other part of the country, in terms anywhere near so precise as those found possible for the Roman invasion of Britain in the first century. But, despite the chronological difficulties, the grave-goods have much else to tell.

Within Kent itself the pattern of Anglo-Saxon settlement generally coincides with the Romano-British pattern. Some of the most important of the settlements, as witnessed by the wealth recovered from their cemeteries, lie close to what had been among the most important Romano-British centres of occupation, such as Canterbury, Rochester, Dover and Faversham. This coincidence is much less marked in the more westerly parts of Kent. West of the Medway, where there had been a number of prosperous Romano-British farms, Anglo-Saxon grave-goods are sparse, and closely related in kind to material found in Surrey and farther up the Thames. Eastern Kent, in contrast, shows evidence of a rapidly developing prosperity, characterised by advanced technical skills in the manufacture of jewellery for which gold was used more freely than in any other part of the country, save perhaps in the workshops which produced the Sutton Hoo jewels, and by the import of luxury goods from the Continent. Among the witnesses of this overseas trade are the gold coin-like jewels from Denmark called bracteates, other kinds of jewellery associated with the Rhineland and northern France, and considerable quantities of glass imported from the Rhenish glass factories. Significant of this economic wealth which is distinctive of Kent, and chiefly of the eastern part, is the fact that it was in Kent that coins of Anglo-Saxon manufacture first came into circulation. Moreover, the great reform of the English currency, which is associated with Offa, king of Mercia, in the eighth century, had its beginnings in the reign of otherwise obscure Kentish kings. Yet this prosperity was manufactured in Kent and did not rise from any distinctive features of the earliest settlements, for what seems to represent the earliest layer of archaeological material from the Kentish cemeteries is marked by the same kind of poor-quality pottery and jewellery that is found in other parts of the country that never came to enjoy the economic wealth acquired by Kent.

Æthelbert who was ruling in Kent when Augustine arrived in 597, was the third of those rulers who, in a later source, are called Bretwaldas (see below, p. 284), but it seems to have been only in his reign that the kingdom enjoyed any political importance. Although Kentish kings continued to rule throughout the seventh century, during much of that time the kingdom was largely dependent upon Wessex, and the dynasty finally came to an end during the Mercian domination in the eighth century. The choice of Canterbury as seat of the archbishopric, the only one in the country until the elevation of York in 735, conferred upon the kingdom a degree of importance in ecclesiastical matters such as it did not maintain in political affairs. The short-lived establishment by Offa of an archbishopric at Lichfield within the boundaries of his own kingdom is a reflection of the difficulties which he had encountered in maintaining control over Kent.

Separated from Kent by the Weald, which the Anglo-Saxons called *Andredesleah*, a name which is related to *Anderita*, the Romano-British name of what is now Pevensey, lay the kingdom of the South Saxons, stretching westwards along the south coast as far as Chichester harbour. Sailors who use Admiralty charts will be familiar with the Middle and Outer Owers, the names of a series of sandbanks lying off Selsey Bill. The Owers now mark a former coastline and it was here, at a place known to the Anglo-Saxons as *Cymenesora*, that the founder of the South Saxon kingdom, Ælle, is said to have landed with his three sons in 477. In 491 Ælle besieged *Andredesceaster*, the Saxon Shore fort at Pevensey, killing all who were inside, 'so that not even a single Briton was left alive'. Beginning a little to the west of Selsey Bill and extending along the coast some little way to the east of Pevensey is the most dense concentration of place-names of the *-ingas* type to be found anywhere in the country, no fewer than 45 lying within the boundary of the modern county of Sussex, more than three times as many as are found in Kent. Angmering, Iping,

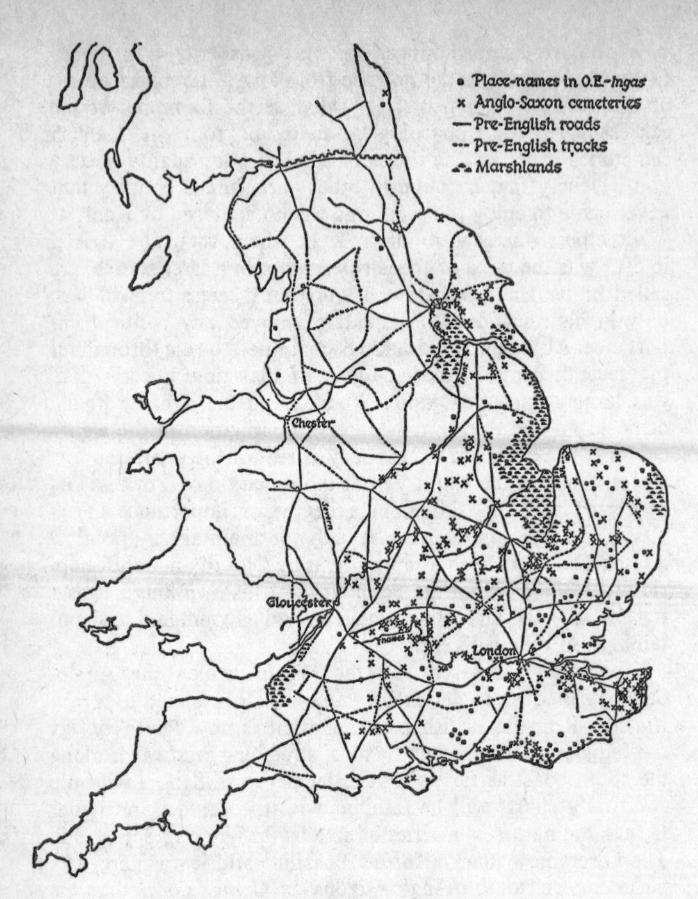

The Anglo-Saxon settlements

Wittering and Worthing are Sussex examples of the type. The name Angmering means 'the followers or dependents of a man called Angenmaer', and in this and other names of the same type, where we find the *-ingas* termination combined with the personal name of an individual, we can at last penetrate beyond the political artificialities of later times to the social units that came into existence during the age of migration and colonisation itself. We have moved away from wars and battles, and are looking instead at small groups of people establishing themselves in new homes and creating the villages which in most instances have remained in continuous occupation from that day to this. It was in this way, not by the building of individual farms, such as had been prominent in the economy of Roman Britain, but by the settlement on the land of groups of people whose leader was commemorated in the name of the village which the group brought into existence, that much of the lowland areas of Britain passed into the hands of the Anglo-Saxons. Although there may have been a number of people within such a group who were blood relations of one another, we ought not to think of them as groups of kinsmen, but as associations of men brought together by their dependence on a common leader, and holding to one another for their own mutual economic and military advantage.

Many of these South Saxon settlements are likely to have been small. The cemeteries of some of them lie on the chalk downs inland from Eastbourne, Brighton and Worthing. There is scarcely any Celtic element at all in the place-names of Sussex. Most even of the river-names of Sussex are English, in contrast with both Kent on the one side and Hampshire on the other where the rivers more commonly retain their old Celtic names, as they do in most other parts of the country. Perhaps the massacre recorded at Pevensey was paralleled in other parts of this area of settlement, resulting in the almost complete extermination of the native population. Although it would be wrong to suppose that the Wealden forest formed an impenetrable barrier between Kent and Sussex, it would be equally wrong to ignore the patent fact that it provided a natural northern boundary to the area of South Saxon settlement and that it tended to isolate this area from influences at work in other parts of southern and eastern Britain. It was this isolation that resulted in the kingdom of the South Saxons being the last of all the Anglo-Saxon kingdoms to abandon heathenism. Politically, the kingdom was of no importance save perhaps in its very earliest days. It was the particular distinction of its founder, Ælle, to be regarded as the first of the Bretwaldas, but we know nothing of the circumstances which won this distinction for him. We can only conjecture that at some time in the second half of the sixth century he was recognised as the leader of the Anglo-Saxon assault against the British in the south-eastern parts of the country as a whole. The eastern part of the modern county of Sussex seems to have lain outside the kingdom of the South Saxons. Between this kingdom and the kingdom of Kent there was a group of people called *Haestingas* who long preserved their separate identity. They were conquered by Offa in 771 and the Latin annal which records their defeat calls them *gens Hestingorum*. This Latin name, together with the Old English *Hæstingas*, implies the settlement in this neighbourhood of a group of people dependent on a man called Haesta. As late as 1011, an annalist describing the areas which had lately been overrun by the Danish army, could write: 'and south of the Thames, all Kent, Sussex, Hastings, Surrey, Berkshire, Hampshire and much of Wiltshire'. The inclusion of Hastings in this list of county names shows that even at that late date the name indicated an area comparable with a county, not simply a town. The name of the people also survives in Hastingleigh, 'woodland of the *Hæstingas*', in Kent, due north of the Sussex Burwash, and in Hastingford, 'the ford of the *Hæstingas*', in the rape of Pevensey in Sussex.

The evidence suggests that the kingdom of the South Saxons grew out of settlements which were taking place about a generation later than the times of Hengest in Kent, with Pevensey remaining in British hands until almost the end of the fifth century. Despite the lack of detail, there is enough continuity in the recorded history of the two south-eastern kingdoms to prove that no part of this corner of Britain was ever regained from English control. Elsewhere south of the Humber, with the exception of Wessex whose origins and early history present problems of considerable difficulty, there is no written tradition to lend even a moderate degree of chronological precision to the distribution of settlement disclosed by cemeteries and early place-names. At the beginning of the historical period, that is during the first half of the seventh century, it is possible to discern three kingdoms lying along the eastern seaboard, the kingdoms of the East Saxons, of the East Angles and of Lindsey. We can also suspect the former existence of two other once independent kingdoms—the Middle Saxons and the Middle Angles. In the midlands lay the kingdom of Mercia which first became prominent during the reign of Penda (*c.* 632–55).

Before *c.* 600, and for long afterwards, London, and presumably the whole of what is now Middlesex, formed part of the kingdom of the East Saxons. Although there is no record of any dynasty of Middle Saxon kings, the name itself suggests that there may once have been such a dynasty. *Middel Seaxe* is exactly analogous in form to *Suþ Seaxe* or *Middel Engle*, and it seems improbable that a people bearing such a name as this would have been confined territorially to an area so small as that of the modern county of Middlesex. The northern boundary of the county is comparatively modern, and Hertfordshire, its neighbouring county to the north, seems not to have existed before the tenth century so that the lands of the Middle Saxons may easily have reached northwards and westwards to the Chilterns. Describing the whereabouts of Chertsey, Bede wrote that it lay *in regione Sudergeona.* This name, the oldest form of the name Surrey, consists of two elements, the first meaning 'southern' and the second deriving from *gē* meaning 'district', 'region'. In the seventh century lordship over Surrey was disputed between Mercia, Kent and Wessex, but if we are right in taking the name itself to mean 'the southern district', there is a suggestion that its connections had at one time lain with more northerly people across the Thames. We may then envisage a group of people called *Middel Seaxe* as occupying land on both sides of the river where now lie Surrey, Middlesex and probably much of Hertfordshire.

The East Saxons are recognisable in historical times as a people forming an independent kingdom governed by their own kings, several of whom are mentioned by Bede. Although it was never of any great importance politically, London lay within its boundaries at the beginning of the seventh century, as if to suggest that by this date the Middle Saxons had already lost such independence as they may once have possessed. The chief problem presented by the evidence relating to the settlement of Essex is to reconcile the marked scarcity of pagan burial grounds with the abundance of place-names indicative of settlement in the pagan period. The coast may have been difficult of access because of the many off-shore shoals and sandbanks, and much of its interior may have been unattractive because of its heavy clays. Perhaps the circumstances which gave a poverty-stricken appearance to large parts of Essex in Romano-British times were still prevalent in the fifth and sixth centuries. Even so, there is a strong archaic element in the place-names, with a number of *-ingas* names second only to those of Sussex. High Roding, White Roding and Aythorpe Roding are three of eight parish names into which there enters the name Roding, or Roothing, deriving from an Old English *Hroðingas*, a people whose lands covered some twenty square miles in western Essex in what later became the hundred of Dunmow. The *Hæferingas*, whose settlement lay in the south-western part of the country and reached to the Thames near Dagenham, have left their name in Havering. Dengie, one of the hundreds of eastern Essex, derives its name from the *Dænningas* who occupied the peninsula between the Crouch and the Blackwater, including the Saxon Shore fort at Bradwell where Cedd built a church in the middle of the seventh century. Another group, the *Gigingas*, are remembered in several surviving place-names, among them Ingatestone, Margaretting and Ingrave.

North of Essex lay the kingdom of East Anglia, embracing the counties of Norfolk and Suffolk within which there are considerable numbers both of cemeteries and early place-names. Like Essex, this area lay within the command of the Count of the Saxon Shore in the late Roman period, with forts overlooking the Wash at Brancaster, the estuary of the Yare at Burgh Castle, and the estuaries of the Deben and Orwell at Walton Castle, a site now lost beneath the encroaching sea. Pottery of the Romano-Saxon type recovered from Burgh Castle and from Walton Castle hints at the settlement of Germanic mercenaries for the defence of this eastern coast after the pattern adopted by Vortigern in Kent. At some inland sites, such as Markshall and Caister-by-Norwich, there are cemeteries so placed as to suggest that they represent communities of hired mercenaries originally settled by authority, not communities sprung from hostile invasion. With no written traditions and without any means of achieving an exact chonology, we can only guess that here in East Anglia, as also in Kent, there came a time when the mercenaries turned against their paymasters and so won the country for themselves.

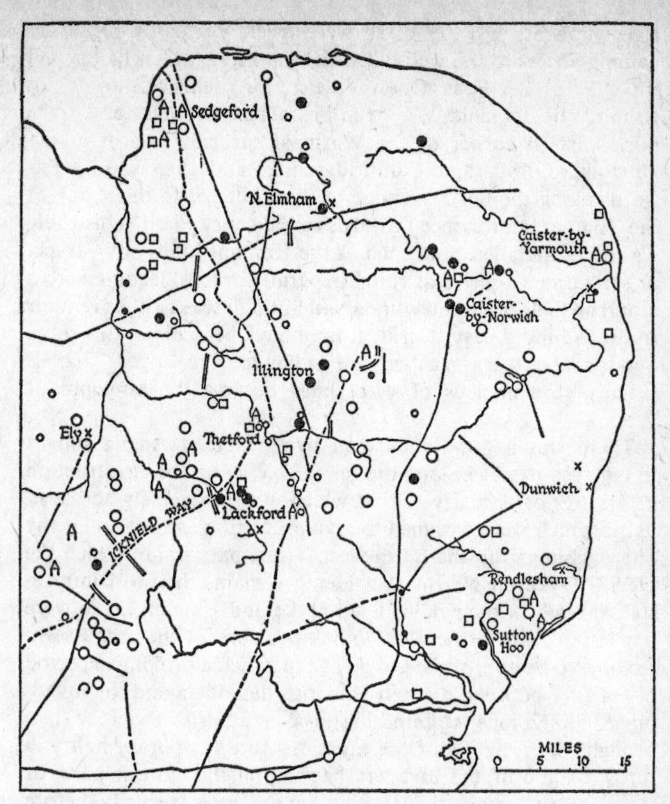

Distribution of Early Saxon cultures in East Anglia

The early settlements lay mainly in Norfolk where there was no lack of sites offering loamy soils and a good supply of water. They could be reached through the harbour at Yarmouth leading up the valleys of the Yare and the Wensum, or through the Stiffkey valley on the north Norfolk coast, or through the Wash. The distribution of cemeteries in western Norfolk and farther south in Cambridgeshire suggests that the rivers flowing into the Wash were freely used as a means of gaining access to the well-drained gravel sites which lie beyond the edge of the Fens. One of the major prehistoric routes of Britain, the Icknield Way, ran from near Brancaster, at the north-eastern corner of the Wash, at first southwards across Norfolk, Suffolk and Cambridgeshire, and then south-westwards along the northern edge of the Chilterns to the valley of the Thames, and thence onwards to Salisbury Plain. This route was not a metalled road such as the Romans built, but a track, or sometimes a series of roughly parallel tracks, leading across a narrow belt of country upon which there was neither fen nor forest to hinder easy transit. It may have been along this route that some settlers reached the valley of the upper Thames to form the nucleus of what later became the kingdom of Wessex.

There was a time when men living in East Anglia sought to bar free passage along the Icknield Way by the construction of a series of defensive dykes which cut transversely across it, dykes which were designed to give protection against an enemy approaching from the south-west. These barriers, of which the Devil's Dyke on Newmarket Heath remains the most impressive, though in their day Fleam Dyke and Heydon Dyke were not less so, still present us with a puzzle. Yet they may seem to some to be appropriate to an age in which a prolonged period of warfare between the native British defenders and the invading Anglo-Saxons, culminating in a great British victory, had brought the progress of the invasions to a temporary halt and thrown some of the invaders back upon the eastern parts of the country, where they might have greater security before moving over to attack once again. Such an age occurred after the British victory at Mons Badonicus.

Immigrants continued to reach the shores of East Anglia during the fifth and sixth centuries, some of them coming to its northern parts, but some of them to the coastal areas of Suffolk and particularly to the neighbourhood of Ipswich. It was this neighbourhood that became the nucleus of the East Anglian kingdom. The first Anglian king who is more than a mere name was Rædwald who was ruling in the early years of the seventh century and who played host to the exiled Edwin of Northumbria. Rædwald was the fourth of the Bretwaldas, succeeding Æthelbert of Kent in that distinction, and so winning for himself a position of sovereignty over all the southern English peoples, a position which was not achieved by any of his successors. At this time a royal seat lay at Rendlesham, now a small hamlet by the river Deben and not very far from Dunwich where the first East Anglian bishopric was established. Close by Rendlesham lay the royal burial ground at Sutton Hoo whose treasures reflect the wealth and political power of the kingdom of East Anglia during the seventh century.

At a time when most of the smaller kingdoms were losing their identities as they became merged in Wessex or Mercia, the kingdom of East Anglia was able to retain a large measure of independence before its ultimate destruction during the Danish invasions of the ninth century. This was largely because the great belt of fenland reaching southwards from the Wash as far as Cambridge served as a protective moat of such width along its inland boundary that the kingdom could enjoy security against aggressive neighbours in the midlands. The Fens themselves, exploited by the Romans for the richness of their soil, have yielded no evidence of settlement during the ages when the less low-lying parts of eastern England were passing into Anglo-Saxon occupation. Whether from the neglect of Roman drainage or through slight change in the levels of land and sea, this large area reverted to the watery waste of which we have such a vivid description in the *Life* of Guthlac, the eighth-century hermit. In Guthlac's age there were small groups of people, the *Gyrwe* for example, whose name means 'fen-dwellers', living along the margins of the fens and in island sites where they could support themselves by the abundance of fish and fowl, but in the age of invasion the fens were avoided in preference for drier sites farther inland. Such were to be found along the banks of the Nene and the Welland some thirty miles upstream from the shores of the Wash itself. Here, in what had formerly been one of the leading centres of the Romano-British pottery industry, are considerable numbers of cemeteries representing people whose arrival is unrecorded, but who later came to be known as the Middle Angles. There is no record of the Middle Angles as occupying an independent kingdom governed by its own royal family. Lacking the protection of any natural frontiers, save that of the fens on the east, they were unable to resist the domination of the Mercians under whose lordship they had already fallen before the middle of the seventh century.

Unless we have been misled by the consequences of coastal erosion, the Lincolnshire coast was not fortified in the Roman period, having neither forts like those of the Saxon Shore to the south, nor signal stations like those of the Yorkshire coast to the north, as though to suggest that its midway position between Britain's northern and southern enemies might itself be a sufficient guarantee of protection against attack from the sea. But even if the coast was left unprotected, there is evidence which suggests that at about the middle of the fourth century the defences of a number of inland urban sites in these eastern areas, some of them quite small, were refashioned on a massive scale which included the provision of bastions for the mounting of artillery comparable with those that are characteristic of the Saxon Shore forts. Such were Caistor at the northern end of the Lincolnshire Wolds and Horncastle at the southern, the latter a small site of barely 5½ acres. Another is at Ancaster which lies on Ermine Street, about eighteen miles south of Lincoln, and a fourth is some twenty-five miles farther south still, at Great Casterton which came to lie within the territory of the Middle Angles. Here, as we have learned by thorough excavation, the old second-century defences were completely reorganised at some period not very long before the great onslaught of 367, probably about 350. A new ditch 60 feet wide was cut through the rock, and stone from it was used to form the foundations of bastions which were added to the external face of the enclosing walls. These measures seem to have given great security to the inhabitants, for neither at Great Casterton itself, nor at a nearby villa, have excavations yielded any sign of destruction in 367. Perhaps this part of the country escaped disaster at this time, partly because of the state of its internal defences and partly because of its remoteness from Picts and Scots as well as from Franks and Saxons.

Late in the fourth century Lincolnshire and the belt of country traversed by Ermine Street as it approaches Lincoln from the south seem to have been prosperous. In 627 Paulinus visited Lincoln and consecrated an archbishop of Canterbury in a church there. On the same occasion he baptised many people in the Trent where the Roman road to York by way of Doncaster crossed the river at *Segelocum*, which had by then changed its name to *Tiowulfingacæstir*, a name whose form is indicative of an early Anglo-Saxon occupation of this site. Both Lincoln itself and *Segelocum* lay within the kingdom of Lindsey governed by a dynasty which, maintaining its identity until the closing years of the eighth century, may have orginated as early as *c.* 500. The cemeteries of the earliest English settlers lie on the Wolds and near the line of Ermine Street both north and south of Lincoln. Although there is no tradition about the way in which the change from Roman to English was effected, there are some hints that the beginnings of the kingdom of Lindsey may have been less violent than those of the kingdom of Sussex, and that perhaps the break with Roman tradition was a little less abrupt.

Save for some parts of Lindsey, all the English kingdoms whose origin we have so far considered lay on the lowland side of what had been the Roman frontier zone marked by the Fosse Way. A line joining the most westerly of the *-ingas* place-names between the Humber estuary and the Bristol Channel would rarely lie to the west of the Fosse Way and then only by a very slight distance. There are, however, some areas in which the cemeteries show a more westerly distribution, notably in the valley of the Warwickshire Avon and in the basin of the upper Trent near Lichfield and Repton. Farther north a number of Saxon burials have been found in barrows in Derbyshire. The rough coincidence of the Roman frontier zone in the middle of the first century with the north-westerly limits of the Saxon penetration, in so far as that is recorded by cemeteries and early place-names, is of course no more than a reflection of the influence of the same geographical conditions in both ages. The Fosse Way frontier has no military or political significance for any period of Anglo-Saxon history, and it does in fact cut clean across what became much the most powerful of the early Anglo-Saxon kingdoms. Unfortunately there is no part of Britain in which the transition from Roman to Anglo-Saxon times is so obscure as in the midland areas out of which the kingdom of Mercia was created. It is not easy to decide whether the *Mierce*, the 'borderers', acquired this name because they occupied a border position between the English and the British, or whether they were so called because they were borderers between the kingdoms of the southern English and the Northumbrians. Although nothing is known about their rulers before the early years of the seventh century, the dynasty itself was of high eminence, claiming descent from men who had ruled in north-western Europe before the migration to Britain, a claim which was not made by any other English dynasty and which moreover seems to rest upon a sound historical basis. It may be that some members of the Mercian royal family had taken a leading part in the invasion of Britain, but if so every record of it has been lost.

CHAPTER TEN

NORTHUMBRIA

The kingdom of Northumbria was created in the early years of the seventh century through the forcible coalescence of two originally separate states, Bernicia the more northerly and Deira the more southerly. These three names suggest at once, by their contrast with such names as South Saxons, East Angles, Middle Angles and the like from England south of the Humber, that the English conquest of northern Britain was not the outcome of invasion and settlement on a scale comparable with what had taken place in the south. Bernicia and Deira are both Welsh names in origin, and Northumbria, though English in its formation, refers only to the people who lived north of the Humber whether they were English, British, Scottish or even Pictish by race. It has a geographical rather than a racial connotation. Just as we may visualise the Brigantes of the first century as a loose confederation of peoples recognising the rule of a single dynasty, so also we may think of the Northumbrians as being not so much people having identity of race, but as people of different races living widely scattered over a very large area and only recognisable as a unit because they were the subjects of one king. The English conquest of northern Britain imposed English government and eventually the English language upon a much larger area than that over which Cartimandua had ruled. Yet it seems likely that there were parts of the kingdom of Northumbria in the seventh century where the predominance of men of English race was less marked than in the kingdoms of the midlands and the south.

The East Riding of Yorkshire is the only area north of the Humber in which cemeteries have been found in numbers large enough to suggest the substantial displacement of the native British population by invading English, and even here, with the notable exception of York itself, they are confined to the Wolds. It is unfortunate that most of these cemeteries were haphazardly excavated and ill recorded and even more unfortunate that much of the material found in them was subsequently lost. Even so, there are some sites on the Wolds which seem to have been in Anglo-Saxon occupation already in the fifth century, and others at which the Romano-British and Anglo-Saxon phases of occupation merged into one another without any perceptible break. Moreover there are signs of settlement at a very early date close beside the legionary fortress at York. When we recall that York was the headquarters of the *Dux Britanniarum* as late as 395, that the signal stations along the Yorkshire coast were in occupation about the years 370–95, and that the defences of the fort at Malton were repaired late in the fourth century, we need to seek an interpretation of the evidence which will explain how it came about that the very area of Britain in which an organised military command is known to have survived longest was among the first part of Britain to have fallen into Anglo-Saxon hands.

The most ready explanation is prompted by the words of Gildas in which he attributes to Vortigern the settlement of Saxons in the eastern parts of Britain. Whether or not Vortigern's authority extended to this part of Britain, York and the Yorkshire Wolds seem likely areas in which to settle Germanic mercenaries intended to give added strength to the northern defences of Britain. Out of this settlement there eventually grew the kingdom of Deira, but we have no record of any of its kings before Ælle who was reigning in the second half of the sixth century and whose name provided Gregory the Great with the subject of one of the series of puns which he is alleged to have perpetrated on meeting a number of young men from Deira in Rome.

The oldest recorded version of the story is found in the *Life of Gregory* which was written by an anonymous monk at Whitby. Struck by the light skin and fair hair of the strangers, Gregory asked them about their origin.

> And when they replied: 'Those from whom we are sprung are called Angles,' he said: 'Angels of God.' Then he said: 'What is the name of the king of that people?' And they said: 'Ælle'; and he said: 'Alleluia, for the praise of God ought to be there.' He also asked the name of the particular tribe from which they came, and they said: 'The Deire.' And he said: 'Fleeing together from the wrath (*de ira*) of God to the faith.'

The author of this work delighted in puns of this kind. He tells how when Gregory himself had once set out to convert the English he had been halted by a locust (*locusta*) which settled upon a page of the book he was reading, and he at once understood the message as meaning that he was to stay where he was—*sta in loco*. It did not escape the notice of the same writer that the name of the Deiran king, Ælle, could by slight manipulation be changed into *Alle* 'which in our tongue means absolutely all. And this is what the Lord said, "Come to me, all ye that labour and are heavy laden." ' Nor did he lose the opportunity of remarking that the name of the first Christian king of Northumbria, Edwin,—or Aeduini in its Old English form—contained three syllables, representing the mystery of the Holy Trinity. We know that the Anglo-Saxons delighted in riddles and puns, and such tales as these were evidently current in Northumbria in the seventh century as part of the body of tradition which had accumulated about the beginnings of English Christianity.

Save for Birling in Northumberland, there are no *-ingas* place-names north of the Tees, though there are a few of the *-ingaham* type which may not be much later. There are virtually no cemeteries either, if, that is, we discount the one or two meagre groups of grave-goods whose poverty when contrasted with corresponding evidence from East Anglia or Kent serves only to demonstrate their insignificance. And yet it was from this northern area that there sprang a dynasty whose successive members achieved such a high degree of military, and later intellectual, success, as to win for it a place of preeminence among the reigning families of England in the seventh and early eighth centuries. It took its origin in what can have been little more than a pirate settlement based upon a rock stronghold on the Northumberland coast at Bamburgh. This is a coast of deep waters and few harbours, as unlike as well could be to the flat lands and sluggish rivers of East Anglia, though Lindisfarne itself offered a fair anchorage and a necessary place of refuge not far from Bamburgh. Here, traditionally in 547, Ida, the first of the Bernician dynasty, began to reign. We know nothing in detail about his achievements and his distinction is only that of having founded a kingdom which later became famous. Welsh tradition, celebrated in song and poetry, remembered that the kings of the northern British peoples joined in a long and bitter struggle against the invaders and that some thirty years after the beginning of Ida's reign one of his successors was closely besieged in Lindisfarne. Treachery amongst the British and their inability to maintain a firm alliance against the enemy was in part responsible for their ultimate defeat. But the threat which the English settlement at Bamburgh presented to British supremacy in northern Britain was less to be feared than the possibility of sudden expansion from the more southerly of the English enclaves in Yorkshire. The situation which confronted the northern British kingdoms late in the sixth century was closely similar to that which had faced their Brigantian ancestors in about the year 70 when Petilius Cerialis had crossed the Humber and established himself at Brough, Malton and York.

A British heroic poem, called *Gododdin*, which is believed to have been written *c.* 600, suggests that on this later occasion, as on the earlier, there was a great gathering of forces from north and west as the British sought to meet and overcome the danger by which their whole position in the north was theatened. Among the British leaders who gathered together in coalition against the enemy was one who had come with his war-band from as far away as Edinburgh, but he and his allies suffered total defeat in a battle fought at a place called Catraeth. The site of this battle, generally accepted as Catterick, lay at no great distance from the site at Stanwick which had been fortified by Venutius in his attempts to hold up the advance of the Roman legions. This was the area, no less for the English *c.* 600 than for the Romans *c.* 70, which held the key to further advance northwards towards the Tyne or westwards across the Pennines to Carlisle. So far as we know, this was the last occasion upon which the British of Lothian collaborated with their kinsmen of Yorkshire, Lancashire and North Wales against the English invaders, and the English victory cannot but have radically altered the whole situation in the north, ensuring that the English themselves would never again be in any danger of expulsion from the lands of which they had now taken possession.

English tradition has recorded no memory of the victory over the British at Catraeth, despite the important consequences which it surely had for the English settlers in the East Riding, but English and Welsh tradition alike remembered one man who did more than any other to bring disaster to the British and triumph to the English. This was Æthelfrith, the last of the pagan kings of Bernicia (reigned *c.* 593–616), whose far-reaching victories over the Scots, as well as over the Welsh, transformed what seem to have been little more than small and isolated settlements near the eastern coast into a kingdom so large and powerful that his successors were able to win and maintain overlordship of the English kingdoms south of the Humber, as well as north, for most of the seventh century. The first of the two great military victories won by Æthelfrith and recorded by Bede was achieved in 603 at *Degsastan*, a place still renowned in Bede's lifetime, but now lost. Æthelfrith's opponent on this occasion was Aedan, king of the Scots of Dalriada which lay on the mainland and among the islands to the north and west of the British kingdom of Strathclyde. Its capital was Dunadd in the Moss of Crinan, a rock stronghold resembling similar natural fortresses at Dumbarton, Edinburgh and Bamburgh. The origin of the kingdom of Dalriada, itself the embryo of the kingdom of Scotland, lay in the settlements of comparatively small groups of Scots who had crossed from north-eastern Ireland towards the middle of the fifth century. Aedan himself succeeded to the kingdom *c.* 574, at about the same time as the British rulers of Strathclyde and Rheged were besieging the English of Bernicia in Lindisfarne. Perhaps it was partly as a result of the British preoccupation in this area, together with their disastrous defeat of Catraeth, that Aedan was enabled to enlarge his kingdom eastwards across the mainland of Scotland a little to the north of the Antonine Wall. This direct conflict between the Scots of Dalriada and the English of Bernicia, between whom there lay a wide expanse of British territory, it not easily explained unless upon the supposition that Aedan's easterly advance had coincided with a northerly advance by Æthelfrith towards Lothian.

The significance of Æthelfrith's victory at *Degsastan* was that it eliminated the Scots as possible contenders for supremacy in northern Britain for a long time to come. From that day to this, wrote Bede, in 731, no king of Scots ever dared to wage war against the English. Æthelfrith's second victory was won over the British in a battle fought at Chester between 613 and 616. Bede regarded the British defeat at Chester and the accompanying slaughter of the monks who had come from Bangor Iscoed to pray for a British victory, as the fulfilment of a prophecy made by Augustine that retribution would surely fall upon the British because of the contumacious attitude adopted by the bishops of the British Church towards Augustine and his fellow missioners. The military and political consequences of the battle are not easy to assess. English armies in the seventh century, like Danish armies in the ninth, often campaigned at considerable distances from their main bases. Since other evidence suggests that the permanent English crossing of the Pennines was not achieved until nearer the middle of the seventh century, it might be wiser to regard Æthelfrith's victory at Chester as the outcome of a passing foray deep into British lands, rather than to see in it a movement of invasion which brought Chester and its neighbourhood into English possession and so began the isolation of the Welsh of Wales from their northern neighbours of Rheged and Strathclyde.

Shortly before his victory at Chester, Æthelfrith overran the kingdom of Deira whose heir, Edwin, was driven into exile, part of which he spent at the court of Rædwald, king of East Anglia. Rædwald, perhaps seeing in the rapid growth of Æthelfrith's power a possible threat to his own position as lord of the southern English kingdoms, the fourth of the Bretwaldas, gave Edwin his full support in an attempt to restore him to his kingdom. In a battle fought in 616 on Northumbria's southern frontier near the point at which the Roman road from Lincoln to Doncaster crosses the river Idle, Æthelfrith was defeated and killed. Edwin was accepted as king in Bernicia as well as in Deira and, in their turn, the Bernician royal family fled into exile, finding refuge for a season in the far north among the Scots and the Picts, where they established relationships which had profoundly important consequences for the later history of Northumbria.

The distinction of Edwin's reign (616–32) was twofold. On the eve of Easter Day 627 he was baptised by Paulinus in a wooden oratory at York, so becoming the first Christian king of Northumbria. Such a momentous event was dear to the heart of Bede, and his accounts of the vision which appeared to Edwin when he was still an exile at Rædwald's court, of his providential escape from the hand of a West Saxon assassin and of the debate in royal council which led to the rejection of the old gods and the acceptance of Christianity, rightly hold a place of such high distinction in English historical literature that they have been familiar to many since childhood. Although the importance of this narrative is primarily for its embodiment of ecclesiastical tradition about the beginnings of Christianity in Northumbria, even so, and despite the hagiographical tinge, it enables us for the first time to observe an Anglo-Saxon king actively and vigorously concerning himself with the affairs of his kingdom.

It is the second distinction of Edwin's reign that he was the first of the Northumbrian rulers whose authority extended southwards beyond the Humber to the kingdoms of the southern English. The reality of his military might is strikingly revealed by his ability to lead a Northumbrian army southwards across the midlands, unobstructed it seems by any Mercian kingdom, even as far as Wessex, to conduct there a successful campaign in vengeance for the West Saxon attempt upon his life, and to return home to Northumbria in triumph. No other Northumbrian king ever did the like. Further evidence of his strength lies in the seeming vigour with which he continued the assault against his British neighbours north of the Humber. He conquered Elmet, the last remaining enclave of British rule on the east side of the Pennines, and thereby opened the way to the western side through the Aire Gap. Towards the end of his reign he invaded North Wales and overran Anglesey, forcing Cadwallon, king of Gwynedd, to seek refuge in the island of Priestholm. He also took possession of the Isle of Man. Nothing has been recorded of his relations with Northumbria's northern neighbours, the British of Strathclyde, and the Picts and Scots, and there is no evidence of any attempt at this time by the exiled Bernician dynasty to return to its homeland.

Edwin, perhaps more than any other Anglo-Saxon king, seems to represent the historical counterpart of Hrothgar, 'the blameless king' of *Beowulf*. Bede, looking back from the troubled times of his own age, perhaps a little oppressed by the uncertainties of the future, described Edwin's reign in terms which, despite his use of Latin rather than Anglo-Saxon, find their echo in the environment of heroic poetry, with something of folklore, and yet something of dignity and strength, generosity and humility:

> They say that there was then such perfect peace in Britain, wheresoever the dominion of Edwin extended that, as the proverb still runs to this day, even if a woman should have wished to walk with her newborn babe over all the island from sea to sea, she might have done so without injury from

any. So much did the same king care for the good of his people that in very many places where he saw clear well-springs breaking out by the side of the highways, he had posts set up and copper vessels hung thereon for the refreshment of wayfarers, which vessels no man dared touch, save for his present use and need, for fear of the king's displeasure, or would wish to touch because of the love they bore him. His dignity was so great throughout his dominions that not only in battle were banners borne before him, but in time of peace also a standard-bearer was accustomed to go before him whenever he rode about his cities, his townships and his shires in the company of his ministers.

Edwin's reign marked an approach to unity such as Britain had not seen since the disintegration of Roman government, and he may have had some consciousness of his position as he had carried before him on his royal progress 'that kind of banner which the Romans call *tufa*', but Edwin's eminence rested upon his own personal achievements. He was king only by right of victories won over his enemies and his rivals in battle. His invasion of Gwynedd provoked the retaliation of Cadwallon who found an ally in Penda, a vigorous warrior of the Mercian royal house. The two invaded Northumbria in 632, engaging Edwin's army at an unknown place in Hatfield Chase, the borderland between Northumbria and Mercia. Edwin was killed and his army totally defeated. Together Cadwallon and Penda proceeded to lay waste the whole of Northumbria which itself now fell apart into its divisions of Bernicia and Deira, but within a little more than a year Cadwallon, after killing Edwin's two apostate successors, was himself defeated by Oswald who with other members of the Bernician royal family and nobility had been in exile in the far north, in the battle of Havenfield, fought late in 633 near the Roman Wall north of Hexham. Cadwallon was overtaken in his flight from the battlefield and killed a few miles farther south.

Oswald's victory over Cadwallon at once restored to Northumbria the position of pre-eminence which had been won for the kingdom by his predecessor Edwin. Oswald himself was related to the Deiran family through his mother and his fate, together with the extinction of Edwin's own descendants, save for a daughter who later married Oswald's brother and successor in the kingdom, removed for the time being any likelihood of a separatist movement which might have led to the breakdown of Deira. Oswald's influence in the far south is suggested by his marriage to a daughter of the king of Wessex and by his confirmation of a grant of land made by that same king for the establishment of the first West Saxon bishopric at Dorchester-on-Thames. Oswald was remembered by historians as the saintly king whose wooden cross set up before the battle of Heavenfield was, according to Bede, the first outward and visible sign of Christianity ever to be seen in Bernicia, remembered also as the man who brought the Columban mission from Iona to Lindisfarne, and as the martyr who met his death at the hands of the heathen Penda. Save for this new power which was now beginning to emerge in the midlands, there was none to rival his authority among the rulers of the English kingdoms, yet it was perhaps in the north, where his long exile during the sixteen years of Edwin's reign had given him opportunities of learning much at first hand about the Scots and the Picts, and also about the Strathclyde British, that the influence of Northumbria now began to be most strongly felt.

Domnall Brecc, whose reign as king of Scottish Dalriada largely coincided with that of Oswald of Northumbria, lost the control over the southern Picts of Fife and Angus which had been won some forty years earlier by Aedan, the opponent of Æthelfrith at *Degsastan*. Bede states clearly that Oswald exercised dominion over both the Scots and the Picts, and although we have no English record of any military expeditions led by Oswald towards the north, Irish annals record a siege of Edinburgh in the year 638. The combatants are not named, but the event is likely to have been of considerable significance, since it would scarcely otherwise have attracted the attention of Irish annalists. The conquest of Edinburgh, a British stronghold, led by the English of Northumbria would mark the final overthrow of all that remained of the kingdom of Manau Gododdin, bringing the English to the southern shores of the Firth of Forth and so face to face with the southern Picts who lived beyond. A longer reign might well have enabled Oswald to consolidate his authority from Wessex in the south to the Firth of Tay in the north, but it was cut short by his defeat and death at the hands of Penda of Mercia in a battle fought at Maserfelth, possibly Oswestry in Shropshire, in 641.

Oswald's overlordship collapsed immediately with his death,

and although his brother and successor, Oswiu (641–70) came to be reckoned among the Bretwaldas, several years passed before he was able to establish Northumbria in the position of supremacy which it had held during Oswald's reign. After the disaster at Maserfelth the kingdom itself fell apart, the Deirans choosing as their king, Oswine, a descendant of the house of Ælle under whom they maintained their independence for ten years. In 651 Oswiu, seeking to reunite the two kingdoms, invaded Deira and brought about the death of Oswine in circumstances which led Bede to reveal plainly enough where his sympathies lay. The move failed in its object, since the Deirans, unwilling to submit to Oswiu's government, took as their king a son of Oswald who then sought the protection of Penda against the Bernicians, thereby making Deira a Mercian dependancy.

Although Penda seems never to have been formally recognized as overlord of the southern English, perhaps because as a heathen he was reckoned outside the pale by those who kept the record of such things, there was no other able to withstand him south of the Humber. He campaigned against Wessex, driving its king into exile for a time, slew Anna, king of the East Angles, and repeatedly invaded and harried Northumbria, even penetrating as far as Bamburgh which was saved from destruction only by the prayers of Aidan, bishop of Lindisfarne, or so at least ran the tradition reported by Bede. In 654 Penda brought together a great coalition in a determined effort to destroy Oswiu and so establish his supremacy north as well as south of the Humber. Supported by Æthelhere, king of the East Angles, as well as by several British princes, the king of Gwynedd among them, he marched against Bernicia with 'thirty legions' to aid him. Some doubt attends the course of his invasion, but it seems as if Oswiu was driven to seek safety in the far north, perhaps near Stirling, but that, in circumstances of which we have no sure knowledge, he was able to recover from an apparently desperate position and to win a great victory in a battle fought near a river called *Winwæd* which cannot now be identified but is believed to have been near Leeds. Penda was killed and by his great victory Oswiu established himself not only as king for the first time of the whole of Northumbria, but also as overlord of all the kingdoms of the English south of the Humber, a position which he was able to maintain for a decade or more, although by the time of his death in 670 Mercia had again risen to prominence under the rule of Penda's son, Wulfhere.

Oswiu was the last of the Northumbrian Bretwaldas. His successor, Ecgfrith (670–85), was faced across his southern frontier by a kingdom now fully recovered from the disaster at *Winwœd* and already dominating East Anglia, Essex and parts even of Wessex. In the autumn of 672 he was in southern England attending an ecclesiastical synod which was held at Hertford under the presidency of Theodore, archbishop of Canterbury, but Eddius, Wilfred's biographer, tells how only two years later Wulfhere, king of Mercia, 'proud of heart and insatiable in spirit roused all the southern nations against our kingdom, intent not merely on fighting but on compelling them to pay tribute in a slavish spirit'. The Mercian invaders were defeated, though the whereabouts of the battle is not known, and Wulfhere's kingdom was laid under tribute to Northumbria, he himself dying shortly afterwards. Eddius has nothing to say of what proved to be the final episode in the long and bitter struggle which had continued for more than forty years since the first alliance between Cadwallon and Penda had led to the overthrow of Edwin in 632. Ecgfrith and Æthelred, Wulfhere's brother and now king of Mercia, met in battle near the Trent in 678 and the Northumbrians were defeated in this their last attempt to secure control over any of the southern English kingdoms.

The death of Ecgfrith's brother in the battle at the Trent might, as Bede suggested, have led to even more prolonged and bloody warfare as the duty of exacting vengeance for his dead brother in accordance with the customs of the blood feud now lay fairly upon Ecgfrith, but a new factor, and one which was to prove of great importance in overriding provincial antagonisms, now came into play. Theodore, who had come to England from the Mediterranean a few years before as archbishop of Canterbury and who could see how greatly the welfare of his church depended upon peace among the English themselves, brought the two opposing families into reconciliation with one another. Ecgfrith lost all control of Mercia and Lindsey but, more important than this, the Mercians agreed to pay in full compensation for Ecgfrith's brother so that, as Bede puts it, 'the life of no man perished for the death of that king's brother, but only a due amercement of money was given to the king that was the avenger'. For a full generation there was no more warfare between the Mercians and the Northumbrians. The boundary between these two kingdoms, marked by the Humber estuary and the wide belt of low-lying marshland which extends westwards from the inner limit of the estuary itself almost to the eastern foothills of the Pennines, long remained the most important political boundary of Anglo-Saxon England, separating those of all races who lived to the north of it from the kingdoms of the southern English, as they came to be called when the lesser states on the southern side of this border began to lose their separate identity. Even after the Danish invasions and the total breakdown of the older political system, it was still remembered that the Humber marked the ancient northern boundary of the southern English peoples.

It was the particular weakness of the kingdom of Northumbria that its rulers were constantly faced with the possibility of having to defend their lands on two widely separated frontiers. Oswald's ability to resist the repeated attacks made by Penda from the south was largely dependent on the continuance of the peaceful and friendly relationships established with the Picts and Scots during the earlier years of exile in those northern parts of himself and his family, as well as numbers of the Bernician nobility. Here, too, the influence of the Scottish monks at work among the Northumbrians, as well as much farther south, was important. It was fortunate for Ecgfrith that Theodore's intervention between himself and Æthelred of Mercia brought peace to Northumbria's southern frontier at a time when the situation in the north was changing for the worse. Even at the very beginning of his reign, the Picts, taking advantage of Ecgfrith's weakness which offered them an opportunity for throwing off the Northumbrian yoke, assembled a great army in preparation for making war upon him. Ecgfrith engaged them with cavalry, defeated them heavily and once more reduced them to subjection. A victory over the northern tribes could bring security for the time being, but there are many episodes in the history of both earlier and later times which show that respite so gained was seldom long-lived and that recovery might follow swiftly for the defeated enemy.

In the spring of 685, despite the attempts of his friends, and particularly of Cuthbert, lately made bishop, to dissuade him from what they evidently regarded as a hazardous and needless enterprise, Ecgfrith led a Northumbrian army across the Forth in an expedition reminiscent of the campaigns of Agricola and Severus against the same threat. His enemies, simulating flight, drew him on through Strathmore, waiting until the Sidlaw Hills were at his back before they engaged him. On 20 May in a disaster which marks a decisive stage in the history of northern Britain, Ecgfrith was killed and his army destroyed at Dunnichen Moss close by Forfar. The Picts recovered their independence and were never again subject to the domination of the Northumbrian or any other Anglo-Saxon kings. During the next twenty-five years there are scattered references to intermittent warfare on this northern frontier between Picts and Northumbrians near the eastern end of the old Antonine Wall, but shortly after 710 Nechtan IV, king of the Picts, sent envoys to Ceolfrith, abbot of Monkwearmouth and Jarrow, to consult him about the right way of calculating the date of Easter, and the friendly relations which were thereby established with the Northumbrians were still unbroken when Bede brought his *History* to its close in 731.

Bede died in 735 and the kingdom of Northumbria then stretched all along the eastern coast from the Humber to the Forth. In the west it included Lancashire north of the Ribble, Westmorland, Cumberland and a large part of south-western Scotland. Although it has been maintained on the basis of place-name evidence that the English occupation of these western regions had begun as early as the end of the sixth century, there is no archaeological or historical evidence to support such a claim. Eddius seems to suggest that several places near the Lancashire Ribble which were given as endowments to Wilfrid's new church at Ripon *c.* 670 had only passed out of British hands a comparatively short time before. Land at Cartmel in Lancashire-north-of-the-Sands is alleged to have been given to Cuthbert by Ecgfrith, and Cuthbert himself was in Carlisle visiting Ecgfrith's queen there when her husband was killed at Dunnichen Moss. Beyond the Solway, Whithorn became the seat of a Northumbrian bishopric shortly before 731, and had presumably been under English control for some time previously. The great sculptured cross at Ruthwell and lesser fragments of crosses sculptured in the Anglian fashion at Hoddom provide further evidence of Northumbrian influence in these areas in the early years of the eighth century.

Beyond the Galloway hills the British kingdom of Strathclyde reached northwards to its capital at Dumbarton, its boundaries fluctuating according to the fortunes of its rulers and the strength of its opponents. It was reduced to narrow straits in 750 when Eadbert, a king of Northumbria who revived some of his kingdom's earlier military distinction, conquered Ayrshire from the Britons, and in 756 he laid Dumbarton itself under siege, but most of his army was destroyed while making its way home from this expedition. The kingdom of Strathclyde later recovered all, and more than all, that it had previously lost, as the power of Northumbria was weakened at first by the decadence of its rulers and later by the attacks of the Danes.

CHAPTER ELEVEN

CONSOLIDATION IN WESSEX AND MERCIA

The history of Northumbria in the seventh century is known to us primarily from the pages of Bede, and we cannot now, except in rare instances, penetrate beyond that narrative to the original material out of which it was constructed. When we turn southwards again across the Humber to examine the development of Wessex and Mercia during the age of Northumbrian hegemony, we find ourselves using different kinds of material which never underwent in early days that process of fusion which leads to a narrative of events. There is something both of gain and of loss, gain in that we still have for southern English history some of those laws, charters and other documents such as are totally wanting for Northumbrian history, and loss in that some events which seem to have been of considerable importance and whose significance was doubtless plain to near contemporaries, were so enigmatically recorded that their proper interpretation must now remain in doubt. A Northumbrian annalist writing in the seventh century might well have recorded Æthelfrith's victory over Aedan at *Degsastan* as no more than *bellum Aedilfridi* and, had it not been for Bede, we should have been left completely ignorant not only of the whereabouts, but also of the combatants and the significance of the battle itself.

Something of this sort characterises the material out of which we must seek to reconstruct the history of Wessex and of the midlands in the seventh century, and if we are sometimes faced with seemingly insoluble problems and are left in the end with an overall impression of obscurity and confusion which seems to contrast with the greater clarity of Northumbrian history in the same period, we ought to remember that this is very largely because no West Saxon historian was found to interpret events at a time when they were still held fresh in the common traditions of the people. Yet, even allowing for differences in the nature of the sources, we can see that there were other factors tending to distinguish the history of the Northumbrians from that of the southern English. The geographical factor remained potent, the distinction between the Highland and the Lowland Zones, between what had been the military and the civil zones of Roman Britain. The inhabitants of the Highland Zone had been used for centuries to military government, and the military prowess, as well as the stability, of the Northumbrian kingdom during the seventh century, although depending largely upon the distinction of its dynasty, may have owed something to the traditions of Roman military government, as well as to the direct rule of British kings after Britain had ceased to be a Roman province. North of the Humber, although there were times of rivalry between Bernicia and Deira, the issue was not one to be waged primarily between different English kingdoms, but between the English, the British, the Picts and the Scots. South of the Humber, and despite the local importance of fenland and forest, the Lowland Zone formed a geographical unit which was likely in time to achieve political unity as well, but here the Anglo-Saxon invasions had brought much more fundamental changes, involving the settlement and colonisation of wide areas, and not merely the achievement of military conquest with the subsequent imposition of foreign government upon a conquered people.

The real wealth of Roman Britain in the fourth century had lain in the areas which were remote from the exposed eastern coasts, in the lands belonging to the Dobunni, the Atrebates and the Belgae. Here were the largest and most prosperous of the towns, Cirencester and Bath, Silchester and Winchester, and here too the signs which reflect prosperity in the countryside lie most thickly on the map of Roman Britain. These were the lands which were reshaped to form the kingdom of Wessex by whose royal dynasty the political unification of England was eventually achieved. The history of the kingdom of Wessex can be told with a fair approach to continuity from *c.* 550, but as soon as we try to discover how the areas which in some respects formed the very heart of Roman Britain passed into English control we at once meet formidable difficulties. The time of transition was a long one, at least a century and a half. The difficulties arise in part from the lack of evidence, although we have more for this area than we have for East Anglia, but in part also from the interpretation of different kinds of evidence which sometimes seem to be in conflict with one another.

The fact, if fact it be, that Vortigern was able to take what he, at least, regarded as measures for the security of Kent, by the establishment of Hengest and his followers there, ought to mean that the whole of southern and western Britain from Kent as far as his homeland in the Wroxeter area was at that time, *c.* 450, under his controlling hand. Ambrosius Aurelianus, to whom Gildas attributes military measures some time after the Saxons had revolted against Vortigern, is not associated with any particular area, but, inasmuch as Gildas regarded him as the last of the Romans, we should expect him to be operating from a base which could still be regarded as part of Roman Britain. This might have been the case in western Britain by *c.* 475, but it could hardly have been so in eastern Britain at that date. The British victory at Mons Badonicus, if it is correctly placed at Badbury Rings near Wimborne, argues that Dorset was still securely in British hands *c.* 500, and we are surely entitled to suppose that in consequence of that victory there was a time during the sixth century when the British exercised control of parts of southern Britain which lay well to the east of Dorset.

According to a persistent tradition, the kings of the West Saxons were descended from two chieftains, called Cerdic and Cynric, who landed near Southampton Water in the fifth century and made their way inland in a series of battles fought in the early years of the sixth. The name Cerdic is commonly thought to be Welsh in origin, not Anglo-Saxon. The different forms in which the tradition has been preserved are inconsistent with one another both chronologically and in what they tell about the family relationships of the men to whom they refer. Moreover they sometimes seem to represent as consecutive events what were in fact no more than variant traditions of the same events. On these and other grounds we may think that great care is needed in seeking to extract a consecutive historical account from the source which is the chief embodiment of these West Saxon traditions, namely the series of annals in the *Anglo-Saxon Chronicle* extending from 495, when Cerdic and Cynric are said to have landed in Britain, until 534 when Cerdic is said to have died. But whatever may be the difficulties of interpreting these annals, and there is no adequate archaeological evidence to give ground for thinking that they represent the historical record of a major invasion of southern Britain from the direction of Southampton Water, the fact remains that Alfred the Great believed himself to have been descended from these men.

The written evidence about the origin of the West Saxon kings relates mainly to Hampshire, but the archaeological evidence makes it plain beyond doubt that the principal area of Germanic settlement in southern England outside Kent and Sussex, lay in the basin of the upper Thames. Along the banks of the Thames itself and of the many streams which join it, there was open well-drained country which had prospered greatly in Romano-British times and which would undoubtedly have proved attractive to Anglo-Saxon settlers. In these areas, at such places as Abingdon, Dorchester, Sutton Courtenay, Frilford, Long Wittenham, East Shefford and Reading, there have been found cemeteries containing some objects which suggest that they were in use well before 500. In some places there seemed to have been no perceptible break between the Romano-British and the Anglo-Saxon periods. In one or two particular instances it has been claimed that burials of a Germanic, rather than a Romano-British character, may be dated as early as *c.* 395. The settlers represented by these cemeteries could have reached the upper Thames either by moving up the river itself from the estuary, or by the Icknield Way leading south-westwards from the Wash. No written record contains any hint of these movements and at present we can do little more than conjecture about their date and about the circumstances in which they took place. It is possible that this was an area in which Vortigern had established mercenaries whose function might have been to defend his own position against those who disagreed with his policy and wished to get help from Gaul.

Whatever may have been the nature and the date of the earliest settlements in the upper Thames basin, it is difficult to believe that they resulted in the permanent occupation of this area by the Anglo-Saxons. One clue to the problem may lie in the scarcity in this area of that other kind of evidence which characterises the settlements in the more easterly part of Britain, the *-ingas* place-names. Such names are likely to be found only where initial settlement had been followed by continuing occupation and the consequent displacement of the British language by the English language. In an area long in dispute between two opposing sides, when first one side and then the other was victorious, as Gildas tells us was the case in the days of Ambrosius Aurelianus before the British victory at Mons Badonicus, we might expect to find a larger proportion of surviving Celtic names and a smaller proportion of archaic Old English names. We recall that the battle at Mons Badonicus was probably within five or ten years of 490 and that the ensuing peace was still unbroken when Gildas was writing *c.* 550 or a little earlier. It may be conjectured that one consequence of the British triumph was the recovery of the upper Thames basin, a recovery based on military supremacy and not necessarily involving the expulsion of the Anglo-Saxon settlers from all of the areas which they had previously taken into their possession.

Such a conjecture would imply that during the years from *c.* 490 to *c.* 550 the boundary between the British and the Saxons across the midlands was marked approximately by the line of Watling Street from London to St Albans, Dunstable, Towcester and High Cross. Four centuries later, in about 886, Alfred the Great, after expelling invading Danish armies from the kingdom of Wessex, made a treaty with the Danish king in which it was agreed that the boundary between them should run up the river Lea to its source, then in a straight line to Bedford and then up the Ouse to Watling Street. Alfred's position in the ninth century was not unlike that of Ambrosius Aurelianus in the fifth. The final conquest, which carried Anglo-Saxon rule across the midlands to the Severn and the Bristol Channel, seems to have taken place in rather more than twenty-five years from *c.* 550 and to be marked by the series of Saxon victories which we have noted above. The first were at Old Sarum in 552 and at Barbury near Swindon in Wiltshire in 556. In 571 the Saxons won a victory at a place called *Bedcanford* or *Biedcanford.* It has not been certainly identified, and the latter of the two alternative forms of the name makes the equation with Bedford difficult. Wherever the battle itself may have been fought, it resulted in the conquest by the Saxons of four towns of which two, Benson and Eynsham, lay in Oxfordshire, one, Aylesbury, in Buckinghamshire, and one, Limbury, in Bedfordshire. Finally, in 577, a Saxon victory at Dyrham won the towns of Gloucester, Cirencester and Bath. It is significant that this age of conquest coincides with the reign of Ceawlin, the first king of the West Saxons known to Bede and the second of those called Bretwalda.

At a time when the authority of Edwin of Northumbria was

recognised both north and south of the Humber, the English of Mercia and Wessex were still taking possession of new lands towards the west, and coming into conflict with one another as they did so. It was not until this westerly expansion had brought the Mercians towards the hills of Wales and the West Saxons to the edge of Dartmoor that we can begin to see the wave as it were recoiling upon itself and political consolidation beginning to take place. Two West Saxon kings of the seventh century are prominent in tradition, Cynegils who reigned *c.* 611–43 and his son, Cenwalh, whose reign (643–72) was almost as long as that of his father. Although there is little archaeological evidence which seems to show that the West Saxons had pushed beyond Selwood and had by *c.* 600 reached, and in one or two places crossed, the line of the Fosse Way as it runs south-westwards towards Ilchester and the estuary of the Axe, the beginning of the main assault on the kingdom of Dumnonia in the south-western peninsula belongs to the early years of the seventh century. In 614 the West Saxons defeated the British on *Beandun*, inflicting heavy casualties upon them. Although the site has not been identified with certainty, there is a strong case for believing the name to be represented now by Bindon in east Devon, a commanding position overlooking the estuary of the Axe, with a ready means of access provided by the Roman road running westwards through southern Dorset from Dorchester. This identification is supported by the evidence of place-names which indicate that the southern part of Devon was colonised by settlers who advanced along the south coast from Dorset and whose habits of nomenclature were different from those of the settlers who entered north Devon from Somerset.

Although the issue of the battle was in victory for the West Saxons, its lasting consequences are difficult to assess. It may be that the western boundary of Wessex was now advanced to the Axe and maintained there. On the other hand, it is certain that during the middle years of his reign Cynegils suffered some severe setbacks which may have adversely affected his strength in relation to Dumnonia. It was one of his sons who plotted the assassination of Edwin of Northumbria, and there was a tradition that in the punitive campaign which Edwin led against Wessex shortly before his baptism five West Saxon kings were killed. There is some evidence that the title 'king' might be enjoyed simultaneously by more than one male member of a royal family and we should therefore interpret this tradition as indicating an attack directed against the West Saxon royal family itself. Northumbrian sources leave no doubt of Edwin's triumph on this occasion. At the same time Cynegils had to contend with Penda against whom he fought at Cirencester in 628. The annalist who recorded the battle in the *Anglo-Saxon Chronicle*, although using words which imply the formal conclusion of a peace treaty between Cynegils and Penda, characteristically thought it unnecessary to state which of the two contending sides was the victor, and we are left to infer from the later history of the lands by the lower Severn that the outcome was a heavy defeat for the West Saxons.

This area, rich and prosperous during the later days of Roman rule in Britain, had first come under West Saxon control in 577 when Cirencester itself, as well as Bath and Gloucester, fell into the hands of the Saxons after they had overthrown a coalition of British kings at Dyrham. A century later it was not any part of Wessex, but comprised the kingdom of the *Hwicce*, governed by a succession of minor rulers who were subject to Mercian overlords. Since there is no further trace of West Saxon kings exercising authority in Gloucestershire during the seventh century, it seems very probable that this whole area, extending eastwards to part of Oxfordshire, where the name survives as Wychwood, came under Mercian domination after the battle at Cirencester in 628, and furthermore that the kingdom of the *Hwicce* was itself established by Penda. A recent survey of the great Wansdyke, an impressive linear earthwork running east and west across much of Wiltshire and Gloucestershire, has suggested to its authors that its western section which runs parallel with the Bristol Avon, was built at this time to mark the boundary between the Mercians and the West Saxons. Although the stretch of the earthwork which runs from near Bath in the west to near Mildenhall in the east may originally have been built to serve some other purpose, it too is likely to have been accepted as representing the more easterly extension of the dividing line between their two kingdoms. Nothing further has been recorded of the reign of Cynegils save that he became a Christian in 635 and that he gave land for the establishment of a bishopric, the first in Wessex. The choice of site, Dorchester-on-Thames, suggests that it was here in the basin of the upper Thames, an area which first fell into Saxon hands before the British victory at

Mons Badonicus, that the heart of his kingdom lay, but if this was indeed the case, it did not remain so for long.

Cynegils was succeeded by his son Cenwalh in 643 when Penda was at the height of his power. If the marriage of Cenwalh to one of Penda's sisters was designed to secure the continuance of peaceful relations between the two kingdoms, it failed in its purpose, since Cenwalh later repudiated his wife and Penda thereupon invaded Wessex, driving Cenwalh into exile among the East Anglians for three years (645–8), a fate in which Bede saw fitting punishment for his earlier refusal to follow his father in accepting the Christian faith. Anna, Cenwalh's host in East Anglia, persuaded him to be baptised, and although on his return to his kingdom Dorchester-on-Thames continued for a while to be the seat of a West Saxon bishopric, it may be significant of the deteriorating position of Wessex in relation to Mercia that Cenwalh chose Winchester, a site more remote from possible Mercian interference, as the seat of a second West Saxon bishopric. A further hint that he was anxious to secure himself as best he could against further invasion by Penda may be implicit in the statement in the *Chronicle* that in 648, the year of his return from exile in East Anglia, he made a grant to a kinsman of what is called 'three thousands of land by Ashdown'. The area conveyed by this grant is represented now in part at least by the line of the Berkshire Downs, and although the chronicler's figure gives no real indication of the exact amount of land concerned, we should be right to regard it as a very large area, perhaps even corresponding with the whole of Berkshire, rather than as a mere estate such as a king might normally confer on a member of his family. When, shortly after Cenwalh's death, we find the Mercians in control of Dorchester-on-Thames and also of Abingdon, we may be justified in regarding Cenwalh's massive grant of land along the Berkshire Downs as marking the West Saxon withdrawal from the upper Thames basin in the face of strong Mercian pressure, and the establishment of the Berkshire ridge as a frontier province whose holder was expected to oppose any further attempts by the Mercians to encroach upon West Saxon territory.

The continual preoccupation of the West Saxon kings with the defence of their lands against the Mercians is sufficient explanation of the absence from the *Chronicle* of any reference to warfare between the West Saxons and the kingdom of Dumnonia for almost half a century after the Saxon victory at Bindon in 614. Whether we are to believe that Cynegils and Cenwalh were able to maintain their frontier with the British as far west as the Axe, despite the difficulties with which they had to contend along their northern boundary, depends partly upon the interpretation which we place on certain enigmatical entries in the *Chronicle* during the second half of the seventh century. In 652 Cenwalh was fighting at Bradford-on-Avon, but we are told nothing either about his opponent or about the outcome of the battle. Although many historians have regarded it as marking a renewal of the West Saxon drive towards the west and have interpreted it as a victory for Cenwalh over the British, such an interpretation is difficult to reconcile with the suggestion that after 628 the only borderland in this area was one which ran east and west between the Mercians and the Saxons along Wansdyke. Perhaps it might be wiser to regard the episode as a border dispute between these two antagonists than as a West Saxon victory over the British who had long since lost control of this part of the country.

Six years later, in 658, Cenwalh was fighting *æt Peonnum*, and we know that on this occasion his opponents were the British of Dumnonia, that he defeated them, and that after the battle he drove them in flight as far as the Parret. The problem here is the identification of the name *æt Peonnum* which many generations of historians have equated with Penselwood in eastern Somersetshire close by the border of Wiltshire. If this identification is accepted, the significance of Cenwalh's victory is that it marks the Saxon penetration of Selwood, locally known as the Great Forest, the opening-up of eastern Somerset and the extension of the western limits of English settlement as far as the river Parret. Yet the identification is not supported by any direct evidence. It has recently been argued that the scene of the conflict lay very much farther to the west and that the site is to be identified with Pinhoe near Exeter, the argument being in part, but only in part, that if the West Saxons were already as far west as the Axe estuary in 614, they are not likely to have been fighting against the British as far east as Penselwood more than fifty years later. Whatever may have been the site of the battle there can be no doubt that the West Saxons were moving deeply into Devon shortly after the middle of the seventh century. A further victory over the British was

The seventh-century kingdoms

won at Posbury near Crediton in 661. The monastery at Exeter in which St Boniface received his early education, is believed to have been founded by Cenwalh himself in 670, and Cenwalh was also making grants of land at Meare and near Taunton at about the same date. Cenwalh died in 672. Ten years later one of his successors drove the British in flight as far as the sea, but we do not know where this took place and can only suppose that the reference is to some point on the north coast of Devon or perhaps of Cornwall. Geraint, king of Dumnonia, was defeated by the West Saxons in 710, and his kingdom gradually shrank westwards within the fastness of Cornwall. For many years to come the Cornish continued to fight for their independence and it was not until the ninth century that Cornwall finally came under West Saxon domination.

There was no relaxation of Mercian pressure against the northern frontier of Wessex after the death of Penda. His son, Wulfhere, conquered the Isle of Wight and gave both it and a stretch of the opposing mainland east of Southampton Water to the South Saxons. Wulfhere's successor, Æthelred, was able to dispose of land in south Gloucestershire and northern Wiltshire, while Dorchester-on-Thames became the seat of a Mercian bishopric. It almost seems as if the expansion of the West Saxons towards the west was being forced upon them by the close confinement of their lands on their northern and eastern borders. Certainly their strength was insignificant in comparison with that of Mercia and their power of quite a different order from that of far distant Northumbria. It was not until 685, the year in which Ecgfrith of Northumbria was defeated by the Picts at Dunnichen Moss, that a change began to take place with the accession in Wessex of a king called Cædwalla. He traced his descent from Cerdic, but his British name, an anglicised version of the name borne by Edwin's opponent in 632, Cadwallon king of Gwynedd, suggests a mixed ancestry. He reigned for only three years but throughout this time he was constantly at war, and perhaps it was the British element in his ancestry that caused him to turn his back on the southwest and strive to give new strength to the kingdom of Wessex by seeking to include within its borders or bring under its control all of England that lay south of the Thames. He conquered the Isle of Wight and brought about the death of the surviving representatives of its Jutish dynasty. He then overran Sussex and invaded Kent, but he had been severely wounded during the fighting in the Isle of Wight and in 688 he left England for Rome where he was baptised in the following year, dying there only a few days later. His brief and violent reign marks a significant turning-point in the fortunes of Wessex. Although there was another century to pass during which it was the Mercians and not the West Saxons who dominated England, even so it was by consolidating their hold on southern England that the West Saxons, first under Egbert at the beginning of the ninth century, and later, after the Danish invasions, under Alfred the Great, eventually moved towards the conquest of the whole country.

Cædwalla's journey to Rome, not undertaken with any expectation that he would return to rule over a Wessex enlarged and invigorated by his successes in the field of battle, but in the pious hope that death and entry into the next world would follow swiftly upon his baptism, may be regarded as symbolic of a change which overtakes the character of English history in the later years of the seventh century. Superiority of equipment and training had enabled the Romans to carry out their conquest of Britain with great speed in a matter of three or four years where the Lowland Zone was concerned, and during the succeeding centuries of Roman rule warfare was normally confined to the frontier areas, save for the rare occasions when there was a breakdown of the defensive system. Despite the development of institutions of local government among the *civitates*, that is to say the tribal cantons in whom had been vested authority in local affairs during the Roman occupation, the security of the province and the maintenance of peace within its borders rested in the last resort on the continuing presence of a foreign army, subject to the orders of a foreign power. Indeed it was largely because the *civitates* were not concerned with frontier defence that their civilisation was able to develop. Chaos quickly followed when the army withdrew and the *civitates* were left to look to their own defence. In contrast, the Anglo-Saxon invasions constituted a military undertaking only in the very limited sense that new lands could not be won unless previous occupants were either driven out or brought into subjection by the use of greater force. The migration of people, the dispossession of many of the natives and the establishment of a wholly new political and social system were processes which were bound to take time.

The development of English history would have taken a very

different course if the presence of some external power had prevented the kingdoms of Mercia and Wessex, Northumbria and East Anglia, Kent and Sussex from waging war upon one another. But there was no *pax Romana* and it is for this reason that the earliest centuries of English history inevitably seem at times to consist of a catalogue of wars and battles. Whatever may be the changes of fashion in historical studies, this aspect of early Anglo-Saxon history is inescapable, since wars and battles are the historical expression of the process which the Vikings later called *landnám*, 'the taking of land', and what we should call settlement. As the seventh century reached its close this process had been largely completed. The limit had been reached in the north and there were no more than minor variations still to take place in the west. For rather more than a hundred years after Cædwalla's abdication, although there were still some battles to be fought between the English kingdoms, there was a more settled order of society in which farmers were able to concern themselves with their lands, kings with the organisation of the means of government, and churchmen with the pursuit of spiritual life and the book learning which was its accompaniment. It was not until almost the end of the eighth century that the security of Britain was once again broken by Viking attacks against such renowned centres of Christianity as Iona, Lindisfarne and Jarrow.

The example of abdication and subsequent journey to Rome, which had been set by Cædwalla, was followed by his successor in Wessex, Ine, but not until he had reigned for close on forty years (688–726). Although we know that Ine was engaged in battle with the Mercians on at least one occasion and that he was several times harassed by the rival claims of other members of the West Saxon royal family, his reign is significant rather for the occurrence of the earliest ecclesiastical synods in Wessex, for the interest he took in the better organisation of the Church in his kingdom by the creation of a see at Sherborne for the areas west of Selwood, and for his code of laws which reveals his close concern with matters agrarian, social and ecclesiastical. Ine and Aldhelm, the first bishop of Sherborne and a man of immense, if somewhat sterile, learning, were contemporaries of Aldfrith and Bede in Northumbria. Aldfrith (685–704), an illegitimate son of Oswiu, probably by an Irish mother, was necessarily concerned at first with recovery from the situation which had been brought about by the disastrous defeat of Ecgfrith by the Picts, but historians remembered him rather as a scholar of high distinction. After early schooling in Wessex, he spent many years studying among the Irish who later recalled his skill in composing Irish verse. He corresponded with Aldhelm, then at Malmesbury, and it was he who had copied for use in Northumbria the book *On Holy Places* which was written by Adamnan, abbot of Iona and biographer of St Columba. For his own use, and perhaps some effort of the imagination is required before we can visualise a seventh-century Northumbrian king being possessed of his own library of learned works, he acquired from the monastery at Monkwearmouth a treatise on cosmography which had been brought from Rome by Benedict Biscop, the purchase price paid by Aldfrith being a grant of land to Monkwearmouth itself. His death was followed by a period of regnal confusion in Northumbria, but a later Northumbrian king, Ceolwulf, was scholar enough to be able to help Bede by criticising the first draft of his *History*. After reigning for some eight years (729–37) Ceolwulf, like Cædwalla and Ine, abdicated, taking himself not to Rome, but to the community of Lindisfarne where he lived as a monk for many years to come.

'On the Present State of the English Nation, or of all Britain'—such is the title of the last chapter but one in Bede's *History*, and the description which it contains relates to the year 721. The beginning and subsequent course of Ceolwulf's reign in his own Northumbria, he writes, had been filled with so many grievous commotions that he could not tell what ought to be said about them or what their eventual outcome might be. The Picts were at peace with English and rejoicing in their fellowship with the universal Church. The Scots, resting content within their own borders, were not busy plotting any further attack upon the English. The British, though ill disposed towards the English and still wickedly resisting the Catholic Church, were yet their own masters in some places, although elsewhere they had been brought into subjection. In these peaceful conditions, many of the Northumbrians, noblemen and others as well, were laying aside their arms, preferring to devote themselves and their children to a monastic life, rather than to follow the pursuits of warfare. 'What the outcome of this will be, the next age will see.' South of the Humber all the kingdoms of the southern English with their several rulers, were subject to Æthelbald, king of the Mercians.

There are two points of particular interest in this account of Britain as it appeared to Bede only a few years before the close of his own life: first his comments, with their manifest sense of foreboding, upon the alacrity with which the Northumbrians were finding a kind of monastic life, in which their families could participate, so much more to their liking than the more strenuous pursuits of war, and secondly his reference to the supremacy of the Mercian king over all the kingdoms of the southern English. Bede further developed the first point in a letter which he wrote to bishop Egbert, shortly to become archbishop, of York, making plain his concern was not with genuine monks, but with the adoption of a spurious form of monasticism which enabled its adherents to avoid the duties, military service among them, and the payment of taxes which would otherwise have fallen upon them. He feared greatly for the effects which this practice might have upon the military strength of the kingdom, because, in addition to the evils arising within such monasteries themselves, there was the further consequence that their encroachment upon land was so great that the sons of some noblemen were being driven to seek their fortunes abroad because there was no land at home upon which they might maintain themselves. Bede's fears were wholly justified. There can be very little doubt that the political and military weakness of Northumbria in the eighth and ninth centuries had one of its roots in this flight from secular responsibilities to what may have been, in the conditions of the age, a more comfortable and secure form of life, and certainly one that held out hope of greater rewards in the life to come. But it was not only in Northumbria that men and women of royal or noble race, enjoying conditions of peace which contrasted strongly with the almost ceaseless warfare of earlier times, found themselves strongly attracted by monasticism. The widespread growth of religious houses for men and women among the kingdoms of the southern English, accompanied by the sudden outburst of missionary activity which took many of the better educated and more adventurous to work among the heathen Germans, can scarcely have failed to weaken the secular element south of the Humber in somewhat the same fashion as Bede observed the undermining of Northumbria's secular strength. Yet this very process may have made it easier for a strong ruler to assert his authority over his own as well as neighbouring kingdoms, and it was at this time that the ancient and distinguished house of Mercia produced two powerful rulers in close succession, each of whom ruled for some forty years, Æthelbald and Offa.

It is significant that Æthelbald himself was not, or at least not willingly, a supporter and protector of the Church in England. After he had been reigning for about thirty years, he was solemnly rebuked by Boniface and a group of bishops who wrote to him from Germany where they found themselves being embarrassed in their missionary work by the scandalous reputation which Æthelbald had gained for himself by his immoral living and his impatience with churchmen. In particular, he was accused of interfering with ecclesiastical privileges, and it was only under the pressure which was brought to bear upon him in this way that he seemed more ready during the later years of his reign to adopt a less high-handed attitude towards the Church. We know little enough in detail about the course of his reign, but that little does not gainsay the verdict of a contemporary who described him as a royal tyrant. He died a violent death in 757 when he was murdered in the night by one of his own bodyguard. His reign was important because it was long and because for almost the whole of it he was the undisputed overlord of England from the Humber to the Channel.

Offa who succeeded to the kingdom of Mercia after a brief period of civil war arising from disputed succession, was unquestionably the most eminent Anglo-Saxon ruler before the days of Alfred the Great himself. It is a sad misfortune that no early biographer was found to give an account of a reign whose course, so far as it can be discerned from diverse and scattered sources, was enlightened by some of the qualities of statesmanship, even though it was also pursued with a vigorous, and at times ruthless, authority. The most prominent and abiding monument of his reign, the great dyke by which he defined the boundary between his own people and the Welsh, discloses an engineering skill in the choice of the line which it followed and a command of resources for its execution which calls to mind the Antonine Wall, if not its Hadrianic predecessor. Offa's Dyke was never intended to be a defensive barrier, but merely a boundary, and as such it could scarcely have been bettered. His reign is distinguished also for its clear indications of growing commercial activity between England and the continent. Trade, both internal and external, will have been stimulated

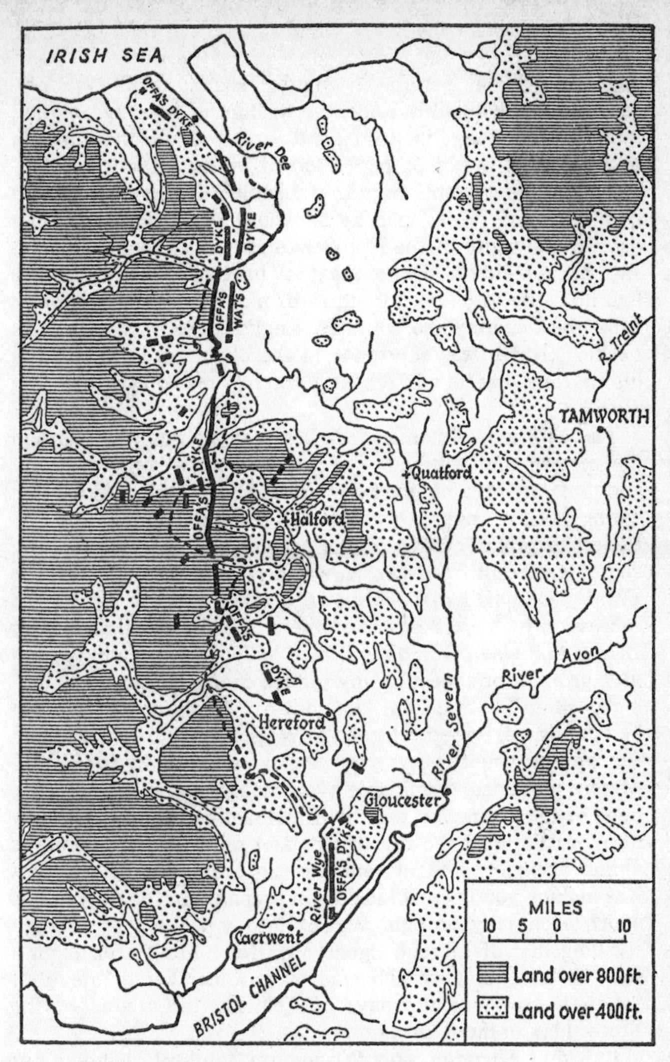

The Mercian frontier with Wales. The modern boundary of Wales-and-Monmouthshire is shown by a broken line

by the great currency reform, first initiated in Kent, which introduced a silver penny of high quality and of a character which remained basically unchanged even beyond the end of the Anglo-Saxon period. In matters ecclesiastical Offa perceived, as Æthelbald did not, the wisdom of keeping on good terms with the pope in Rome, and perceived also that his own political ends would be better served by the establishment of an independent archbishopric at Lichfield in the heart of his own kingdom, rather than by allowing the whole of the English Church south of the Humber to remain in spiritual obedience to an archbishop whose seat lay in Kent, where the people had no cause to be friendly towards him. Although there were still others among the southern English who could claim to be kings, there was substance in the claim made by Offa in his charters that he was *rex Anglorum* or *rex totius Anglorum patriæ*.

The dynasties of some of the lesser kingdoms which lay on the eastern and southern fringes of Mercia—Lindsey, Kent and Sussex—became extinct during Offa's reign. Æthelbert, a king of East Anglia, was beheaded at Offa's command in 794. Egbert, a representative of the ancient house of Wessex and claiming descent from Cerdic, was driven into exile among the Franks. Offa had made his own arrangements to secure the succession in Mercia by having his son consecrated as king in 787, so that when Offa himself died in 796, there can have been little ground for expecting any sudden change in the commanding position in which the kingdom of Mercia now seemed to be established. Egbert returned to Wessex from exile in 802 and for the next twenty years, while we can see that the strength of Mercia remained formidable even though her rulers achieved none of the distinction won by Æthelbald and Offa, the history of Wessex and of the rest of England south of the Thames is almost completely blank, and we can only guess that Egbert was making good use of his time in preparation for the exploits which eventually brought Wessex into a position of strength rivalling that of Mercia. Egbert won for himself a distinction such as had not been achieved by any member of the West Saxon house since the days of Ceawlin, the second of the Bretwaldas, in the sixth century.

In 825 at *Ellendun*, now Wroughton, south of Swindon, not far from the scene of earlier conflicts between the West Saxons and the Mercians, Egbert defeated Beornwulf, king of Mercia, and so overthrew the Mercian supremacy. He promptly dispatched his victorious army to Kent whose Mercian puppet ruler was expelled, and the people of Kent, Surrey, Sussex and Essex all submitted to him. Beornwulf, who had escaped alive from the battle at *Ellendun*, was killed by the East Anglians, who thereupon sought West Saxon protection against any possible Mercian attempt to seek vengeance. After a pause for recovery and further preparation for more distant compaigning, Egbert invaded Mercia in 829 and advanced as far north as the southern border of Northumbria at Dore near Sheffield where he received the submission of the Northumbrian people. In the next year he invaded north Wales. A West Saxon chronicler, choosing, perhaps deliberately, to ignore the great Mercian rulers of the eighth century, hailed Egbert as the eighth of the Bretwaldas, placing him in succession to Oswiu, the last of the Northumbrians who had reigned more than a century and a half earlier. The claim was exaggerated. Egbert never exercised such authority as Offa. Moreover the kingdom of Mercia very soon recovered its independence and it was a long time before West Saxon rulers were able to wield any real authority over the Northumbrians. Even so, Egbert's achievement was of great importance in that it gave solidity to the kingdom of Wessex and brought fresh strength to England south of the Thames at a time when it was sorely needed. Egbert was the first of the long and distinguished line of West Saxon rulers upon whom fell the main burden of defending England against the Vikings.

The first Viking attacks had already fallen upon the exposed coasts of Britain. Lindisfarne was sacked in 793, Jarrow in 794 and Iona in 795, and even before Egbert's accession three Viking ships had come to land on the Dorset coast near Portland and killed the royal officer who went down to discover who the strangers were. These episodes mark the beginning of a movement whose ultimate consequences for the history of Britain were of the greatest importance, a movement which takes its place in that long succession of invasions by Celt, Roman, Saxon, Dane and finally Norman. Danes and Norwegians between them took possession of half England from Essex, Suffolk and Norfolk in the south-east, to Lancashire, Westmorland and Cumberland in the north-west. They occupied Shetland and Orkney as well as much of the Scottish mainland. They seized the western isles, established many settlements in Ireland and set up a kingdom on the Isle of Man. And with them they brought their language, institutions and social customs, as well as their heathen beliefs, all of which remained to influence the character of their settlements long after the settlers themselves had become subjects of the kings of England who were descended from Egbert and his predecessors in the house of Wessex. But all this was a gradual process which continued for more than two hundred years and which on a wide view seems not wholly separable from the Norman Conquest itself, for the Normans were ultimately of Scandinavian origin themselves.

The monasteries lying in isolated positions on unprotected coasts or islands were the first victims of the Viking attacks, from Coldingham in the north to Thanet and Reculver in the south. An attack upon Sheppey in 835 marked the beginning of a long series of raids which ranged all along the eastern and southern coasts of England and against which there were no coastal defences. It was the usual practice of the raiders to come with the easterly winds of spring, campaign for a season and then return to their homes before the onset of autumn, but occasionally they would winter in England so that they might start their spring campaigns the sooner. We have record of only one notable English victory over the Vikings in this age and it was achieved by Egbert's successor, Æthelwulf, when, in 815, he defeated a large heathen host which had previously been assaulting Canterbury and London. Fifteen years later sporadic raiding aimed at the winning of booty gave way to organised invasion with conquest and settlement as its objectives. A great army landed in East Anglia in the autumn of 865 and in a series of swift campaigns fought during the next five years it destroyed the ancient kingdoms of Northumbria, Mercia and East Anglia. Late in 870 it left Thetford in preparation for its first attack against Wessex, but here the invaders found a greater state of military preparedness and they were quickly engaged, at first in minor skirmishes, but later, in a pitched battle on the Berkshire Downs, or Ashdown as it was then called, they were driven back in flight.

Alfred himself played a major part in this engagement which, though it was not decisive for subsequent events, at least showed that the Danes were not invincible. In April 871, under conditions which left him with no choice but to buy time from his enemies, he succeeded to the kingdom of Wessex. It had been held before him by three of his brothers. He became the father of Edward the Elder and the grandfather of Athelstan, two kings whose military achievements between 900 and 939 went far towards creating the kingdom of England.

CHAPTER TWELVE

THE CONVERSION OF THE ANGLO-SAXONS

The Anglo-Saxon invaders of Britain were pagan in their beliefs. Their burial customs give plain evidence of pagan ways of thought, and however widely Christianity may have been diffused in the Lowland Zone of Britain late in the fourth century, there can be no doubt that by *c.* 500 England south-east of the Fosse Way was predominantly, if not wholly, a pagan country once more. Yet if the evidence is adequate to demonstrate the fact, it tells us nothing about the manner in which the worship of the pagan gods was conducted. This is in part because the Anglo-Saxons normally built in wood and their pagan temples were in consequence much less durable than the solidly built stone structures of the Romano-British period, and in part because of the deliberate suppression of heathen memories by the Christian Church in later times. One of the complex of buildings which formed the royal palace at Old Yeavering in Northumberland is believed to have been a heathen temple which had subsequently been adapted to Christian use. We know that the principal centre of heathen worship among the Deirans lay at Goodmanham on the Yorkshire Wolds, and Bede has left us a vivid account of the destruction of the temple and its idols by Coifi, the heathen high priest. Eddius tells how Wilfrid and his companions, cast ashore by a storm on the coast of Sussex, found themselves confronted by the chief priest of the South Saxons who stood before them on a mound and sought to confound them by his magical arts.

Gregory's instructions to his emissary, Augustine, were that the heathen temples should not be destroyed, but only the idols which they housed. The temples themselves were to be purified and consecrated to Christian use. If these instructions were followed, a number of heathen temples are likely to have become centres of Christian worship. Such was very probably the case at Goodmanham itself, at Harrow-on-the-Hill, later crowned with a Christian church, but once called *Gumeninga hearh*, 'the holy place of the Gumeningas', and perhaps also at St Pancras, Canterbury. Such words as *hearh* meaning 'hill sanctuary', *weoh* 'idol' or 'shrine', and *ealh* 'temple' are found as elements in a considerable number of English place-names, and these, together with others which embody the names of such deities as Thunor and Woden are widely distributed over the midland and southern counties of England. The counties of Essex, Surrey and Sussex in particular show evidence of a deeply rooted heathenism which endured until the late seventh century. Three of the seven names now used for the days of the week are ultimately of Roman origin, but the other four—Old English *Tiwesdæg, Wodnesdæg, þunresdæg and Frigedæg* —embody the names of four Anglo-Saxon deities—Tiw, Woden, Thunor and Frig. Easter preserves the name of a heathen goddess *Eostre* and the old pagan name for the season of midwinter, the name *Giuli* which was applied to the last and the first month of the year, survives as Yule. The gods worshipped by the Anglo-Saxons were members of the Germanic pantheon and some of them figure prominently in later Scandinavian mythology.

The mission sent by Gregory and led by Augustine reached Thanet early in the year 597. It was directed towards the conversion of the heathen Anglo-Saxons whose conquests had now given them possession of most of the Lowland Zone. If, however, we are to visualise the situation by which the mission was confronted, and if we are to understand the course of ecclesiastical history among the English during the seventh century, we must look far beyond those parts of the country which had already been occupied by the invaders and even beyond the uttermost limits of the Roman province itself. Upon a superficial view, the remains of the Roman roads and of their frontier works may strike many people as the most obvious and enduring relics of the Roman occupation, but those who look more deeply may well come to believe that the most fruitful legacy bequeathed by the Roman occupation to later ages was not in material things, but in the Christian faith. Whatever changes may have accompanied the isolation of Britain from the Empire, the extinction of the Christian faith was certainly not among them. There are few more remarkable occurrences during the early centuries of Britain's history than the vigorous growth of Christianity in the age which followed the end of the Roman occupation, despite the isolation of most of the country from Rome itself. In Welsh history the sixth century has been called the age of the saints. In the fifth century St Patrick, deeply engaged in missionary work in Ireland, was concerned also with the conduct of a king of Strathclyde whose behaviour seemed to St Patrick ill suited to that of a Christian ruler of a Christian kingdom. There is a hint that Christianity had reached the more southerly Picts, those by whom Ecgfrith was defeated in 685, if not already within the Roman occupation, then very soon after its end. The Church prospered so greatly in Ireland that it was able to send its own missioners overseas. Columba, who was born in Donegal *c.* 520, established himself in Iona *c.* 563 and from there he directed a mission to the more northerly Picts. Gildas, a British monk who is believed to have been writing at about the middle of the sixth century, was not concerned with heathenism, but with the failure of a number of British kings to conduct their lives according to the principles of the Christian faith which they professed.

On this wide view, embracing Ireland as well as all the rest of Britain, the Anglo-Saxon settlers are seen as heathen intruders upon a civilisation which certainly by the end of the sixth century, and perhaps considerably earlier, had become predominantly Christian. The task of conversion was rendered the more easy since it could be approached from two sides—from Canterbury and from Iona—working independently of one another, but the subsequent creation of a well-ordered Church among the Anglo-Saxons was made the more difficult because of the ways in which the Celtic Church in Britain had developed during its period of isolation from Rome. Despite these latter difficulties, which proved formidable enough, the erratic ebullience of Celtic saintliness combined with the more orderly and methodical ways of Rome to create a Church whose achievements rank among the great contributions to the civilisation of western Europe in the early Middle Ages.

Although the villa at Lullingstone came to a violent end some two centuries before the arrival of Augustine, the nearness of Kent to Gaul and the passage of traders to and fro across the Channel may have prevented the obliteration of Christianity from this corner of Britain. Certainly Æthelbert, the king of Kent, knew something about Christian practices before Augustine's arrival in 597, because his Frankish wife was a Christian who had been accompanied to Britain by a Frankish bishop, and Christian services had been held in a church in Canterbury which was believed by Bede to have been built during the Roman occupation, the church which we now know as St Martin's. The conversion of Æthelbert was achieved within the year and this first success was swiftly followed by others which may have encouraged Augustine to think that his task was going to prove less formidable than he had feared when he was travelling through Gaul on his way to Britain. He was himself consecrated as bishop and later made archbishop with his seat in Canterbury. A second Kentish see was established at Rochester and a third in London as a base for a bishop among the East Saxons whose ruler, a nephew of Æthelbert, had been converted.

The security of the mission was dependent upon the security of the base from which it worked, and this was why Augustine established himself in Canterbury where he was assured of royal protection and support, rather than in London which was an East Saxon and not a Kentish city. Later events both in London and in Essex suggests that the hold of heathenism was much stronger there than in Kent where further witness to the strength of Romano-British Christianity may be seen in Augustine's choice of site for his cathedral in Canterbury. Bede tells us that he restored within the city 'a church which he had learned had been built there of old by the work of Roman believers, and consecrated it in the name of the Holy Saviour, our Lord and God, Jesus Christ, and established there a residence for himself and all his successors'. In this fashion Canterbury Cathedral had its beginning, and by preferring to restore an old site rather than to build on a new one, it seems almost as if Augustine was conscious that his task was not so much to win a new province for the Church, as to recover a lost one. Nothing is known about this oldest cathedral. In successive additions and rebuildings all traces of the earliest period have been lost or so deeply embedded in the present fabric that nothing can be learned about them.

There are, however, extensive remains of the settlement in which the missioners themselves lived their communal life on a site which then lay a little way outside Canterbury to the east. This settlement, now commonly known as St Augustine's, came to embrace several churches within its precincts, one of them, St Pancras, being alleged by medieval tradition to have been built on the site of a centre of heathen worship. The most prominent of the remains, preserved through their incorporation in the foundations of the Norman abbey built by Abbot Scotland at the end of the eleventh century, are those of the church

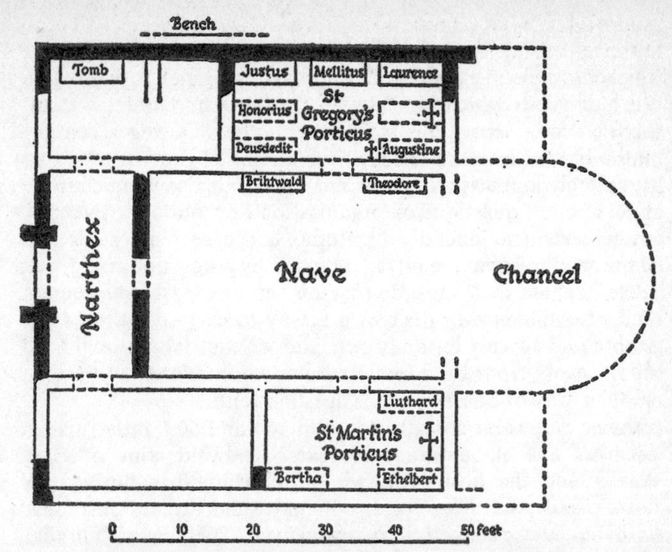

Plan of the church of St Peter and St Paul at Canterbury

of St Peter and St Paul, which was erected at the instigation of Æthelbert and served as the burial place of the early archbishops of Canterbury, including Augustine himself, and of several members of the Kentish royal family. Late in the eleventh century the relics of the early archbishops were translated to an appropriate place in the new abbey, but the original tombs can still be seen.

When a secure base had been won, the tasks which lay ahead were first to complete the overthrow of Anglo-Saxon heathendom by sending missionaries to other parts of the country, second to come to some agreement with the Celtic Church and third to establish the mechanism of ecclesiastical government. None of these formidable tasks came even near to completion during Augustine's lifetime. When he wrote to Gregory in Rome to ask about his relations with the bishops of the Celtic Church in Britain, he was told that they were all committed to his charge. On two separate occasions Augustine met in conference with members of the Celtic episcopacy, but no understanding was reached between them. According to Bede, Augustine's failure to stand up when the Celtic bishops approached was the occasion of breakdown at the second conference, but such a tale, though it may reflect some measure of tactlessness in Augustine's approach, reveals nothing of the deep divisions which lay between the two Churches as a result of their long separation from one another. During a century and a half of isolation the Celtic Church had gone its own way not merely in matters of form and ritual, but also in much more fundamental questions of organisation and outlook. Even so, its achievements, unaided by Rome, had been remarkable and those who rejected the advances made by Augustine could well have justified their attitude by their sense of past achievement and of confidence in their own ability to carry out their tasks with equal success in the future, and without the unsought aid of strangers from the Mediterranean who understood nothing of their way of observing the Christian faith.

After Augustine's death, between 604 and 609, little further progress was made for some years. Rædwald, king of East Anglia and the host of Edwin of Northumbria during the latter's exile, was converted, but under the persuasion of his wife he later relapsed into heathenism, keeping within one temple an altar for the sacrifices of Christ and a second small altar for offerings made to 'devils'. On the death of Æthelbert in 616, the mission received such a severe setback that it was all but extinguished and its influence thereafter greatly reduced. Æthelbert's son, though he lived to build another church within St Augustine's, reverted to pagan ways, and at about the same time there was such a severe reaction in Essex that the bishopric in London had to be abandoned.

The marriage of a daughter of Æthelbert of Kent to Edwin, king of Northumbria, gave the Canterbury Church an opening which enabled it to achieve a notable success in the north. It had been a condition of the marriage contract that the Kentish princess and her attendants should be allowed to practise their own religion, and even Edwin himself, presumably with some knowledge of Christianity gained from his visit to Rædwald's court, had expressed a readiness to adopt his wife's beliefs if his councillors thought fit. The bride was accordingly accompanied on her journey north by Paulinus, one of a group of missioners who had arrived in England in 601 and who, before he set out for Northumbria, was consecrated bishop in Canterbury in 625. For a year Paulinus had no success in his efforts to secure converts, but in 626, after escaping from the knife of a West Saxon assassin, Edwin agreed to the baptism of his infant daughter, a ceremony which took place at Pentecost when several other members of the royal family were likewise baptised. Finally, after he had successfully completed his campaign of vengeance against the West Saxons and after long debate with his councillors, the heathen sanctuary at Goodmanham was overthrown and Edwin was baptised on the eve of Easter Day in a little wooden oratory built specially for the purpose in York. At the time of his baptism Edwin was much the most powerful ruler in the country, and the example which he set was quickly followed by many of the nobility and others among his subjects.

Paulinus then travelled widely over Northumbria, visiting in particular the royal estates where he might expect that many of the people would be ready to follow the example which had been set by their king. In the far north he went to the royal palace at Old Yeavering where he stayed for thirty-six days with the King and his Queen, preaching to the many thousands who had flocked to hear him from the neighbouring farms and villages, and later baptising them in the river Glen. In Deira, apart from York itself, the scene of Edwin's baptism, he worked at Catterick, baptising his converts in the nearby river Swale, and at Dewsbury in the West Riding, both of them royal estates. At Dewsbury he built a church whose stone altar, escaping the fire which soon afterwards overwhelmed the church, was still preserved in Bede's time. He journeyed from Northumbria to visit Lindsey where he baptised a royal officer in Lincoln and saw to the building of a church within the city. Many of the people of Lindsey were baptised by him in the Trent near the Roman fort called *Segelocum*, then known as *Tiowulfingacæstir*, and now called Littleborough.

One of those who received baptism in the Trent from the hands of Paulinus remembered him as a tall, slightly stooping figure, with black hair, hooked nose and emaciated face, and his memories eventually came to the ear of Bede who recorded them for posterity. The rapid progress made by Paulinus in the north encouraged Pope Honorius to set up a new archbishopric in York, with Paulinus as its first holder, but before this could be done Edwin was defeated and killed by Cadwallon and Penda. Paulinus took flight by sea to Kent, accompanied by Edwin's widow, her infant daughter and several other members of the Northumbrian royal family. He was also able to bring with him some of King Edwin's plate, including a gold cross and a gold chalice. These precious objects which were still kept at Canterbury in the eighth century suggest that the wealth and splendour exemplified in the jewellery recovered from Sutton Hoo may have been no less characteristic of Edwin's court than of the court of East Anglian kings. Amid this disaster, only one member of the mission remained in Northumbria. This was James the deacon who, remembered later especially for his skill in the Roman chant, continued steadfastly preaching and baptising in a village near Catterick.

A century later the evil year which followed the death of Edwin was still remembered among the people of Northumbria both for the apostasy of the English kings and for the cruel tyranny of Cadwallon. For Penda it could at least be said that he was a pagan ignorant of Christian ways, but the savagery displayed by Cadwallon towards his fellow-Christians among the English of Northumbria moved Bede to denounce him in terms of uncommon vigour. As soon as Oswald had secured his position in Northumbria he sent to Iona for help in re-establishing Christianity among his people, and in 635 Aidan came with a small company of monks who settled themselves on the island of Lindisfarne where they could enjoy a fair measure of security against the possibility of hostile attack, with ease of access to the mainland for their missionary work which they now began to pursue with the vigour characteristic of the Celtic Church in this age. Others followed them from Iona to give help in founding churches and monasteries, as well as instruction in the observance of monastic life. Within a generation the kingdom of Northumbria had become wholly Christian.

The documents and early traditions which enabled Bede to record in some detail the history of the conversion in Kent and Northumbria have no counterparts from the midlands or Wessex, and for these areas we have little more than the record of isolated incidents, with here and there some early ecclesiastical relics testifying to otherwise unrecorded missionary activities. Penda remained heathen to the last, but in 653 his son, Peada, was baptised by Finan, Aidan's successor at Lindisfarne, on the occasion of his marriage into the Northumbrian royal family, and a bishopric was subsequently established among the Mercians. In East Anglia, after earlier attempts had failed to yield any lasting results, Christianity was established during the reign of Sigebert, principally through the work of two men whose origins were very different—Felix, a Burgundian who was consecrated bishop in Gaul and then travelled to Kent, in the hope that the archbishop might be able to find missionary work for him to do, and Fursa, a distinguished Irish ascetic. While the Northumbrian Oswald was exiled in the far north, the East Anglian Sigebert had been driven to seek refuge in Gaul whence he later returned to his own kingdom already a Christian and with a reputation for learning which bore fruit in the establishment of a school organised upon lines similar to those followed by the Roman mission in Kent. Felix was given an episcopal seat at Dunwich where he continued in office for many years. Soon after the arrival of Felix in East Anglia, Sigebert was visited by a wandering Irish saint, one of the many Irishmen who left their homeland in this age to lead the life of a pilgrim and whose wanderings took them far and wide across Europe. Prompted by a vision he decided to remain in East Anglia for a while and the King gave him a site upon which to establish a monastery wherein others might be instructed. The site upon which Fursa settled was that of the old Saxon Shore fort known to the Romans as *Garrianonum*, though it was then called *Cnobheresburg*, now Burgh Castle overlooking Breydon Water. The monastery which he founded there was later generously endowed by Anna, king of East Anglia. An early Christian cemetery and the remains of some ecclesiastical buildings have lately been identified within the fort. After remaining there for some years Fursa resumed his pilgrimage, crossing the sea to Gaul where he died.

Following the relapse to heathenism in Essex in 616, Christianity was restored to the kingdom shortly after the middle of the century by Cedd who was English by origin but Celtic by training. Like Fursa, he settled in one of the Saxon Shore forts, building a church within *Othona*, the Anglo-Saxon *Yþancæstir*, and the modern Bradwell-on-Sea between the Crouch and the Blackwater. The church which he built still survives beside its recently acquired neighbour, an atomic power station. Cedd remained in contact with Northumbria, later building a monastery at Lastingham in Yorkshire where he died. If some of the early records of the monastery at Peterborough had survived it is likely that we should have been able to recognise it as the fountain-head of an important evangelising movement in the south-east midlands. A magnificent church of seventh-century date at Brixworth in Northamptonshire, and a rich collection of early sculptured stones at Breedon-on-the-Hill in Leicestershire testify to the existence of prosperous Christian communities of whose early history nothing is known, save that they were believed on good evidence to have been founded by an abbot of Peterborough in the second half of the seventh century. Monks from Peterborough are also believed to have founded other monasteries in Surrey and even in Kent. At about the same time as Felix reached East Anglia, Wessex was visited by a certain Birinus who came to Britain from Italy with the intention of preaching among the heathen in the remoter parts of the country, but when he found that the West Saxons, on whose shores he had landed, were still heathen he decided to remain with them.

In 635 Cynegils, king of Wessex, was converted, and Birinus was established as bishop at Dorchester-on-Thames, though it is doubtful whether Christianity became at all widespread among the West Saxons until some years later. As the boundaries of the kingdom moved out towards the west, they overran two important centres of Celtic Christianity, one at Malmesbury founded by an Irishman called Maildubh and later renowned in the days of Aldhelm, and the other at Glastonbury of even earlier origin. The kingdom of the South Saxons, off the track of those who travelled between England and Gaul, and largely isolated from its northern neighbours by the Weald, was the last to be converted. On one occasion when Wilfrid and his companions were returning to England from Gaul, a south-easterly gale blew them off their course and they narrowly escaped slaughter at the hands of the pagan host that hastened down to the shore to seize their ship which had gone aground. Some years later, in 680, rejected by his own Northumbria, Wilfrid found refuge with a king of the South Saxons, himself a Christian though his people still remained heathen. Wilfrid was given an estate at Selsey and during the next five years he converted the South Saxons. There remained the Isle of Wight, and after it had come into the possession of Cædwalla of Wessex in 686, Wilfrid was able to make a start with its conversion, leaving the work to be completed by a nephew when he himself returned to Northumbria.

Although we can find references in later documents condemning those who worshipped idols or followed other iniquitous practices, England had become a Christian country well before the end of the seventh century. No doubt the complaint made by some Northumbrian rustics to Cuthbert, that men had robbed them of their old ways of worship and there were none who knew how the new ways should be conducted, might have been echoed in many other parts of the country. But even if there was still a very lively world of witchcraft, black magic and malicious monsters, the organised public worship of heathen gods had everywhere ceased, though there was a brief return to heathen ways in some parts of the country under the stress of plague, and a more widespread return of heathenism after the Viking invasions of the ninth and tenth centuries. In place of heathen shrines, outward signs of Christianity were becoming widespread over the country, not only churches and monasteries, but also, and particularly though perhaps not exclusively, in Northumbria, wondrously worked, free-standing, stone crosses which first became in the seventh and eighth centuries a characteristic feature of the English countryside.

Even before the conversion had been completed, at a time when Sussex and the Isle of Wight were still heathen, the dispute between the Roman and the Celtic Churches, foreshadowed in the fruitless meetings of Augustine and the Celtic bishops, came to a head. Canterbury and those parts of the country over which the archbishop exercised control naturally conformed with Roman ways, but there were many areas in which the successes achieved by the Celtic missionaries had led to the adoption of Celtic beliefs and practices. The conflict might issue in such practical difficulties as faced the Northumbrian court when a king celebrated Easter at a time when his queen was still engaged in the Lenten fast. There were other matters of ritual upon which the two Churches were divided, and we need not be surprised to find that the bitterness of the discord which such matters provoked was no less great in the seventh century than it still remains in the twentieth. Perhaps more important for the future of the Church in England was the deep difference between the Roman and the Celtic Churches in their attitude towards the episcopacy. In the seventh century a bishop in the Celtic Church was invariably a monk, and as such he was subject to the authority of his abbot. He exercised particular spiritual functions, but he was not concerned in matters of jurisdiction or administration which lay in the control of the abbot, and in particular he was not confined within precise diocesan boundaries, for none such existed.

The Celtic missionaries who worked among the English were almost all of Irish or Scottish origin—and for the seventh century these two terms are almost interchangeable. According to Bede the Welsh Church had taken no part in the conversion, but relations between the English and the Irish were not then coloured by such prolonged and bitter fighting as had taken place between the British and the English in the sixth and seventh centuries. The British are not likely to have forgotten the slaughter of the monks of Bangor by the pagan Æthelfrith of Northumbria, any more than Bede forgot the slaughter of the Northumbrian Christian Edwin by the British Cadwallon.

At a gathering which was held at Whitby in 663 the two sides argued their case in the presence of Oswiu, king of Northumbria, and the decision went in favour of Rome. In addition to Oswiu and Hild, the Celtic view was supported by Cedd, bishop among the East Saxons, and Colman, bishop at Lindisfarne. Opposing them was Oswiu's son, Alchfrith, Agilberht, a bishop of Frankish origin who was then at work among the West Saxons, James the deacon who had now been labouring in Northumbria for almost thirty years since he had first travelled north with Paulinus, and Wilfrid. Such a gathering was by no means representative of the two Churches. Indeed it was little more than a meeting of Northumbrian churchmen, for the presence of Agilberht was due to the accident of a chance visit to Northumbria at the time, and Cedd was himself of Northumbrian origin. Even so it seemed to be in the eyes of Bede an occasion of the very greatest importance, and looking back over the centuries we cannot find fault with that sense of historical judgement which caused him to lay so much emphasis upon a gathering which even now seems to mark the beginning of an epoch in the history of the Church in England, an epoch which ends only with the Reformation.

The decision taken at Whitby, though decisive for the English Church, marked neither the beginning nor the end of the movement which eventually brought all the Churches of Britain, Celtic and Anglo-Saxon alike, into conformity with Rome. The Church in southern Ireland had already conformed some thirty years earlier. It was followed later by the northern Irish, the Pictish Church, the Church of Iona, and finally, though not until 768, by the Welsh Church. But a mere decision could not by itself produce a Church ordered upon the principles of Roman ecclesiastical government. Shortly after the synod of Whitby, England experienced a particularly severe outbreak of the plague which caused the death of many leading churchmen and resulted even in a brief resuscitation of heathenism among the East Saxons. Chance and a wise choice made by the Pope brought to England at this time, as holder of the archbishopric of Canterbury, a man of the highest intellectual distinction and great administrative ability, Theodore, a native of Tarsus. Arriving in England in 669, he found men rebuilding their heathen temples, but nowhere in the whole country so far as we can see was there a single bishop, with the exception of Wilfrid at Ripon, who had been consecrated in a manner of whose validity the Roman Church could have no doubt, or who was not otherwise in disrepute. Theodore held the see of Canterbury for more than twenty years, and during that period, beginning with a general assembly of the whole Church in England at Hertford in 672, he created a diocesan organisation and made provision for the proper government of the Church by the holding of regular conciliar assemblies.

Theodore was accompanied on his journey to Britain from Rome by Benedict Biscop, a Northumbrian nobleman who, like a great many of his kind, devoted himself to the monastic life and is remembered as the founder of two famous monasteries, Monkwearmouth and Jarrow. Bede, their most distinguished son, was born a year or so after Theodore reached Canterbury and near the beginning of one of the great ages in the history of the Church of England. The remarkable achievements of this age owed much to the vigorous and enlightened enthusiasm with which many men and women who were of royal or noble birth devoted themselves to monastic life, finding therein an outlet for their activities and a fresh source of inspiration at a time when the turbulent centuries of Romano-British collapse and Anglo-Saxon conquest had at last given way to an age of relative peace. Monkwearmouth and Jarrow, founded by a nobleman, were richly endowed by Northumbrian kings. Hartlepool and Whitby became the homes of those who in other ages would have been called princesses. Wilfrid, the founder of monasteries at Hexham and Ripon, was of noble birth. Ely was founded by a woman who was the daughter of one king and had been the wife of another. Minster-in-Thanet had several royal nuns among its company and Wimborne in Dorset was founded by two sisters of a West Saxon king.

The rapid growth of monastic life throughout the country produced a class of people who, though they may not have been large in numbers, yet achieved a high level of education and learning. Knowledge of Latin became widespread, serving both the needs of scholarship and of correspondence between people living in different parts of the country. Canterbury under Theodore, Malmesbury under Aldhelm and Jarrow in the days of Bede became centres of monastic learning of high distinction by any standards. To their age also belong the saintliness of Cuthbert, the inspired beauty of the Lindisfarne Gospels and the restrained dignity of the Ruthwell and Bewcastle crosses. If, from the viewpoint of modern times, we tend to regard the lifetime of Bede (*c.* 671–735) as spanning the greatest age of the Anglo-Saxon Church, although one which was already beginning to show signs of decadence before his death, we ought to remember that Alcuin who became master of the school at York in 767 could in later life look back from his position at Charlemagne's court to a time after Bede's death which seemed to him to be one of the greatest distinction.

It is not easy to reach any conclusions about the state of the Church in England in the years between the death of Bede and the accession of Alfred. In a letter which Bede wrote in 734 to his pupil Egbert, shortly to become archbishop of York, he commented on a number of points which seemed to him to require urgent attention. There were not enough priests or teachers and it was wrong to demand material support for the Church when nothing was done for the spiritual salvation of the people. More bishops were needed, even though there might be difficulties in securing adequate endowments of land to support them. In particular the monastic ideals were being gravely abused by those who set themselves up in spurious monasteries, not wishing or intending to devote themselves to a religious life, but merely seeking an escape from their obligations in the secular world. Although Bede was referring specifically to the Church in Northumbria, it is unlikely that the weaknesses which he observed there were peculiar to Northumbria alone. Rather less than a century and a half later we find Alfred lamenting the decay of learning in England, saying how once men had come to England from abroad in search of learning and wisdom, but that Englishmen who wanted such things now would need to seek them abroad. Yet Bede was looking for faults, not seeking to commend what was good, and perhaps Alfred painted his picture of the decay of learning in too sombre colours. That there had been great changes, as a result of which monasticism had disappeared from the land by the time of Alfred's accession, there can be little doubt, yet there is much to suggest that, at least in parts of the country, the Church continued throughout the eighth century to be inspired by the high ideals which seem to be characteristic of it in the age of Bede. This was the age of the Anglo-Saxon mission to the heathen Germanic peoples of western Europe, a movement which took many Anglo-Saxon men and women away from the security of England to lives of difficulty and danger, ending sometimes in martyrdom. Their fortunes were followed with close interest by those who remained at home and who sent them letters of encouragement or copies of the books for which they asked.

The very success of this continental mission, undertaken by those who were well aware that they were returning to lands from which their own ancestors had once come to invade Britain, itself deprived the Church at home of many of those who would have been its natural leaders. Although we know very little about the state of the Church in England during the first half of the ninth century, we do at least know that the monasteries along the east coast of England were the first victims of the Vikings, and we must surely conclude that there was still such life within their walls as to make them worth the attacking. Moreover we know also that the monks of Lindisfarne clung to what had become a dangerously exposed position for almost a hundred years after the first assault, and that as late as *c.* 850 a Gaulish abbot was in learned correspondence with both an archbishop and an abbot in York.

CHAPTER THIRTEEN

THE NATURE OF EARLY ANGLO-SAXON SOCIETY

(1) KINGS AND MEN OF NOBLE BIRTH

Although we cannot learn anything about the nature of Anglo-Saxon society from documents written by the Anglo-Saxons themselves until the seventh and eighth centuries, there is a little understanding to be won from taking note of some of the contrasts with the dominant characteristics of the preceding Romano-British age. And the most striking of these characteristics was the enforcement of the *pax Romana*. The inhabitant of Roman Britain was not normally concerned with warfare, unless he happened to be one of those conscripted for service with the Roman army, and in that case he would, at least in the early days, have been sent for duty overseas. Although he may have had to bear a heavy weight of taxation as his contribution to the support of the armies by which he was protected, the protection which he received in return was very real, so much so that there were successive generations of men living in parts of Britain between *c.* 65 and *c.* 365 who may have experienced local disturbances but to whom warfare on anything approaching a national or even tribal scale was unknown. In this respect the contrast with the earlier, and even with the later, centuries of Anglo-Saxon England could scarcely have been more pronounced. Without the *pax Romana* the civilisation of Roman Britain could not have flourished as it did, and at least some measure of peace and security was a necessary condition for the development of Anglo-Saxon society in a similar way. Each of the Anglo-Saxon kingdoms had first to be established in a hostile land and subsequently to be defended against the attacks of its neighbours, whatever their nationality, and a successful king needed to be first and foremost a warrior who could attract others to his service by his own success in battle.

Reges ex nobilitate, duces ex virtute sumunt wrote Tacitus, describing Germanic custom. They take their kings on the ground of birth, their generals on the basis of courage. The principle of heredity, though not that of primogeniture, was of the first importance in the Anglo-Saxon conception of kingship, yet, save in one instance we do not know to what extent the early Anglo-Saxon kingdoms were founded by adventurers whose prowess in war enabled them to maintain a band of warriors—*duces ex virtute*—or by men who had already established themselves as kings before the invasion of Britain—*reges ex nobilitate*. The great Offa who ruled Mercia for most of the second half of the eighth century could claim descent through many generations from ancestors, one of them likewise called Offa, who ruled near Slesvig while Roman government had not entirely ceased to function in Britain, but it seems unlikely that such remarkable continuity would have been common in conditions so disturbed as those prevailing in the age of migrations. Other Anglo-Saxon royal families also acquired long pedigrees, but beyond the point at which we can bring independent evidence to check the historical reality of the persons to whom they refer, we do well to regard them mainly as indications of a growing pride in royalty, and as giving more eminence to the institution of kingship by seeking to demonstrate its greater antiquity. Whether or not the means used to demonstrate that antiquity were fictitious was beside the point. We shall not nowadays be deceived by the inclusion of Beornic in the Bernician pedigree, nor by the descent of Edwin of Northumbria in the seventh generation from Seabird (*sæfugl*). Nor need we believe that Æthelwulf of Wessex, father of Alfred the Great, really supposed, as his pedigree-makers claimed on his behalf, that his descent could be traced all the way back to Adam. This was no more than a pleasant fiction intended to deceive no-one, but nevertheless perhaps proving a little helpful to morale at a time when Alfred saw his kingdom reduced to the Somerset marshes and the outlook dark indeed for the future of this West Saxon dynasty. But whatever the uses of pedigrees, and human nature has not yet changed so much as to put the pedigree-makers out of business, once the Anglo-Saxon kingdoms had been established, succession was hereditary in the sense that the throne was expected to pass, and normally did pass, to a member of the royal family, though within that limitation there was sometimes room for choice.

The power, wealth and dignity which became attached to the office of king later in the Middle Ages make it difficult for us nowadays to realise the small, almost miniature, scale upon which the affairs of government were conducted in the early centuries of Anglo-Saxon England. The change from Romano-British canton to Anglo-Saxon kingdom was marked by a real break in the practical methods of government, and led eventually, under the influence of the Church, to the development of ideas about the functions and duties of rulers which were quite foreign to the age when Britain was governed by an imperial legate. Yet there were parts of Britain in which the new kingdoms were no bigger than the old cantons. We do not find elsewhere that degree of geographical coincidence that may be seen between the cantons of the Cantiaci and the Regnenses and the kingdoms of Kent and Sussex, yet the area occupied by the Iceni, the Trinovantes and the Catuvellauni was little, if at all, larger than that covered by the kingdoms of East Anglia and Essex, and also inhabited by the Middle Angles and the Middle Saxons who may also have once held the status of independent kingdoms. It is only with the emergence of the larger states—Northumbria, Mercia and Wessex—that the unit of Anglo Saxon government became substantially greater than the old Romano-British canton.

A king of Kent or Essex whose subjects numbered only a very small fraction of the present-day inhabitants of these two counties, could exercise a very high degree of direct, personal control and needed no elaboration of subordinate offices of government. There is some evidence that, even within such relatively small areas, there might be two or even three members of the royal family holding the title of king at the same time. A seventh-century king of Kent was known simply as *rex Cantuariorum* or, in Old English, as *Cantwara cyning,* and when we find a charter hailing such a king as *dei gratia rex Anglorum* we know at once that this part at least of the charter is a forgery reflecting royal styles of a much later age. And so also a Northumbrian king of the same age was called *Norþanhymbra cyning,* a Mercian king *Miercna cyning.* A century later, during Offa's reign, we find that official documents, coming from the royal court, are beginning to reflect the political changes which have taken place through the suppression of some of the smaller dynasties and the concentration of wider authority in the hands of the king of Mercia himself. Offa might still on occasion call himself *rex Merciorum,* but he might also call himself *rex Anglorum* or *rex totius Anglorum patriae* or even *rex Britanniae.* These experimental titles have some constitutional significance in their reflection of the political changes which were taking place and in their implication of a belief that the English were a single people who might be made subject to a single ruler. In fact, however, there were still at this time four effective kingdoms—Northumbria, East Anglia, Mercia and Wessex—and although Offa's was the dominating figure, these four kingdoms still possessed a much greater degree of independence from one another than did the four provinces of Roman Britain in the age of Diocletian. The Church was the only authority which overrode political boundaries, and we may see the importance which Offa attached to its influence in his efforts to secure greater control over it by establishing an archbishopric at Lichfield within the boundaries of his own kingdom. Early in the ninth century Wessex was already beginning to acquire the power and influence which had been wielded by Mercia in the eighth and Northumbria in the seventh, but it was the Danish invasions which, by the destruction of all the other English dynasties, left the house of Wessex without a competitor among rulers of English race.

Although there were many kings ruling England in the seventh and eighth centuries, there is a strong tradition that from very early times there had been one amongst them who held a position of pre-eminence among his fellows, a position which was not hereditary to any one royal family or kingdom, but which was won and maintained by military prowess. This position, for which an entry in the *Anglo-Saxon Chronicle* for the year 827, uses the title *Bretwalda,* was held at different times by kings of Sussex, Wessex, Kent, East Anglia, Northumbria and Mercia. Bede, though not himself using the title *Bretwalda,* writes of such kings as exercising an *imperium* which was in some way distinct from the degree of authority normally exercised by a ruler within the limits of his own kingdom. We do not know what particular advantages the *Bretwalda* enjoyed by virtue of his distinction, although we need not doubt that they were real and substantial. In particular we are left to wonder whether the title itself was an invention of the ninth century in which it is found recorded, or whether it had a longer history, perhaps preserving some lingering memory of a time when Britain had been a single country under Roman rule, a legacy passed from Magnus Maximus to Vortigern and inherited, or more probably acquired in battle, by Ælle, king of Sussex in the second half of the fifth century.

At the end of the Anglo-Saxon period the monarchy stood at the apex of a variety of institutions which served the purposes and met the needs of local government with such efficiency that they continued to form the framework of administration for long after the Norman conquest. National affairs, on occasion involving even succession to the throne itself, were discussed in the king's council. Local affairs came within the purview of the shire court attended by the bishop and the ealdorman, and at a lower level still were the monthly meetings of the hundred court or, as it was called in the Danish areas of the country, the wapentake court. The sheriff acted as the vital link between the central government and these local institutions. He had become the king's chief executive officer in local affairs and he was there as the king's agent within the territories even of the greatest landed magnates. The king's writ was the means by which the king's pleasure was made known on a variety of judicial, administrative and financial matters in different parts of the country. But this elaborate, and on the whole efficient, system of government came gradually into being over several centuries, and it is not easy to see how far it had developed by the time of Alfred's birth. We know that there were no wapentakes in England before the Danish invasions in the second half of the ninth century, since the word wapentake itself, like riding, is of Scandinavian origin, and we cannot see the sheriff securely in his office before the beginning of the eleventh century. There can be little doubt that some sort of royal council existed in each of the Anglo-Saxon kingdoms from the very earliest times, but difficulties at once arise if we seek to define its functions and membership or when we begin to look more closely at the history of shire and hundred.

Negatively we can be sure that the primitive king's council was neither an elected nor a representative body. Its roots lay in Germanic custom untouched by Roman law, and many centuries of practical experience were necessary before the eventual formation of more formal, constitutional ideas about methods of procedure and about functions. The king's council in Northumbria or in Kent in the seventh century was little more than a gathering of the king's principal friends and advisers. Edwin of Northumbria thought it right to consult *cum amicis principibus et consiliariis suis* before yielding to the demand made by Paulinus that the time had now come for him to redeem the promise, made in exile at Rædwald's court, that he would accept Christian baptism. Bede's well-known account of the discussion which followed gives us a vivid picture of a royal council assembled in deliberative discussion, and yet the term 'council' applied to a gathering of this kind may seem a little too formal in its implications. King, friend, nobleman, high priest, councillor, ealdorman, thegn—these are the English words to be equated with the Latin terms used by Bede to describe those who were present, and together such men made up a royal court not markedly dissimilar from the band of men who assembled for their nightly feasting in Heorot, the great hall of *Beowulf*. Despite the difference of the subject debated, the participants in the discussion about Christianity at Edwin's court were essentially the same kind of people who discussed how to meet the attacks of Grendel upon Hrothgar's court. Both gatherings resemble the Germanic *comitatus* described by Tacitus.

Security against attacks, if not of monsters, at least of warlike neighbours, would be an ever-present concern of an Anglo-Saxon king, and matters of defence and military expeditions would frequently be the subject of discussion between kings and their councillors. The maintenance of an army, the apportionment of land, the exaction of tribute from a defeated enemy or perhaps the payment of tribute to a *Bretwalda*—such matters as these were of direct and immediate consequence from the very earliest days of the Anglo-Saxon settlements in Britain, and we must not suppose that they were not discussed merely because we have no written record of such discussions. It is, however, the written record itself which first begins to lend an air of greater formality to the proceedings of a king's council, and here the influence of the Church was of the first importance.

A full and formal record was kept of the proceedings of the synod of Hertford which was held in 672 under the presidency of Theodore, archbiship of Canterbury, and although this was an ecclesiastical council concerned only with the affairs of the Church, nevertheless the advantages of embodying decisions in a formal written document would be obvious enough, at least to those who stood to benefit from them, whether their concern was with the law, with grants of land or with remission of taxation. The two earliest Kentish law codes are represented as the personal decrees of the kings themselves, although Bede states that Æthelbert's was enacted *cum consilio sapientium*, but the prologue to the third, dating from 695, states that the code was issued after the holding of a deliberative assembly of the clergy and the nobility. At about the same date Ine, king of Wessex, similarly consulted his bishops, his ealdormen and his chief councillors before issuing his own law code. Throughout the Anglo-Saxon period, advising the king in the revision and promulgation of laws continued to be one of the important functions of the king's council, and we are entitled to suppose that it acted in this way in Mercia and Northumbria at an early date though no early laws survive from either of those kingdoms.

Perhaps of greater, and certainly of more frequent concern, were matters affecting the king's lands and the revenues arising from the land and from other sources. Such might be of relatively minor importance, as when Æthelbald, king of Mercia, granted the bishop of Rochester the remission of tolls on one ship entering the port of London, tolls which would otherwise have been collected by the king's tax-gatherers. The charter recording this grant is only one of a number of documents showing the concern of the king's council with fiscal matters. Of immensely greater importance were decisions which affected the king's revenue by the creation of privileged estates. In particular, the transfer of large areas of land to the Church, for the foundation and further endowment of monasteries reduced the royal revenue by exempting such lands from the secular burdens which would otherwise have lain upon them, and, if carried to the point of abuse, as happened in Northumbria in the eighth century, the defence of the kingdom might itself have been imperilled because of the lack of land upon which the sons of the nobility could be maintained. The majority of surviving Anglo-Saxon charters deal either with gifts of land or with disputes about its ownership and it is a sure assumption that this topic was at all times one of the major concerns of royal councils.

Some of the decisions reached at meetings of the king's council were embodied in royal charters, but no charters contain a complete record of the proceedings of any single meeting of a council. Those whose names were appended to the charters as witnesses of the transaction in question give some idea of the people present when the business was discussed, but we are not entitled to suppose that any list of witnesses represents the entire body of those present at a council meeting. During the period of Mercian hegemony in the eighth century those present at council meetings include members of the royal family, leading churchmen and several members of the nobility, men who witnessed documents with the title *dux* or *ealdorman*. On one occasion, a meeting at Brentford in 781, where the matter at issue was a dispute between Offa and the church of Worcester about the possession of certain lands, every single bishop south of the Humber and Mersey was present. The influence of such gatherings as these undoubtedly extended far beyond the frontiers of Mercia itself, but further advance towards some more truly national council was cut short by the Danish invasions, and it is not until the reign of Athelstan in the first half of the tenth century that we see the king's council developing into a body of truly national importance.

So profound were the changes taking place in almost every aspect of life in tenth-century England that it is often difficult to know how far features which are characteristic of some aspects of this later age were themselves recent innovations and how far they represent merely a continuing development of institutions and ideas of earlier origins. The Anglo-Saxon invasions of Britain completely overthrew the Romano-British state. The Danish and Norse invasions of the ninth and tenth centuries fell far short of overthrowing the Anglo-Saxon state in a similar way, but they did profoundly alter the course of its development, and not least in matters of local government. Although local government through shire and hundred or wapentake was almost universal in England in the late tenth and the eleventh centuries, there are large areas of the country, particularly those settled by the Danes, where it is by no means clear whether this system was wholly new in the tenth century or whether it rested partly upon methods of local government employed in the old kingdoms of Northumbria, Mercia and East Anglia. On the whole the evidence suggests that in most of the midlands, as well as in the north of England, shire and hundred, as well as riding and wapentake, did not take their medieval form until after the Danish invasions.

The Danish military incursions into Wessex were not followed by permanent settlements, and there is in consequence less likelihood that the system of local government prevailing there in the days of Alfred's sons and grandsons was fundamentally different from that familiar to his father and grandfather. There is enough evidence to make it appear reasonably certain that before *c*. 850 the kingdom of Wessex had been subdivided into shires, corresponding broadly with those which still exist and that by that date meetings of the shire court were being held under the presidency of an ealdorman, a royal official of noble birth who held considerable administrative and judicial responsibilities, who led the shire levies in times of war and who enjoyed a social status which allowed him to be equated for some purposes with a bishop. We can even catch a glimpse of the ealdorman exercising judicial functions as early as the seventh century, but there is no evidence to show whether the shires were already in existence by that date.

The history of the hundred in early times is even more obscure. We know that the hundred court was the ordinary local criminal court of the country in the eleventh century, holding its meetings once every four weeks, and we can be sure that it was working in parts of the country by the middle of the tenth century. A court such as this, with its relatively frequent meetings held in the open air, would have had a much more immediate impact upon the countryside and its inhabitants than the more august assemblage of important dignitaries which came together only twice a year for the meetings of the shire court. In the tenth century the concern of the hundred was largely with the apprehension of thieves and the recovery of stolen property, especially cattle. We have no reason for thinking that the farming people of this age were either more or less law-abiding than they had been at earlier times. The need for some small, local court for the adjustment of local disputes, and perhaps also for the local apportionment of taxation, would come into existence as soon as reasonably settled conditions were reached after the invasions, and it may well be that the hundred or something like it had already a long history before it figures in official documents.

The most powerful bond in this new society, whose being depended upon the security which had to be won and maintained by its own strength, and could not be bought for a price from others, was that which united lord and man in a close relationship which was neither national nor tribal but personal. It is this principle of personal allegiance which is the most dominant characteristic of early Anglo-Saxon society and which fulfilled for the smaller units of which it was composed some of the functions which in a society with more highly developed forms of government would have lain partly with the army and partly with judicial officers: Tacitus had been struck by the manner in which Germanic chieftains and their retainers were so closely united in bonds of loyalty that any who sought to win their own safety by withdrawing from battle after the death of their own chieftain would do so only at the cost of incurring lifelong reproach and infamy. The oath of allegiance which they had sworn to him required them not only to defend and protect him, but also to ascribe to him the glory won by their own exploits, as well as to continue fighting even after their chieftain himself had fallen.

At the time of which Tacitus was writing, the Roman occupation of Britain had scarcely yet begun, but these same principles were still forcefully at work in the Anglo-Saxon age, and even as late as the end of the tenth century the loyalty of a follower towards his lord was still regarded as among the greatest of virtues. It was a loyalty which looked for rich material rewards, although the tie went much deeper than the merely material, and if loyalty was the chief virtue of the retainer, generosity, perhaps even more than personal bravery, was the chief virtue of the lord. The joys and delights of those who were able to share in the fulfilment of these ideals, as well as the wretchedness and misery of those who, whether deservedly or through some unkind chance of fate, had become outcasts from the society of lord and man, are most vividly portrayed for us in works of poetry, especially in *Beowulf*.

Heorot, the great hall symbolising the prosperity of Hrothgar's reign, richly decked for banqueting with golden tapestries and other objects of splendour, was the setting wherein Hrothgar's faithful followers received gifts of treasure and arms as rewards for their services, and the setting also wherein they shared with their lord the long years of misery brought about by the attacks of the evil monster Grendel. When Beowulf went back home, after killing the monster, he surrendered to his own king, as custom demanded that he should, the rich gifts which the king of the Danes had given him as a reward for his exploits, but he then received in return from his own lord a great estate, a hall in which to live and a position of high rank in the country. The fate of a man who failed to stand by his lord in time of need finds expression in the bitter reproaches uttered by Wiglaf, Beowulf's young kinsman, against the cowardly traitors who deserted the aged Beowulf in his last and fatal fight. They would no longer be able to share in the receiving of treasure and all their joys would cease. When word of their infamy had spread to the nobles of other nations, they and all their families would be left to wander landless and destitute. Better for them if they had died with Beowulf, than to live such a life of dishonour.

The fate of the lordless, landless man also finds its most vivid expression in poetry, particularly in *The Wanderer* whose theme is of the transitory nature of merely human ties in a world where security is to be found only by those who put their trust in God. The joyous life which had once been shared with fellow-men has given way to the paths of exile wherein the dawning of each new day brings only sorrow. The exiled wanderer has none to whom he can turn for the joys of the feast, for rich reward or for good counsel. He lies down in sorrow to sleep and to dream of happier days when he gave faithful allegiance to the lord whose bounty he enjoyed and who now lies buried in the darkness of the earth. The faces of his dearly loved companions rise vividly before him, but as he gives them joyful greeting, they vanish at his awakening sight of the harsh, cold realities of life, the grey sea swept by winter storms, the falling snow and hail.

The Seafarer which tells of a man impelled by his restless spirit to set out on a voyage across the stormy waves, in the manner, as some would think, of those who felt themselves driven to go on a pilgrimage 'for the love of God', exchanged the laughter of men for the cry of the gannet, the joy of life in great halls for the lowering storm-driven winter's night. The sight of a tumbled Roman building, its roofs collapsed and its walls undermined by age, moved another poet to meditate upon the fate of those who had once shared in the now vanished splendour of its courts. Such poems, though perhaps primarily concerned with persuading men of the evanescent quality of the purely human, give us real insight into the age to which they belong. They take us away from hypocausts and mosaic floors to the world of human thoughts and emotions which, for all its wealth of material relics, Roman Britain remains stubbornly reluctant to disclose. And there is a sense in which they point the contrast between the two ages, the one given security under the yoke of the *pax Romana,* the other learning that the world gives security to none and that consolation must be sought elsewhere. These poetic expressions of the bond between lord and man, with the obligations of protection and reward on the one side, and of faithful service on the other, are very far from being merely literary conventions. So to interpret them would be to mistake the part played by minstrelsy and poetry in Germanic society. The theme is one which can be abundantly illustrated from historical sources.

The young Edwin, after being driven into exile by Æthelfrith, wandered for many years before he at length came to the court of Rædwald, king of East Anglia, whose protection he sought. When Æthelfrith learned where Edwin was he sought to bribe Rædwald to kill him, and although his efforts almost succeeded Edwin was saved by Rædwald's wife who shamed her husband into nobler conduct by reminding him of the dishonour which would mark a man who had taken gold in exchange for the life of a homeless refugee such as Edwin. And Edwin himself, when warned that his life was in danger and advised to seek safety in flight, refused to do so because he would thereby have broken the pact into which he had entered with Rædwald. On another occasion Edwin's life was saved by Lilla, one of his retainers, who, with no shield to protect him, thrust his own body between Edwin and the assassin's knife. While Edwin was reigning, it was the turn of the Bernician royal family to seek safety in exile, and many of the young Bernician nobility accompanied Oswald to his place of refuge among the peoples of the distant north. Oswine, king of Deira, is portrayed by Bede as a handsome man and tall of stature, courteous in his manner and generous to all whether of high or low degree. His royal qualities won for him the love of all, and men of the noblest birth came flocking to his service from all the neighbouring kingdoms. For seven years he reigned in peace and prosperity, loved and greatly honoured. Here are all the hallmarks of the ideal king of the Germanic heroic age, surrounded by his band of loyal fighting men. His story took a different twist when Oswiu, king of Bernicia made war upon him. Seeing that his forces were greatly outnumbered, Oswine thought it best to disband his army and await a more favourable time for engaging battle. Accompanied only by Tondheri, the most faithful of all his retainers, he took refuge in the house of Hunwold whom he also believed to be faithful to him, but Hunwold betrayed Oswine who together with the faithful Tondheri was murdered in a manner to be abominated by all men.

The betrayal of a king by a trusted companion was among the most detestable crimes known to Anglo-Saxon society.

Oswiu the instigator of this particular crime, sought to make atonement by founding a monastery upon the site, but the detail of Bede's narrative, even to the day of the week on which the crime was committed—20 August 651—is evidence enough that the story had been long remembered and often told. Scarcely less important than the bond between lord and man was the tie of kinship upon which the security of the individual very largely depended. The interaction of these two fundamental conventions of Anglo-Saxon society is illustrated in the instructive account of the death of a West Saxon king more than a hundred years later. The beginning of the story which found a permanent record by its inclusion in the *Anglo-Saxon Chronicle*, was in a West Saxon revolt led by Cynewulf against the unjust rule of Sigebert, the West Saxon king. Sigebert lost by the revolt the whole of his kingdom save for Hampshire whose ealdorman remained faithful to him, but in the end Sigebert killed the faithful ealdorman and was himself driven to seek refuge as an outcast in the Weald. He lived there for some time, but he was eventually hunted down and killed by a swineherd seeking to avenge the death of the faithful ealdorman. We hear little of individuals among the low orders of Anglo-Saxon society and it is therefore of interest to note that even a swineherd recognized the obligation of taking vengeance upon one who had killed his own lord.

The story then passes over some thirty years during which Cynewulf continued to rule the West Saxons, but at the end of that time a brother of the dead Sigebert, a man called Cyneheard, began to plot against Cynewulf's life. His opportunity came when he learned that the king was paying a visit to a mistress, accompanied only by a small band of his retainers, most of whom had been left behind elsewhere. In a surprise attack Cyneheard slew the king before his men were aware of what was happening. When the woman's cries raised the alarm, they ran hastily to the scene. Among the king's retainers were some of the kinsmen of Cyneheard's followers and Cynheard, after trying bribery, offered to let the kinsmen go free, but they refused, and although they were outnumbered and although their king was already dead, the king's men fought until every one of them had been killed, save only for a Welsh hostage, and even he had been wounded. On the next morning the main body of the king's retainers heard of what had happened and rode up to the scene to find that Cynheard and his rebels had barricaded themselves within the house. Again the same situation arose. Among the rebels inside were some of the kinsmen of those who were attacking the house from the outside. But those who were outside said that no kinsman of theirs was dearer to them than their lord and they would never take service with his slayer. They offered to let the kinsmen within go free, but those within refused and they fought until all within had been killed, save for one man who was a godson of one of those who were outside. In this instance the bond between lord and man had proved stronger than the ties of kinship when the two came into conflict with one another. And there is some reason for thinking that this may have become generally so, partly under the influence of the Church which had no quarrel with the bond of loyalty uniting lord and man, but which sought to replace the ancient duty of the kindred of a slain man to exact vengeance by a payment of money.

The security of a kingdom depended on the ability of its king to win his battles and overawe his neighbours, thereby ensuring payment of the tribute which would enable him to provide for his followers and his subjects the kind of life idealised in *Beowulf* and in Bede's account of the 'perfect peace' which marked the reign of Edwin. The security of the individual, on the other hand, rested very largely upon his position within a family upon whose help he could rely in time of need. There is no doubt that the ties of kinship were very strong throughout the Anglo-Saxon period, even though they might, as we have seen, be overridden by the bond between lord and man. In an age which had no institution comparable with a modern police force, and which was no longer subject to the rule of Roman law, fear of provoking the kindred into action could be an effective restraint upon crime, particularly upon the crime of homicide, but also upon lesser crimes against both property and the person of the individual. It was the bounden duty of the kindred to seek redress for any one of its members who had received insult or injury, and in the case of death to exact vengeance or compensation. This was not simply a matter of personal satisfaction but a binding convention which was recognised by all the Germanic peoples.

For a man to die by the hand of another and for his death to remain unatoned could be a cause of grief no less bitter than that experienced by the man who lost both lord and land. Again it is to *Beowulf*, and to what is perhaps the saddest passage in the whole poem, that we may turn for the poetic expression of this tragic situation. Towards the end of the poem, before setting out to slay the dragon by whom he was himself killed, Beowulf looks back over his past life. He recalls the joyful days he had spent as a young man at the court of king Hrethel, until the time came when the king's eldest son was accidentally killed by an arrow shot by one of his brothers. The bitterness of the tragedy was not that the king's eldest son had been killed, but that he had died a death for which there could be no atonement nor any vengeance taken, since this was homicide within the kindred for which there was no remedy. Hrethel's grief was likened by the poet to that of an old man who had to watch his son swinging on the gallows, an executed criminal for whom, too, no vengeance could be taken. Such a man could not but feel himself heartbroken by the desolation of the deserted hall which had once been his son's home. And so Hrethel himself, deprived of all means of consolation, withdrew from the society of men and died in lonely grief.

This episode, revealing a reaction wholly remote from such as would be aroused by a similar tragedy in modern times, illustrates two of the many legally sanctioned conventions which controlled the procedure of the kindred in a case of homicide. In the first place there could be no compensation for homicide within the kindred, since those to whom compensation was due and those by whom it must be paid were the same. Secondly there could be no compensation for a man who had died as a legally convicted criminal. Beyond this, the kindred could not seek vengeance or compensation until the accused man had been proved guilty. Further restraint forbade pursuit of the blood feud against anyone who had killed while fighting in defence of his lord, his man or his own kin against any who had made an unlawful attack, and also in certain other circumstances. The exact extent of the kindred in degrees of relationship is uncertain, though it is known that at least in the time of Alfred it included the family of both the father and the mother. All its members were liable to contribute towards the payment and also to share in the receipt of the wergild, the sum of money by which proper atonement could be made to the kindred for the death of one of its members and which could be honourably received by those to whom offence had been given.

The amount of an individual's wergild varied according to his rank in society, but it was a fixed sum established in law, not simply the largest sum which could be extracted. In early Kentish law what is called the ordinary wergild is placed at one hundred shillings. The wergild of a Kentish nobleman was three hundred shillings and there were lower orders, possibly including manumitted slaves or subject Britons whose wergilds were eighty, sixty or forty shillings. Kentish law prescribed that part of the wergild should be paid at the open grave and the remainder within forty days, also that if the slayer left the country the kinsmen were to pay half the wergild. Early West Saxon law recognised wergilds of two hundred shillings for the ceorl and twelve hundred for a nobleman, but these sums are not directly comparable with the Kentish wergilds, since they were reckoned in units of different value.

There was a wide variety of circumstances other than homicide in which payment of the wergild might be exacted for offences committed. West Saxon law provided that a thief caught in the act might escape from execution by the payment of his wergild and that those who harboured fugitives must pay the wergild appropriate to their rank if they could not clear themselves of the accusation by other means. A man who was accused of sharing in a hostile raid, in which more than thirty-five had taken part, was also to redeem himself by payment of his wergild or by other means. In all these different circumstances—plain homicide, theft, protecting fugitives from justice or making hostile raids—the liability of the criminal for payment of the wergild made the crime the concern of the kindred and not merely of the individual himself. There were also many less serious matters in which a man who was unable to look to his kin for support might find himself in a sorry state. The ordinary method by which a free man would clear himself of a charge that had been brought against him was by appearing in a court and taking an oath in which he was supported by an appropriate number of companions who would take a similar oath in his defence. The number of 'oath-helpers' required to rebut a particular accusation varied with the gravity of the offence with which the man was charged. But it was first and foremost to his kinsmen that a man so placed would turn for help.

(2) FARMERS AND TRADERS

The society depicted in Anglo-Saxon poetry, and to a lesser extent in the other written sources, is an aristocratic society of kings and noblemen, and although we do right to draw heavily upon this kind of evidence for an understanding of the social conventions of the Germanic Heroic Age, we can easily exaggerate the importance of the aristocratic element and so present an archaic picture of a society which was in fact undergoing rapid change. Ties of loyalty and kinship undoubtedly remained important, but once the days of invasion and settlement had passed, the gradual development of institutions of government brought into operation other forces whose end was the maintenance of order. Moreover a seventh-century churchman, archbishop Theodore, whose background was Mediterranean, though he might condone killing at the command of one's lord, imposed heavy penance upon a man who killed merely as an act of vengeance for a kinsman. We hear much in heroic poetry about the rich rewards expected and received by those who were the faithful followers of a prosperous king. The jewels discovered in the ship burial at Sutton Hoo show the kind of treasures which might belong to a seventh-century Anglo-Saxon ruler, and show also that the poet of *Beowulf* was not merely indulging his poetic fancies in his description in the opening lines of the poem of the splendid treasures which accompanied the dead Scyld on his voyage into the unknown. Yet for all this poetic emphasis on wealth, supported now both by the jewellery from Sutton Hoo and by the grandeur implicit in the royal halls at Old Yeavering, we may well suspect that this was more often the wealth for which men longed than the wealth which they possessed.

The collapse of the *pax Romana*, arising from the breakdown of the Roman imperial defences in the west, was followed by the collapse of the monetary system which had supported the economy of Roman Britain throughout the occupation, and herein we may recognise the second great contrast between the age of Roman Britain and the earlier part of the Anglo-Saxon period. Throughout the Roman occupation there had been an abundant supply of currency, some of it copper, most of it silver. Britain's own silver, won by extraction from her lead, was an important source of the raw material for silver coinage struck under the control of the imperial treasury, but the supply of silver from the British mines ceased shortly after 400, and the import of copper coins into Britain stopped at about the same time. Some of the output of the Gallic mints continued to reach Britain, but it is believed that by about 430 the circulation of coins had entirely ceased in Britain. The complete collapse of the currency system in a society which had lived by it for centuries could not but have had the most far-reaching consequences for the country as a whole. The kind of life which had been lived by the owners of the villas at Lullingstone, North Leigh and Woodchester, or by the citizens of Canterbury, Silchester and Cirencester was no longer possible, and we are perhaps right to think of the end of Romano-British town and villa life not so much in terms of the destruction of the sites by war, although this may have happened often enough at the villas, nor even in terms of physical abandonment, but rather in terms of economic collapse. Even apart from the lack of security which led men to hide in the earth such precious belongings as the great silver treasure found at Mildenhall, industry and trade could no longer be conducted as they had been when currency had been freely available for all the purposes of business. Yet not all parts of the country will have been equally affected. Town and villa life had never taken root in the north where the need for currency was primarily as a means of paying the soldiery and where native wealth could be reckoned by bushels of grain or head of cattle as well in Romano-British as in Anglo-Saxon times.

The Anglo-Saxon settler who was neither nobleman nor slave is the man known to us from the documents as the *ceorl*. The modern English 'churl' reflects fairly closely the pronunciation of the Old English word *ceorl*, but unfortunately 'churl' conveys an image of an ill-favoured surly fellow little better than the brutes placed in his care, and since this image is a false one, it seems better to keep the Old English spelling *ceorl*. Such men as these normally gained their living by farming. Two distinct kinds of evidence, the *-ingas* place-names and the pagan cemeteries, imply that they usually lived and worked not as individual farmers with none but their own immediate household about them, but in close association with numbers of others belonging to their own class of society. In origin many of the *-ingas* place-names imply a direct personal relationship with a particular individuals—such as Cooling in Kent, Godalming in Surrey, Reading in Berkshire, Blickling in Norfolk, and many more similarly formed names in which the first element is the name of an individual, presumably that of the founder of the settlement. The sense of other names of this general type is that of geographical association with reference to the inhabitants of a particular area—such as Epping and Nazeing in Essex, the former referring to men who lived on the 'upland' and the latter to those who lived on the 'ness'. Many of the *-ingas* names are compounded with *hām*, the element denoting a collection of individual dwellings which together constituted a village. This element, *hām*, though widely distributed, is commonest in the primary areas of Anglo-Saxon settlement, the south-eastern counties, the Thames valley and East Anglia.

The pagan cemeteries also point to settlements in village communities. The 500 cremation burials recovered from Lackford in Suffolk are believed to represent less than half the total number in that cemetery, and the cemetery at Loveden Hill in Lincolnshire seems to have been of comparable size. The cemetery at Caister-by-Norwich is reckoned to have contained between 700 and 1,000 burials ranging in date over about 250 years. The recorded burials, certainly no more than a fraction of the totals, from such cemeteries as Girton and Wilbraham in Cambridgeshire or Sarre and Kingston in Kent are in each case more than 200. These and many others of comparable size undoubtedly represent the burial grounds of village communities. The cemetery at Wilbraham in Cambridgeshire lay on open chalkland beside the Street Way and about half a mile from the modern village of Great Wilbraham to which the earliest documentary reference dates from *c.* 975. The remains of the houses inhabited by those who were later buried in the cemetery may be assumed to lie beneath the modern village, and if this is true of Great Wilbraham, it is likely to be no less true of scores of other villages which we may believe to have been inhabited without a break since pagan Saxon times. A slightly different kind of community seems to be implied by the cemetery at Finglesham in Kent. There were some 38 graves extending over about three generations from *c.* 550. Some of the graves, both of the men and the women, were very richly furnished with jewels and other objects. They may represent successive generations of a single family which had achieved prosperity and which had a number of workpeople in its employment. Cloth weaving was one of the sources of this family's wealth.

Apart from churches and the remains of some monastic communities, very little is known about Anglo-Saxon buildings. This is partly because the village houses probably lie beneath medieval and modern successors, and partly because wood, not stone, was the ordinary Anglo-Saxon building material. Before the ninth century, stone seems to have been used only for ecclesiastical buildings, and even then only on sites where nearby Roman buildings provided quarries of stone already cut to shape. It is only in exceptionally favourable circumstances that wooden buildings leave remains which are apparent on the surface and so invite excavation, yet, once discovered, the site of a wooden building can be made to disclose its history in considerable detail, as at Old Yeavering, the royal township where a Northumbrian palace lay in the seventh century. The place was dominated by an immense timber hall which was built in the early years of the century and was associated with a number of smaller halls set about it, one of them possibly used initially as a temple for pagan worship, and also with a large timber grandstand for assemblies held in the open air. During the occupation of the site which lasted for about three-quarters of a century, the great hall and its associated buildings were more than once destroyed by fire and more than once rebuilt with great technical skill. The royal palace at Old Yeavering, like the royal hall in *Beowulf*, called Heorot, represents the highest level of society, but in its essence it was only a more elaborate form of the kind of dwelling which seems to have been characteristic of north-western Europe for many centuries, the so-called longhouse, a rectangular wooden building varying greatly in its overall dimensions, but commonly being three or four times as long as it was wide. Houses of this kind have been found at several sites in the Saxon and Frisian areas of the North Sea coasts. The principal dwelling-houses of a Saxon village at Warendorf, near Münster in Westphalia, occupied *c.* 650 to 800, were large longhouses varying from 14 to 29 metres in length and 4·5 to 7 metres in width. In some cases the side walls of these houses were bowed outwards in the manner which can be seen in the houses within the Viking Age fortress at Trelleborg in Denmark. A small group of rectangular wooden buildings has been found at Maxey near Peterborough, the largest of them being approximately 16 metres long by 7 metres wide. They were constructed of timber, with wattle and daub, and were associated with circular pits which may have been used for storage. Other houses of timber construction have been found at St Neots in Huntingdonshire. The plan of the longhouse seems to be reflected in the long, narrow and lofty proportions which are characteristic of the nave of a number of Anglo-Saxon churches.

Village communities which lived by agriculture and stock farming would require a wide variety of buildings which could be used as barns, stables, byres and storehouses, as well as for the specialised trades of smith, carpenter, weaver and potter, but only the discovery of an Anglo-Saxon village which had already been abandoned before the Middle Ages, and its subsequent excavation could supply the evidence which is at present lacking. Such a site might be expected to give valuable information about the agricultural practices of the earliest Anglo-Saxon settlers, but for the present there is no counterpart in the Anglo-Saxon period to the Iron Age farm at Little Woodbury. We know that barley, oats, wheat, flax and woad were among the crops cultivated in the Cambridge region, and it is probable that of the cereal crops barley was the most important, since it was used by the brewer as well as the baker. No Anglo-Saxon plough has yet been discovered, nor is there any written evidence about it in the centuries before the Danish invasions. There is no positive evidence that the settlers brought with them either implements or better agricultural practices than had already been familiar in Britain for some centuries, but we may surmise that the insecurity of the age, as well as the lack of capital, would tend towards a greater degree of communal practice than is implicit in the villa economy of Roman Britain. Undoubtedly the life of the Anglo-Saxon ceorl was one of arduous and continuing effort to secure a livelihood for himself and his family. Over the centuries the farmers gradually spread from the more easily worked soils and from the alluvial tracts along the river banks where many of the earliest settlements had been made, moving on to the heavier clays and clearing scrub and forest to bring new fields into cultivation. This was a long and slow process mainly unrecorded in its detail and visible only when we compare a map of habitation sites at the time of Domesday with those known in the same area five centuries earlier. At Old Windsor the remains of a large water-mill, with three vertical wheels in parallel and driven by water drawn from the Thames along a leet 20 feet wide, are evidence of increasing yields of grain in the ninth century as fresh arable was won from what had formerly been forest land, possibly in this instance under royal direction.

It seems unlikely that we shall ever be able to recover enough evidence to disclose the fortunes of the towns of Roman Britain during the fifth and sixth centuries. The few sites which are still accessible to excavation can scarcely be regarded as typical, because their very accessibility now is an indication of failure within or soon after the Roman period. Those in which some continuity of life seems most probable on general grounds are for that very reason inaccessible now, at least on a sufficiently large scale. Even though the problem cannot be advanced beyond conjecture, there are some general points which are beyond dispute. No-one will claim that the later English borough in its administrative and judicial aspects owes anything to a heritage bequeathed from Romano-British times. The constitution of *colonia, civitas* and *vicus* vanished completely after the withdrawal from Britain of the whole machinery of Roman civilian administration. It is equally certain that, although there is evidence of some new building at St Albans in the fifth century, the investment of capital in towns on a scale such as had been seen during the Roman occupation had no parallel in the Anglo-Saxon period. Even the comparatively modest reorganisation of urban defences which seems to have taken place in the fourth century required capital resources and technical skills which lay beyond the experience of the Anglo-Saxons.

If by town life we mean the kind of life which could have been experienced at about the middle of the second century by a citizen of Canterbury, St Albans, Silchester or Cirencester, then we can only conclude that the town life of Roman Britain was completely destroyed by the Anglo-Saxon invasion. But this is not to say either that all the towns were destroyed or that they were deserted, becoming places such as may have inspired the poet who composed the work which we now call *The Ruin* to meditate on the transitory nature of human prosperity. The conditions prevailing over much of Britain during the fifth and sixth centuries are more likely to have encouraged those who could to live in the old towns where the company of men and stone walls would have given a far better protection than the open countryside. Some of the British of Kent after being defeated by Hengest fled to London, and surely London's walls offered them greater security than, for example, the villa at Lullingstone.

Enough archaeological evidence has now come to light in Canterbury to show that the city was never without inhabitants between the departure of the Romans, if the phrase may be used, and the arrival of Augustine, and if there was this degree of continuity in such an exposed area, we should hardly expect to find less in areas more remote from the invaders. Recalling what we know of the appearance of Gloucester, Cirencester and Bath, as they existed in the fourth century, it is difficult to imagine them as nothing but empty and decaying ruins at the time when they passed into Anglo-Saxon hands after the battle at Dyrham in 571. Some continuity seems more likely at such sites as these, as also at Carlisle whose Roman walls and fountain were shown to Cuthbert when he visited the place in 685. There are other places, such as Lincoln, York, Caister-by-Norwich and Great Chesterford at which early Anglo-Saxon cemeteries have been found in what seem to be significant relationship to the Roman sites. Three of the the Saxon Shore forts—Reculver, Bradwell-on-Sea and Burgh Castle—were the scenes of Christian activities in the seventh century.

Two factors tended towards the growth of a life in towns which was something different from the merely static or decadent continuation of that of the old Romano-British towns. The arrival of Christian missionaries brought back to Britain at least some men who were familiar with the city life of the Mediterranean countries, and with the development of a diocesan organisation some of the old Roman centres were chosen as seats for the newly created bishoprics. Episcopal sees were established in Canterbury, Rochester, London, Winchester, Dorchester-on-Thames and York in the seventh century. But more important than this was the revival of trade with the return of more stable conditions, and particularly of maritime trade. London had become one of the main ports for shipping to the Continent in the time of Bede who describes it as the market of many nations coming to it by sea and land. It was here that Boniface embarked when he set sail for the Rhine in 716. London, Canterbury and Rochester which were well placed to benefit from North Sea and cross-Channel trade provide the earliest evidence of an Anglo-Saxon town life which was in active growth. Another important route went from the Solent to the mouth of the Seine. On the right bank of the

Itchen, lying between the Romano-British *Clausentum* and medieval Southampton, was the river settlement of *Hamwih* whose inhabitants traded with Rouen. On the east coast, in addition to London, ports at Ipswich and Caister-by-Yarmouth served to link East Anglia with the Rhine and other parts of north-western Germany and the Low Countries. But away from these coastal areas, towns did not play a prominent part in the life of Anglo-Saxon England before the times of the Danish invasions. The real stimulus to fresh growth came with the building of fortified centres first in southern England, during the reign of Alfred the Great, and later in the Danelaw as well as in English Mercia, but this development belonged to the second half of the ninth century and to the tenth century.

No coins of Anglo-Saxon manufacture were found at Sutton Hoo and this is one of several arguments which have led to the view that, despite the circulation of limited quantities of foreign currency in England in the seventh century, no Anglo-Saxon coins were struck before *c.* 675, though others have dated the earliest Anglo-Saxon coins almost a century earlier. The first Anglo-Saxon coins were struck in gold, some of them copies of Merovingian types and some of them derived from Roman imperial types which had been in circulation in the third and fourth centuries. The gold coinage had a short life and there was a rapid change to the rather thick silver coins called *sceattas* which were circulating in considerable number by the end of the seventh century. With rare exceptions, the *sceattas*, which show great variety of design, were anonymous, having upon them the name of neither king nor moneyer, as if to suggest that coinage was not yet regarded as a royal prerogative, but merely as a means of facilitating growing trade. Near the end of the eighth century, following upon a reform of the coinage in Gaul, the *sceattas* were displaced by new silver pennies which bore upon them the name both of the king by whose authority they were issued and of the moneyer by whom they were struck. This great reform, symptomatic of reviving wealth, took place in Kent *c.* 775. About ten years later, when the kingdom of Kent came to be dominated by Mercia, Offa took the Canterbury mint under his own control and caused his name to be placed on the obverse of coins struck by moneyers, some of whom had been working previously for Kentish kings. Shortly afterwards the design of the coins was radically altered, and after some further variations, the new silver penny conformed to a pattern which continued in use without further fundamental change throughout the Anglo-Saxon period. The obverse of the coin bore the king's name and usually, though not invariably, the king's bust, and on the reverse was the moneyer's name. Offa's coinage which is distinguished both for its high artistic merit and for the excellence of its quality, came into general circulation, superseding the old *sceattas* everywhere save in Northumbria where the older type continued in use, but gradually degenerated into copper.

The high quality of Offa's coinage is the best evidence for the return of a considerable degree of wealth to Britain before the end of the eighth century, but long before Offa's reign some of the new Anglo-Saxon communities had passed beyond the stage at which they could do no more than meet their own immediate needs. In the sixth and seventh centuries goods of different kinds were being imported into England, not merely as the personal belongings of migrants but as objects of trade, from Sweden, Denmark, the Rhineland and Gaul, as well as from much more distant lands. This was an age in which the North Sea and the Channel were not the barriers which they later became with the growth of nationalism, but the bonds which united those who lived on their opposing shores in a manner which allowed men and goods to cross from side to side with a freedom which sometimes seems surprising in the present age of artificial boundaries.

Anglo-Saxon pottery is known to us principally from the cinerary urns in which were placed the ashes of those who had been cremated after death. There is some evidence that in the sixth century these urns were being made by professional potters whose products became fairly widespread in the east midlands, but it is likely that ordinary domestic needs were met by individual households. All of this pottery, whether intended for domestic or funeral purposes, was hand-made, coarse in its execution, unshapely in its design and ugly in its ornament. Wheel-thrown pottery of a better quality was imported into Kent from the Rhineland where the techniques of pottery manufacture had descended without a break from late Roman times. A small quantity of wheel-thrown pottery was also imported into East Anglia and came later to be manufactured at Ipswich where the techniques employed were those of the Rhineland. Outside Kent and East Anglia the old tradition of hand-made pottery survived even into late Saxon times. In the eighth century and later, Rhineland pottery was imported in increasingly large quantities, some of it in the form of large amphorae in which Rhenish wine was being carried in the ninth century to Canterbury, London, Ipswich, Southampton and as far down the Channel as Jersey. Duurestede at the mouth of the Rhine, and Quentovic, on the Channel coast, were the main ports from which these Rhineland goods were shipped to England. Wine was also coming to Southampton from Rouen. Far away in the south-west wheel-made pottery manufactured in the Mediterranean was coming direct by sea in the fifth and sixth centuries to Cornwall, south Wales and southern Ireland, probably serving as carriers for Mediterranean wine and oil which were used partly for the table and partly to meet liturgical needs. It is possible that these imports should be associated with a continuing export trade in Cornish tin.

Glass was a rare and costly item which is likely to have been found only on the tables of the rich, and even then seldom outside Kent and the adjacent parts of south-eastern England. Although it is possible that some glass may have been manufactured at Faversham in Kent, the Anglo-Saxons as a whole had no knowledge of glass making, and supplies had to be imported from the various continental centres of production which were scattered westwards from the Rhine as far as the Somme. Since this imported glass is known to us now almost entirely from interments, we know very little about its use by the Anglo-Saxons in the days when the practice of burying goods with the dead had ceased, but even as late as 756 an abbot of Monkwearmouth wrote to the archbishop of Mainz asking him to send a good glass-maker since the English themselves had no skill in the art. Among other imports to reach England from the Rhineland were the millstones brought from the lava field near Mayen in the Eifel.

Although we have little detailed knowledge about iron mining in Anglo-Saxon England, there is no doubt that the metal was in widespread use not merely for weapons of war but also for common farm implements. An iron spearhead is frequently found in graves which seem not to be those of men in any way distinguished for their wealth, and iron swords and shield bosses are by no means rare. The more elaborately fashioned swords, sometimes with blades manufactured in the technique known as pattern welding which produced an iridescent surface on a polished blade, and with richly decorated hilts, the ornamental helmets and coats of mail were expensive items which belonged only to the aristocracy. The Anglo-Saxons themselves were probably not so skilled in the manufacture of sword blades as the swordsmiths of the Rhineland, but they were unrivalled in their decorative metalwork, using gold, silver and bronze to produce ornaments which at their best may stand comparison with the finest jewellery of any age and which even at their worst show great technical skill. The Derbyshire lead mines were certainly being worked in the ninth century as we know from documentary evidence, but we do not know whether the Anglo-Saxons were able to extract silver from the lead, as had been done in Roman Britain, or whether loot was the main source of their supply of silver, as it almost certainly was of their gold. India is believed to have been the ultimate source of the cut and polished garnets of which large numbers were used for brooch settings in cloisons, that is to say in small cells of metal, usually gold, somewhat resembling the wax cells made by bees as containers for their honey. It is in the skilful and variegated shaping of these cloisons, in the use of twisted or plaited gold wire and in the inlaying of bronze with patterns of silver wire, that the Anglo-Saxon jewellers showed their greatest skill. Most of the gold and garnet jewellery has been found in Kent, but the East Anglian kings employed jewellers some of whose products surpassed even the finest of the Kentish jewellery, and the surviving fragments of metal ornaments from book covers found at Whitby suggest that the case which Wilfrid had made for his Ripon Gospels, and the jewelled cover which was made for the Lindisfarne Gospels were not inferior either in technique or in artistry to the Sutton Hoo and Kentish jewellery.

We have no reason for thinking that the treasures of gold, silver and precious stones with which Acca's church at Hexham was adorned were not of native manufacture, even though some of the raw materials may have come from distant sources. Some graves of the pagan period have yielded bronze vessels of Coptic manufacture, Indian cowry shells and amethyst beads. African goatskin was used for the binding of the Stonyhurst Gospel, and the artists of Lindisfarne extracted their purple from *folium*, then a Mediterranean plant, and their blue from crushed *lapis lazuli* whose nearest source was India. Benedict Biscop brought back from Rome, in addition to books and pictures, two silk cloaks which he gave to Aldfrith in exchange for three hides of land. The coffin to which the relics of St Cuthbert were translated in 698 contained a richly figured silk of eastern Mediterranean origin. These, however, were articles of luxury which no doubt reached the country only in small quantities, some of them perhaps coming as gifts rather than as articles of trade.

Objects imported into England from the fifth to the ninth centuries show remarkable variety in their nature as well as in their places of origin. We have much less information about exports in this period, although there is some evidence for an export trade in two commodities, slaves and cloth. St Patrick wrote from Ireland in the fifth century rebuking a British king whose soldiers carried off prisoners from Ireland with the intention of selling them in the foreign slave markets. English boys were being sold as slaves in Gaul in the sixth century, and according to a tradition recorded by Bede there were English slaves to be bought in the slave market in Rome at about the same date. In the seventh century a Northumbrian prisoner of war was sold to a Frisian merchant in London. Seventh-century Kentish law allowed a freeman caught in the act of theft to be sold as a slave overseas, although this practice was forbidden by Ine in Wessex. It is certain that slave labour was widely employed in England itself and these scattered documentary references suggest that the number sold overseas may have been considerable.

Clothing, no less a necessity of life than food and shelter, is likely to have been produced by individual households to meet their own needs, although there may have been some specialisation at an early date in village communities, such as that at Sutton Courtenay in Berkshire where the weaving huts were set apart from the ordinary living-quarters. Spindle whorls and loom weights are common objects of Anglo-Saxon sites of the pagan period. Textile remains, or the impressions made by textiles on other objects with which they had lain in close contact for centuries, have been found in a number of Anglo-Saxon graves. Flax was certainly being grown and woven into linen in the pagan period. Fragments of broken-diamond twills in linen have been found in Cambridgeshire at Barrington, in Suffolk at Sutton Hoo and in Kent at Finglesham. Other sites, including Sutton Hoo, have yielded broken-diamond twills in wool. Tablet-woven braids have been found both as separate bands and as the border of a twill cloth. Although the total number of finds is not large, the cloth itself is evidence that Anglo-Saxon women were highly skilled in the art of weaving in the pagan period. A small number of richly furnished women's graves have yielded iron 'weaving swords' used as beaters for cloth. These objects, which were normally made of wood, are rare and may perhaps reflect the source of the wealth which is made evident by the richness of the accompanying grave-goods. It was regarded as a mark of particular sanctity in Æthelthryth, wife of Ecgfrith king of Northumbria and foundress of the monastery at Ely, that after she became a nun she never wore linen but only woollen garments. Extravagance in dress, not only among the aristocracy but also among the common people was, in Alcuin's beliefs, one of the sins which called forth the divine wrath manifested in the sack of Lindisfarne by the Vikings in 793. Evidence that at least some English cloth was being sent abroad in the eighth century is contained in a letter which Charlemagne wrote to Offa in 796. There had previously been a quarrel between the two kings as a result of which Charlemagne closed his ports to English merchants, an action indicating that in normal conditions there was a regular trade between the two countries. When negotiations were reopened, each of the two rulers agreed that traders would have formal protection by public authority when visiting the country of the other. Charlemagne had taken note of an earlier request by Offa that the 'black stones', possibly Tournai stone used for the making of fonts, which he had promised him, should be cut to the right length, and in his turn he forwarded to Offa a complaint that his people were not satisfied with the *sagae* that were being sent from England and would he see that they were of the same length as had been customary in former times. It is not clear whether the *sagae* were simply woven lengths of woollen cloth, such as those to which Tacitus refers in connection with the *Germani*, or manufactured cloaks, but the trade was evidently an established one and Charlemagne seemed to think that Offa was able to exercise some control over it.

*

A medieval doctrine, known in England in the days of Alfred the Great, taught that there were three orders of men—those who fought, those who worked and those who prayed. Such doctrine belongs rather to the world of book learning than to the realities of a society in which kings and noblemen might give up the profession of arms for that of monastic vows, and in which ceorls might so prosper that they were enabled to enter into the ranks of the nobility. An Anglo-Saxon poet perceived that God in His divine wisdom had so distributed an infinite number of gifts among men that none might be brought to his downfall by excessive pride in his own endowments. Some were blest with physical strength, some with skill in determining the customs of the people in a gathering of councillors. Some knew how to secure a lofty building against sudden fall, some were skilled workers in gold and jewels, and some could make weapons for the use of men. Some were clever horsemen, some pious and generous in the giving of alms, and some witty in their cups. And some were men of learning, versed in books and deft of hand in writing mysteries of words.

Those who fought did so because bravery was a virtue in itself, and because victory in battle was the foundation upon which the household of kings and noblemen rested while society still lived in a Heroic Age. Their motives as well as their methods were very different from those of the diversity of Spaniards, Syrians, Gauls, Rhinelanders and Frisians who maintained the *pax Romana* in Britain, fighting for a soldier's pay in ultimate obedience to an emperor who lived in far-off Rome. When Anglo-Saxon England moved out of the kind of Heroic Age which is characterised by warfare, into a more settled state, the country was largely defenceless against any attack which might come from abroad, and at the time of Alfred's birth it was at the beginning of an age no less violent than that which had brought Roman Britain to an end. During the interval between these two ages of invasion—the Anglo-Saxon and the Viking—those who worked had recovered at least some of the wealth and prosperity lost to Britain with the collapse of Roman trade and industry, and of the monetary system upon which they rested. Offa's coins minted at Canterbury were both more beautiful and of better quality than the money in circulation in Britain during the fourth century. Even so, Alfred's England had none of the capital resources which were at the command of those who had ordered the affairs of Roman Britain. Yet, for all its security and for all its material wealth, Roman Britain remained a small part of a great Empire, an occupied country subject to foreign rule, important as a frontier province and exploited for its mineral and other kinds of wealth. It made no original contribution in spiritual or intellectual matters to the Empire to which it belonged. Although Roman roads remain today as the most strikingly visible legacy of four centuries of occupation, there is substance in the claim that the most precious legacy of Roman Britain to posterity was the Christian faith. The first seeds were sown in Roman times, but the first harvest was not gathered until a later age. It was the achievement of the third order of men—those who prayed, the clergy and the monks—to create in Anglo-Saxon England a civilisation richly active in a kind of growth which found no counterpart under the sterile transience of Roman rule in Britain.

We cannot explain that sudden burgeoning of the spirit which gave to men and women, whose recent forefathers can only be called barbarians, an understanding of intellectual and spiritual values which at once carried them to heights of achievement such as had never been reached during the Roman occupation. 'No man,' wrote King Alfred, translating the *De Consolatione Philosophiae* of Boethius, 'can bring forth any craft without wisdom, for whatever is done in folly cannot be accounted as a craft.' It was a combination of wisdom and good fortune that brought to England in 669 the Greek monk Theodore, who was to govern the English Church for the next twenty-one years. He was accompanied on his journey to England by Hadrian, an African born and abbot of a monastery near Naples, and by Benedict Biscop, a Northumbrian nobleman who is remembered as the founder of the monasteries at Monkwearmouth and Jarrow. This is how Bede described the age of Theodore:

> And soon he travelled over the whole island, wherever the peoples of the English dwelt, for he was most willingly received by them all and also heard, and, everywhere accompanied and assisted by Hadrian, he spread the right rule of life and the canonical custom of celebrating Easter. And this was the first of the archbishops whom the whole Church of the English agreed to obey. And because, as we have said, they both were amply instructed in sacred as well as secular literature, they gathered a crowd of disciples, and rivers of wholesome knowledge daily flowed to water the

hearts of their hearers; and, together with the books of the sacred writings, they delivered to them also the knowledge of the metrical art, of astronomy, and of ecclesiastical computation. It is a testimony of this that until today some of their disciples are still living who know the Latin and Greek languages even as their own, in which they were born. And certainly there were never happier times since the English sought Britain; for, having very powerful and Christian kings, they were a terror to all barbarous nations, and the desires of all were bent on the joys of the heavenly kingdom of which they had recently heard, and whoever wished to be instructed in sacred studies had matters at hand to teach them.

There had already been a school at Canterbury before the arrival of Theodore. It was the source whence Sigebert secured teachers for the school which he established after his conversion in his own kingdom of East Anglia. But this was a new kind of school whose teaching was based on the ancient learning of the Greco-Roman world, and it quickly attracted scholars in large numbers, many of them Irish. Its most famous pupil, Aldhelm of Malmesbury, likened the Irish scholars who went to hear Theodore to a pack of Molossian hounds surrounding a fierce boar. They sought to bite him with the sharp tooth of grammatical inquiry, but the old boar was more than a match for his assailants, and he drove back the attacking host so that they had to seek refuge in dark caves. The teaching at Canterbury was based on the seven liberal arts—the *trivium* of grammar, rhetoric and dialectic, and the *quadrivium* of arithmetic, geometry, astronomy and music—but the expounding of Holy Scripture lay at the heart of all teaching, and to this end both Greek and Latin grammar were studied. Even at this early date Irish men of letters and learning held that mastery of vocabulary which they have ever since retained, and the new learning taught at Canterbury gave them fresh opportunities for adding more strange and bizarre words to that kind of 'western speech' which is called *Hisperica Famina.*

Through the influence of its pupils the Canterbury school was able to bring about a synthesis of Greco-Roman and Celtic scholarship which, with the intermingling of a third element, the Anglo-Saxon, created that full flowering of intellectual and artistic life which distinguishes the age of Bede as one of the great creative ages of European history. Aldhelm, the most learned of Canterbury's pupils, had received his early schooling under Irish discipline at Malmesbury, the foundation of the Irish scholar Maildubh. He returned to Wessex to become abbot of Malmesbury, and later the first holder of a new bishopric at Sherborne in Dorset. For more than twenty years he maintained a close friendship with Aldfrith, king of Northumbria, who had passed a time of exile among the Irish where his reputation for learning and scholarship later achieved legendary fame. Another of the pupils of Theodore and Hadrian at Canterbury was Albinus, abbot of St Augustine's monastery and the man at whose instigation Bede wrote his *Ecclesiastical History of the English Nation*. The books wherein Bede acquired the learning which entitles him to a place among the great scholars of the Middle Ages, were gathered into the libraries at Monkwearmouth and Jarrow by Benedict Biscop, himself not only the founder of the two monasteries, but also Theodore's travelling companion on his journey from Rome to Canterbury, and for two years abbot in Canterbury before returning to his native Northumbria. The Anglo-Saxon contribution to this civilisation was not merely that there were many men and women among them apt and ready to learn when an opportunity was given to them. Their skill in producing intricate patterns and designs in metal or upon vellum was matched by a like skill in manipulating words. The Anglo-Saxons shared the common Germanic love of minstrelsy, an art which already had long traditions behind it when the Roman legions first invaded Britain. The ancient skills were put to the service of the new teaching. Hild's monastery at Whitby, where several bishops received their early education, was one centre at which religious poetry was composed as the vehicle for conveying to the illiterate the stories told in the Old and in the New Testaments. And beside Bede, whether of his own immediate age or not, must stand the unknown author of *Beowulf* whose poem conveyed in the ancient idiom the new doctrine that, in the ceaseless struggle between good and evil, men were not dependent on themselves alone.

APPENDIX A

TABLE OF DATES

55 B.C.	Caesar's first invasion of Britain
c. A.D. 10–41	Cunobelinus ruling over much of south-eastern Britain
A.D. 43	Roman invasion under Aulus Plautius
49	Foundation of the *colonia* at Colchester
60	Rebellion of the Iceni under Boudicca
78	Agricola reaches Britain
84	Agricola's victory at *Mons Graupius*
c. 122–33	Building of Hadrianic frontier
c. 143	Building of Antonine frontier
196–7	Clodius Albinus defeated and killed in Gaul. Hadrianic frontier overthrown
208–11	Severus in Britain; dies at York, 211
287–93	Carausius ruling in Britain
296	Allectus defeated by Constantius Chlorus. Hadrianic frontier overthrown for second time; restored by Constantius Chlorus
367–70	Assault on Britain by Picts, Scots and Saxons. Hadrianic frontier overthrown for third time; restored by Theodosius
383	Magnus Maximus seizes western empire
388	Magnus Maximus killed
410	Honorius writes to the *civitates* of Britain
411	Constantine III killed
c. 425–55	Reign of Vortigern
429	Visit of Germanus to Britain
c. 453	Settlement of Hengest in Kent
c. 455	Saxon rebellion against the British
c. 460–80	Age of Ambrosius Aurelianus
c. 477	Landing of Ælle near Selsey Bill
c. 490	Battle at *Mons Badonicus*
c. 491	South Saxons capture Pevensey
c. 552	West Saxons capture Old Sarum
c. 556	West Saxon victory at Barbury Castle near Swindon
c. 571	Saxons capture Benson, Eynsham, Aylesbury and Limbury
c. 577	West Saxons capture Bath, Gloucester and Cirencester
c. 590	Northumbrian victory over the British at Catterick
597	Augustine converts Æthelbert of Kent
603	Æthelfrith, king of Northumbria, defeats Aedan, king of Scots, at *Degsastan*

627	Paulinus converts Edwin of Northumbria
635	Mission of Aidan to Lindisfarne
663	Synod of Whitby. [Some authorities prefer 664]
669	Theodore reaches Canterbury
672	Council of Hertford
687	Death of Cuthbert (born *c.* 634)
709	Death of Wilfrid (born *c.* 634)
716	Accession of Æthelbald in Mercia
735	Death of Bede (born *c.* 671)
757	Accession of Offa in Mercia
793	Lindisfarne attacked by Vikings
796	Death of Offa
802	Accession of Egbert to Wessex
825	Mercians defeated by Egbert at Wroughton
829	Mercia conquered by Egbert to whom the Northumbrians also submit
839	Death of Egbert of Wessex
851	Vikings winter in Thanet and attack London and Canterbury
865	Great Danish army lands in East Anglia
866–7	Danes attack Northumbria
867–8	Danes move into Mercia
869	Martyrdom of Edmund, king of East Anglia
871	Danes defeated at Ashdown. Accession of Alfred (April)

The Bretwaldas

The title is first used in a ninth-century annal in the *Anglo-Saxon Chronicle* where it is applied to eight kings of whom the first seven are also mentioned by Bede as rulers enjoying a position of particular distinction.

c. 477–91	Ælle, king of the South Saxons
c. 560–93	Ceawlin, king of the West Saxons
c. 560–616	Æthelbert, king of Kent
c. 590–620	Rædwald, king of East Anglia. [Dates very uncertain]
c. 616–32	Edwin, king of Northumbria
633–41	Oswald, king of Northumbria
641–70	Oswiu, king of Northumbria
802–39	The eighth king called Bretwalda by the *Anglo-Saxon Chronicle* is Egbert, king of the West Saxons

But a similar supremacy was exercised by two Mercian kings in the eighth century:

716–57	Æthelbald
757–96	Offa

APPENDIX B

PASSAGES IN OLD ENGLISH

The two prose passages which follow are taken from the A text of the *Anglo-Saxon Chronicle*. They describe the arrival of the great Danish army of invasion and its first campaign against Northumbria. The landing itself was in the autumn of 865 and the entry into York on 1 November 866. The verse passage is from *Beowulf*, ll. 32–52. It describes the burial of the mythical Scyld and should be read in conjunction with the account given above, p. 39, of the Sutton Hoo ship-burial.

(i)

[866] Her feng Æþered Æþelbryhtes broþur to Wesseaxna rice; ond þy ilcan geare cuom micel here on Angelcynnes lond, ond wintersetl namon on East Englum, ond þær gehorsude wurdon, ond hie him friþ wiþ namon.
[866] In this year Æthelbert's brother Æthelred succeeded to the kingdom of the West Saxons. And in the same year a great heathen army came into the land of the English and took winter quarters in East Anglia; and they were provided with horses there and the men of East Anglia made peace with them.

(ii)

[867] Her for se here of East Englum ofer Humbre muþan to Eoforwicceastre on Norþhymbre, ond þær wæs micel unþuærnes þære þeode betweox him selfum, ond hie hæfdun hiera cyning aworpenne Osbryht, ond ungecyndne cyning underfengon Ællan; ond hie late on geare to þam gecirdon þæt hie wiþ þone here winnende wærun, ond hie þeah micle fierd gegadroden, ond þone here sohton æt Eoforwicceastre, ond on þa ceastre bræcon, ond hie sume inne wurdon, ond þær wæs ungemetlic wæl geslægen Norþanhymbre, sume binnan, sume butan; ond þa cyningas begen ofslægene, ond sio laf wiþ þone here friþ nam.
[867] In this year the heathen army went from East Anglia over the mouth of the Humber to the city of York in Northumbria. And there was great dissension of the people among themselves, and they had repudiated their king Osbert and taken a king Ælla who was not of the royal race; and it was not until late in the year that they were sufficiently united to make war against the heathen army. Nevertheless they gathered a great army together and attacked the heathen army in York and broke into the city. Some of them got inside and there was an immense slaughter of the Northumbrians, some inside and some outside. Both the kings were killed and the remnant made peace with the heathen army.

(iii)

Þær æt hyðe stod hringedstefna
isig ond utfus, æþelinges fær;
aledon þa leofne þeoden,
beaga bryttan on bearm scipes,
mærne be mæste. Þær wæs madma fela
of feorwegum frætwa gelæded;
ne hyrde ic cymlicor ceol gegyrwan
hildewæpnum ond heaðowædum,
billum ond byrnum; him on bearme læg
madma mænigo, þa him mid scoldon
on flodes æht feor gewitan.
Nalæs hi hine læssan lacum teodan,
þeodgestreonum, þon þa dydon,
þe hine æt frumsceafte forð onsendon
ænne ofer yðe umborwesende.
Þa gyt hie him asetton segen g[yl]denne
heah ofer heafod, leton holm beran
geafon on garsecg; him wæs geomor sefa,
murnende mod. Men ne cunnon
secgan to soðe, selerædende,
hæleð under heofenum, hwa þæm hlæste onfeng.

The prince's ship with its curved prow lay there at the staithe, rime-crusted and ready to start. They laid down their beloved prince and giver of treasure in the bosom of the ship, a hero beside the mast; many treasures and precious things from distant lands had been brought there. I have not heard of a ship better furnished with weapons of war and raiment of battle, with swords and byrnies. Upon his bosom lay a host of treasures that were to travel far away with him into ocean's power. They adorned him with no lesser gifts, treasures of the people, than did those who in the beginning sent him forth alone across the waves while he was still a child. They set besides a golden standard high above his head; they let the sea carry him, a gift unto the ocean. Their hearts were sorrowful and mournful were their spirits. No men, whether counsellors in the hall or heroes beneath the heavens, can truly say who received that load.

BOOKS FOR FURTHER READING

Maps

Ancient Britain (Ordnance Survey North and South Sheets, Chessington 1951), a map of the major visible antiquities of Britain prior to 1066
Map of Roman Britain (3rd ed., Ordnance Survey, Chessington 1956)
Map of Britain in the Dark Ages (Ordnance Survey 1966)

Roman Britain

During the last thirty years excavation and aerial photography have won a great deal of new evidence about almost every aspect of Romano-British life. The results achieved by such work are usually reported either in national journals such as the *Journal of Roman Studies*, the *Antiquaries Journal* and the *Archaeological Journal*, or in one of the many volumes published by local archaeological and antiquarian societies. The *Journal of Roman Studies* contains a year-by-year summary of excavations and chance finds in Britain, but in general the reader must learn to find his own way to detailed information about the areas and topics which interest him. Anyone in need of help, advice or information on archaeological matters, whether of the Romano-British or any other period, may find his needs met by inquiry directed to the secretary of his local antiquarian society or to the Council for British Archaeology, 8 St Andrews Place, London NW1 4LB. When reading general works on Roman Britain it is of particular importance to note the date at which they were written, since the rate of progress in recent years has been such that a general book is likely to be out of date on some major matters within two or three years of publication. It is for this reason that the following list of works relating to Roman Britain is arranged in chronological order of publication.

D. R. Dudley and G. Webster, *The Rebellion of Boudicca* (1962)
E. Birley, *Research on Hadrian's Wall* (1961)
A. L. F. Rivet, *Town and Country in Roman Britain* (Hutchinson University Library, 1958). This book has a detailed bibliography arranged in relation to the Romano-British cantons.
I. A. Richmond (ed.), *Roman and Native in North Britain* (1958)
I. D. Margary, *Roman Roads in Britain* (2 vols., 1955 and 1957)
G. C. Boon, *Roman Silchester* (1957)
I. A. Richmond, *Roman Britain* (Pelican History of England, 1955)

This book has a detailed biblography arranged chapter by chapter.
J. Liversidge, *Furniture in Roman Britain* (1955)
V. E. Nash-Williams, *The Roman Frontier in Wales* (1954)
A. R. Burn, *Agricola and Roman Britain* (Teach Yourself History Series, 1953)
E. Birley, *Roman Britain and the Roman Army* (1953)
Guide to the Antiquities of Roman Britain (British Museum, 1951)
O. G. S. Crawford, *Topography of Roman Scotland North of the Antonine Wall* (1949)
G. Home, *Roman London* (2nd ed., 1948)
I. A. Richmond, *Roman Britain* (Britain in Pictures Series, 1947)
J. Collingwood Bruce, *Handbook to the Roman Wall* (10th ed., 1947)
R. W. Moore, *The Romans in Britain* (1938). This book contains a selection of Latin texts, and translations of some Greek ones, relating to the Romans in Britain.
R. G. Collingwood and J. N. L. Myres, *Roman Britain and the English Settlements* (Oxford History of England, vol i, 2nd ed., 1937). Books 1–4 of this volume are concerned with Roman Britain, Book 5 with the Anglo-Saxon settlements.
Sir George Macdonald, *The Roman Wall in Scotland* (2nd ed., 1934)
R. G. Collingwood, *Roman Britain* (1932)
A. R. Burn, *The Romans in Britain* (1932). This is an anthology of inscriptions, with translations and commentary.
R. G. Collingwood, *The Archaeology of Roman Britain* (1930)
J. Mothersole, *The Saxon Shore* (1924)
F. Haverfield and Sir George Macdonald, *The Roman Occupation of Britain* (1924)
F. Haverfield, *The Romanisation of Roman Britain* (4th ed., 1923)
J. Ward, *Romano-British Buildings and Earthworks* (1911)
J. Ward, *The Roman Era in Britain* (1911)

The Anglo-Saxons

A number of books mentioned below are concerned with the whole of the Anglo-Saxon period, and not merely with that part of it which precedes the accession of Alfred the Great. More detailed bibliographies will be found in *English Historical Documents*, I (see further below), and in W. Bonser, *An Anglo-Saxon and Celtic Bibliography, 450–1087* (1957). This last does not include material dealing with literature and linguistics. Although there have been many important advances in knowledge about the early Anglo-Saxon period during the last thirty years or so, the amount of new archaeological evidence has not increased in the same proportion as it has for the Romano-British period. For this reason the books which follow are arranged by subject rather than by date of publication.

Sources

(in translation, or provided with translations, unless otherwise stated)

English Historical Documents, I, ed. D. Whitelock (1955), a selection of documents for the period *c.* 500–1042, with detailed bibliographies

R. W. Chambers, *England before the Norman Conquest* (1928), including a section on Roman Britain and extending as far as the Norman Conquest.

Bede, *Ecclesiastical History of the English Nation.* The standard Latin text is still that by C. Plummer (2 vols., text and notes, 1896). A new text with facing translation by B. Colgrave and R. A. B. Mynors is available in the Medieval Text series (Nelson, 1969). There are translations by J. E. King (Loeb Classical Library, 1930); J. Stevenson, revised by L. C. Jane (Everyman's Library, reprinted 1954); L. C. Jane (Temple Classics, 1903); A. M. Sellar (1907) and L. Shirley-Price (Penguin Books, 1955).

Anglo-Saxon Chronicle. The most recent translation is that edited by D. Whitelock with D. C. Douglas and S. I. Tucker (1961). Another reliable translation is by G. N. Garmonsway (Everyman's Library, 1960) following page by page the text edited by C. Plummer, *Two of the Saxon Chronicles Parallel* (1896).

Beowulf. Among many translations of the poem are those by D. Wright (Penguin Classics, 1957); J. R. Clark Hall, revised by C. L. Wrenn (1950); and R. K. Gordon in *Anglo-Saxon Poetry* (Everyman's Library, 1954). Among recent editions of the text are those by Fr. Klaeber (3rd ed., 1951); C. L. Wrenn (1953); and E. van K. Dobbie (1953).

Among other books containing texts or translations, or both, of Anglo-Saxon sources are:

B. Dickins, *Runic and Heroic Poems of the Old Teutonic Peoples* (1915)

N. Kershaw, *Anglo-Saxon and Norse Poems* (1922)

C. W. Kennedy, *Early English Christian Poetry* (1952)

K. Malone, *Ten Old English Poems* (1941)

Two Lives of Saint Cuthbert, ed. B. Colgrave (1940)

The Life of Bishop Wilfrid by Eddius Stephanus, ed. B. Colgrave (1927)

Felix's Life of Saint Guthlac, ed. B. Colgrave (1956)

The Letters of St Boniface, trans. E. Emerton (1940)

The Laws of the Earliest English Kings, ed. F. L. Attenborough (1922)

General and Political History

R. G. Collingwood and J. N. L. Myres, *Roman Britain and the English Settlements* (Oxford History of England, vol. i, 2nd ed., 1937). Books 1–4 of this volume are concerned with Roman Britain, Book 5 with the Anglo-Saxon settlements.
N. K. Chadwick (ed.), *Studies in Early British History* (1954)
R. H. Hodgkin, *A History of the Anglo-Saxons* (3rd ed., 1952)
P. Hunter Blair, *An Introduction to Anglo-Saxon England* (1956)
J. E. Lloyd, *A History of Wales* (3rd ed., 2 vols., 1939)
H. R. Loyn, *Anglo-Saxon England and the Norman Conquest* (1962)
G. O. Sayles, *The Medieval Foundations of England* (2nd ed., 1950)
W. F. Skene, *Celtic Scotland* (3 vols., 1876–80)
Sir Frank Stenton, *Anglo-Saxon England* (Oxford History of England, vol. ii, 3rd ed., 1971)
D. Whitelock, *The Beginnings of English Society* (Pelican History of England, vol. ii, 1952)
F. T. Wainwright (ed.), *The Problem of the Picts* (1955)

Art and Archaeology

A. W. Clapham, *English Romanesque Architecture before the Conquest* (2 vols., 1930–4).
G. J. Copley, *The Conquest of Wessex in the Sixth Century* (1954)
Sir Cyril Fox, *Offa's Dyke* (1955)
D. B. Harden (ed.), *Dark-Age Britain* (1956)
F. Henry, *Irish Art in the Early Christian Period* (1965)
R. Jessup, *Anglo-Saxon Jewellery* (1950)
T. D. Kendrick, *Anglo-Saxon Art to A.D. 900* (1938)
E. T. Leeds, *The Archaeology of the Anglo-Saxon Settlements* (1913)
E. T. Leeds, *Early Anglo-Saxon Art and Archaeology* (1936)
R. L. S. Bruce Mitford, *The Sutton Hoo Ship Buriel, a Handbook* (British Museum, 1972). See also for Sutton Hoo the same writer's appendix to R. H. Hodgkin's *A History of the Anglo-Saxons* (3rd ed., 1952).
D. M. Wilson, *The Anglo-Saxons* (Ancient Peoples and Places Series, 1960)

The Church

C. J. Godfrey, *The Church in Anglo-Saxon England* (1962)
E. S. Duckett, *Anglo-Saxon Saints and Scholars* (1947)
E. S. Duckett, *Alcuin, Friend of Charlemagne* (1951)
J. A. Duke, *The Columban Church* (1932)
W. Levison, *England and the Continent in the Eighth Century* (1946)
A. Hamilton Thompson (ed.), *Bede: His Life, Times and Writings* 1935)
H. Williams, *Christianity in Early Britain* (1912)

Literature and Language

P. S. Ardern, *First Readings in Old English* (2nd ed., 1951)
A. C. Baugh, *A Literary History of England*, Book 1, Part 1 by K. Malone (1948)
A. C. Baugh, *A History of the English Language* (1951).
G. L. Brook, *An Introduction to Old English* (1955)
R. W. Chambers, *Beowulf, an Introduction to the Study of the Poem* (3rd ed., 1959)
R. V. W. Elliott, *Runes, an Introduction* (1959)
K. Jackson, *Language and History in Early Britain* (1953)
C. W. Kennedy, *The Earliest English Poetry* (1943)
M. L. W. Laistner, *Thought and Letters in Western Europe* (2nd ed., 1957)
W. L. Renwick and H. Orton, *The Beginnings of English Literature to Skelton* (2nd ed., 1952)
K. Sisam, *Studies in the History of Old English Literature* (1953)
C. G. Starr (ed.), *The Intellectual Heritage of the Early Middle Ages*, selected essays by M. L. W. Laistner (1957)
H. Sweet, *Anglo-Saxon Primer* (revised by N. Davis, 1953)
D. Whitelock, *The Audience of Beowulf* (1951)
R. M. Wilson, *The Lost Literature of Medieval England* (1952)

Place-names

K. Cameron, *English Place-names* (1961)
E. Ekwall, *English River-names* (1928)
E. Ekwall, *The Concise Oxford Dictionary of English Place-names* (4th ed., 1960)

Coins

R. H. M. Dolley (ed.), *Anglo-Saxon Coins* (1961)

INDEX

THE CENTURY OF REVOLUTION

1603–1714

Christopher Hill

In England between the years of 1603 and 1714 a transformation took place which embraced the whole of life, thought and taste. This book attempts to reassess what happened, penetrating below the surface of seventeenth-century events to show how our modern society began to take shape, and how England's position in the world was considerably altered. It outlines the changes which set England on the path of Parliamentary government, economic advance and imperialist foreign policy, of religious toleration and scientific progress, and shows the century as the greatest age in English literature.

While not setting out to provide an exhaustive compendium of facts, it considerably broadens and enriches our concept of a brilliant and bewildering century of change, heralding the modern world – 'the world of banks and cheques, budgets, the stock exchange, the periodical press, coffee-houses, clubs, coffins, microscopes, shorthand, actresses and umbrellas'.

60p